Business Models
A Guide for Business and IT

ISBN 013062135-8

90000

9 780130 621351

Business Models

A Guide for Business and IT

Haim Kilov

Prentice Hall PTR, Upper Saddle River, NJ 07458
www.phptr.com

Library of Congress Cataloging-in-Publication Data

CIP date available.

Editorial/Production Supervision: *Mary Sudul*
Page Layout: *FASTpages*
Acquisitions Editor: *Paul Petralia*
Editorial Assistant: *Richard Winkler*
Manufacturing manager: *Alexis Heydt-Long*
Art Director: *Gail Cocker-Bogusz*
Cover Design: *Design Source*
Cover Design Direction: *Jerry Votta*

© 2002 by Prentice Hall PTR
Prentice-Hall, Inc.
Upper Saddle River, NJ 07458

Prentice Hall books are widely used by corporations and government agencies for training,
marketing, and resale.

The publisher offers discounts on this book when ordered in bulk quantities. For more information,
contact Corporate Sales Department, phone: 800-382-3419; fax: 201-236-7141; email: corpsales@prenhall.com
Or write Corporate Sales Department, Prentice Hall PTR, One Lake Street, Upper Saddle River, NJ 07458.

Product and company names mentioned herein are the trademarks or registered trademarks
of their respective owners.

Author can be contacted at: *haimk@acm.org*

Printed in the United States of America

10 9 8 7 6 5 4 3 2 1

ISBN 0-13-062135-8

Pearson Education LTD.
Pearson Education Australia PTY, Limited
Pearson Education Singapore, Pte. Ltd.
Pearson Education North Asia Ltd.
Pearson Education Canada, Ltd.
Pearson Educación de Mexico, S.A. de C.V.
Pearson Education — Japan
Pearson Education Malaysia, Pte. Ltd.

To my wonderful wife, Shifra

Contents

Introduction

The goal of information technology (IT) is to support the solution of business problems. Traditionally, businesses and their customers have relied on human intermediaries to "sort things out." However, with the rapid development of e-business, there is usually no human intermediary; if the IT system that supports a business is not what it is supposed to be, then customers will quickly go to a competitor, and the business may "softly and suddenly vanish away" as a result.

The Economist noted in November 2000 (Eric Brynjolffson, MIT) that software and hardware account for only one-tenth of true corporate investment in IT; the rest is in new business processes, new products, and training of employees. Ninety percent is a sizable amount worth looking at.

For IT systems to be successfully used in new business processes and new products to solve business problems, both the business and the IT systems must be understood by all stakeholders. This understanding is demonstrated in business, IT system, and technological infrastructure specifications. These types of specifications are considered by many to be substantially different. This misconception leads to very serious problems—particularly in cooperation, or lack thereof, between groups of people speaking very different and obscure languages. But these languages should be neither very different nor obscure: it is possible to make our specifications simple, elegant, and convincing, which results in effective uses of IT in business. Specifically, business people including decision makers should be able to read the specifications and be convinced that "this is what they do," and "this is what they want," no more and no less. Thus, the main achievement of a good specifier is to provide a 20-page clear and complete specification, instead of a 1000+-page incomplete and vague one.

The **basic** underlying concepts and constructs for all kinds of specifications are the same: "the same materials and phenomena are treated by different theories, at different scales and different levels of complexity and abstraction" (C.A.R. Hoare). Many of these concepts and structuring rules have been around for a long time, but only recently have become well-defined and successfully employed in applications. They were formulated in international standards such as the Reference Model of Open Distributed Processing (RM-ODP); their foundations are in mathematics; and their relationships to the Universe(s) of Discourse are in philosophy. These concepts are neutral with respect to a methodology, technology, or tool(set), and thus will not become obsolete in 12 months. This book shows why and how usage of these concepts makes the following possible:

- To provide clarity and understandability for all stakeholders who could use the same explicitly defined framework for strategy and contracts instead of handwaving or slide shows;
- To use abstraction essential for business and technology leaders, including the Board level, to tame complexity and be in charge, i.e., to stay focused on core competencies at all levels;
- To provide for traceability between and maintainability of specifications (and of products and services that satisfy these specifications) instead of relying on tacit knowledge of gurus;
- To define explicitly the relationships between software artefacts visible to the business and the appropriate fragments of business specifications;
- To understand the potential damage to a business that implementation of a particular IT service or system may inflict, and correct it.

Business modeling picks and chooses those business things, actions, and relationships among them that are of interest and importance to the business stakeholders. These things, actions, and relationships are used to create business models—*simplified* specifications of the business. Such business specifications are often considered to be a given starting point for IT system design and development. In real life they are not given; they have to be discovered, created, and explicitly formulated.

This book describes the foundations of business modeling based on a small set of concepts and constructs. The term "business" does not mean only a traditional business: in addition to traditional and "e-businesses," we may consider, for example, the business of creating and managing an IT project, the business of a technological infrastructure, the business of a relational database management system, and so on. The underlying concepts are the same.

Concepts are not introduced unless absolutely necessary (as is the case with Occam's razor). The emphasis is on continuing relevance of what was achieved earlier: no wheels are reinvented. This book shows how to achieve precision and explicitness in business thinking essential to model and build businesses for the new economy. (Clearly, we need to distinguish between the new economy and the window dressing of the new economy.) The approach shown here applies both to precompetitive (or generic) business models and to (the competitive advantages of) specific business models, and thus to winning in the inevitable business transformations. This book also shows how to construct complex business patterns (such as "exotic option trade") from generic (such as "contract") and basic ones (such as "invariant") using well-defined structuring rules (such as "composition"). We never start from a blank sheet of paper: the basic business patterns and structuring rules, as well as many generic ones, are precisely those that we see in RM-ODP and related standards. In the same manner as businesses in the United States rely on the approach used in the standard Uniform Commercial Code, modelers ought to rely on the approach used in the standard RM-ODP.

As a result, the foundations of business modeling are made explicit, practical, usable, and teachable, in the same manner as foundations of mature engineering disciplines. This book shows how modeling is used both in the analysis of existing systems and in the design of new ones. The emphasis is on analysis —making explicit the parts of the whole and relationships among them— because in analysis we still encounter an abundance of ill-conceived or ill-posed problems, over-reliance on tacit assumptions, on "a few beautiful graphics," etc.

The system of concepts used in a specification should make it possible to express the specification's meaning in an elegant, easily understood manner. The concepts discussed in this book have been around for a long time; for example, some of them were formulated by Aristotle. We try to provide some flavor of the mathematical and philosophical foundations underlying these important concepts. And we provide examples from various areas of human endeavor.

The foundations presented here have been used in many information management projects in various industries (finance, insurance, telecommunications, medical, publishing, human resources, and so on), as well as in business transformation. The same foundations have been used in IT system models and in technological infrastructure models, as well as in metamodeling. Needless to say, the practical usage provided feedback for improving the foundations.

The book you are reading now is not The Ultimate Truth. This book presents business modeling following the approach to software engineering texts proposed in 1969 by B.W. Lampson [SE1970]: "...produce a document of perhaps 150 to 200 pages that would really serve as a standard for the field, in that it would produce a base from which one could teach, and in many cases a base from which one could talk and think. This would eliminate a great deal of our terminological differences and a great deal of the re-thinking that one has to do when one embarks on a new project. The attempt should be to tell what is known, not to break new ground and not to produce a complete or finished work in any sense." In the context of this book, the term "standard" refers to important international standards—the Reference Model of Open Distributed Processing and the General Relationship Model. And the phrase "what is known" explains the abundance of references.

We agree with the present-day mathematicians that the concept of *structure* is the most important one used in specifications: "The primary role in a theory is played by the *relations* between the mathematical objects concerned rather than by the nature of these objects" [D1998]. This was noted not only by mathematicians but also by famous economists. Walter Bagehot in *Lombard Street* observed in 1873: "The objects which you see in Lombard Street, and in that money world which is grouped about it, are the Bank of England, the Private Banks, the Joint Stock Banks, and the bill brokers. But before describing each of these separately we must look at what all have in common, and at the relation of each to the others." [B1873] In the practice of business specifications, we found out that emphasizing *structure over content* [KA1997, K1999] leads us to discover important concepts and conceptual similarities between apparently different business and system frameworks. In this manner, we achieve reuse of concepts and thus intellectual economy that helps a lot in discovering and formulating the structure of a business or an IT system.

Two kinds of structuring concepts are considered in the book. *Generic* relationships—such as composition and subtyping—are encountered in (and are the basic building blocks of) the specification of any business or system. But the most important concepts used in banking, insurance, or finance, as described in books published in the nineteenth and early twentieth centuries, have been successfully reused in present-day business (including e-business) specifications of these areas; only refinements, rather than changes, were needed. When reusing these classic business concepts in specifications, it was also possible to demonstrate that some important business-specific constructs (such as contract) were used in all these business areas.

In order to discover the essential structure (as opposed to the accidentals), we ought to use abstraction, i.e., to suppress the irrelevant details of the subject matter. In doing so, we may determine the essential commonalities among things and relationships that appear to be (perhaps substantially) different. In other words, abstraction helps us to put our knowledge in order. Abstraction has been used in this manner for a long time. The concept of a number is a well-known example; as Aristotle notes, "[t]he investigations of mathematicians have to do with things reached through abstraction, for they study them after eliminating all sense data... retaining nothing but quantity and continuity." The concept of a contract in business is another well-known example: "Then the people of Israel began to write in their instruments, and contracts, in the first yeere of Simon the high Priest" (1611 Bible 1 Macc. xiii. 42). And abstraction is one of the first concepts introduced and used throughout by the RM-ODP, an ISO standard widely used in this book.

This book is based on my substantial experience in modeling (finance, insurance, telecommunications, document management, business transformation), consulting, contributing to national and international standards, serving as Chairman of and speaking at international conferences and workshops, publishing more than a hundred papers and four books, and facilitating many business modeling sessions with subject matter experts including various levels of decision makers. Some early versions of the material presented in this book were published in numerous papers and conference proceedings used and publicly praised by practitioners—analysts and customers.

People of widely varying backgrounds can master the ideas presented in this book. The importance of explicitly using mathematics for effective reasoning was emphasized not only by modelers, engineers, and computing scientists, but also by such successful entrepreneurs as Conrad Hilton: "For me ... the ability to formulate quickly, to resolve any problem into its simplest, clearest form, has been exceedingly useful. ... A thorough training in the mental disciplines of mathematics precludes any tendency to be fuzzy, to be misled by red herrings, and I can only believe that my two years at the School of Mines helped me to see quickly what the actual problem was—and where the problem is, the answer is."

This book helps readers to do just that. The concepts are transmitted by education rather than by osmosis "on the job." Thus, the audience comprises business experts, including strategists and decision makers, as well as modelers, specifiers, business and IT architects, analysts, and designers. Students, especially students of management (including MBA), will also find the book of use.

No knowledge of UML™ is required.

Acknowledgments

The book would be impossible without the inspiration obtained from many ideas and concepts from literature, both in computing science (see the reference list, with a specific emphasis on ideas by E.W. Dijkstra, C.A.R. Hoare, J. Goguen, W. Kent, D. Parnas and others) and elsewhere (Adam Smith, Ludwig von Mises, F.A. Hayek, Yuri Lotman, and, of course, Lewis Carroll and others; most are in the reference list). Thanks go to many colleagues and subject matter experts for a lot of helpful collaboration, and especially to Allan Ash, Ken Baclawski, Othmar Bernet, Bernie Cohen, William Frank, Dave Frankel, David Frankel, James Garrison, Michael Guttman, Ed Hayes, D.Randolph Johnson, Thomas Kudrass, Jason Matthews, Terry Merriman, Joaquin Miller, Donna Muscarella, Ian Simmonds, Oliver Sims, Sandy Tyndale-Biscoe, Kevin Tyson, Steven C. Wolfe, Brian Wood, with whom quite a few ideas presented in the book have been discussed, often in the context of actual projects. Many thanks also go to Paul Petralia and Mary Sudul from Prentice Hall.

Chapter 1

The Purpose of Modeling

Models are created and used for *understanding*. To achieve that, the modelers together with the stakeholders pick and choose those things, actions, and relationships among them that are of interest to the stakeholders. A model includes only the essential characteristics of the modeled world (sometimes also known as the Universe of Discourse[1]) and suppresses everything else. These essential characteristics are formulated using a small set of concepts, and in this manner, the original, often very complicated, situation is translated into its substantially simplified model. (There may be several models of the same situation depending upon the viewpoint, i.e., depending upon which characteristics are considered essential—and which are considered unimportant—by the holders of the viewpoint.)

The essential "business rules" of the modeled situation are formulated as properties of the constructs used in the model. Laws of elementary geometry or elementary physics are well-known examples presented in school; these laws are very widely and successfully used because they and their logical consequences

---

1. The Universes of Discourse in the IT context include not only the business (or application) domain, but also descriptions of it, as well as requirements to software for the application domain, descriptions of these, and also the software being developed or reused [B2000a]. Clearly, the description of a domain, for example, stored in some IT system, may differ from the domain itself. Consider, for example, situations in which the same person "has" several (or no) "identities" in the IT system, or in which the IT system keeps data about persons (or things) that do not exist (yet?). Observations of the same kind have been made in RM-ODP, by William Kent in [K1979], and elsewhere.

1

govern models that accord well with experience. I show in this book that in business (and IT) models the laws are formulated as invariants of the relationships of the model as well as pre- and postconditions of actions of the model.

In the process (and as the result) of effective modeling, we observe that many constructs used in very different business and IT situations are the same, so that we can freely reuse these constructs and get their essential properties, instead of rediscovering these properties for each particular situation. Specifically, we note that an information management system technologically supported by modern computers and an information management system technologically supported by pencil and paper have many essential commonalities, and that, from the business viewpoint, the specifics of the technological virtual machine may be of no interest at all. Thus, the purpose of modeling is *not* to facilitate the usage of computer-based information management systems. (At the same time, some technological virtual machines may provide new business opportunities in the same manner as, for example, railroads did in the mid-19th century.)

We can reason about a simplified model of a very complex situation much more easily than we can reason about the situation itself. In other words, *models help us to manage complexity* and, therefore, to make substantiated decisions based on the well-understood and explicitly formulated essentials of the modeled situation. This is why most engineering or business artefacts—such as buildings, bridges, airplanes, enterprises, and markets—do not fall apart. The work of a modeler is analogous to the work of a physicist who "is trying to correlate the incoherent body of crude fact confronting him with some definite and orderly scheme of abstract relations, the kind of scheme he can borrow only from mathematics" [H1940]. The specifics of the *mathematics* used by a business or IT system modeler may differ from the specifics of the mathematics used by a physicist, but the essence—the structure—remains the same: mathematics is "the art and science of effective reasoning" (E.W. Dijkstra), where "effective" means "reduced to a doable amount" [D1976a]. Mathematics provides the patterns of thinking essential for managing complexity,[2] and the ability to use mathematics is "one of the things that distinguishes professional engineers from technicians"

---

2.   "A mathematician, like a painter or a poet, is a maker of patterns. If his patterns are more permanent than theirs, it is because they are made with ideas." [H1940] F.A. Hayek in "The theory of complex phenomena" [H1964] emphasized the same approach to mathematics. And Yuri Lotman, one of the founding fathers of semiotics, in his last interview (1992) also stressed the importance of mathematics as a method of thinking.

[P2001]. I describe and use these patterns throughout the book. I apply the generic patterns to handle (discover, distill, reuse) business-specific patterns.

Creating good models is not easy;[3] using these models and reasoning about them is much easier. At the same time, the process of modeling is not less valuable than its result, when we model a business, we get insights into its essentials. A good model of a business serves as a framework for making decisions about possible further directions of that business (including business process change), as well as about possible usage (and non-usage) of computer-based information technology systems in order to improve some characteristics of that business. These information technology systems also need to be well-understood, and in order to do that, they also have to be modeled.

In essence, good models provide for clear and explicit treatment of complicated problems.

Success and Failure of Projects and Strategies

A specification should, above all things, be orderly in arrangement, precise in diction, full and complete in all respects, and without repetition, excess of description, or elaboration of verbiage.
Specification for architects, surveyors and engineers [S1904]

We treat business modeling—following Dines Bjørner and others—as an essential part of software engineering. Mastery of software engineering *concepts* is one of the most important prerequisites for the success of an information management project.

It is very instructive to recall how the term "software engineering" first appeared. The NATO Science Committee established its Study Group on Computer Science in Autumn 1967, and this Study Group recommended a working conference on Software Engineering. This first Software Engineering working conference was held in Garmisch in 1968, resulting in a superb 230-page Proceedings volume [SE1969]. The Editors emphasized that "[t]he phrase 'software engineering' was deliberately chosen as being provocative, in implying the need for software manufacture to be based on the types of theoretical foundations and

---

3. Creating a model of a situation may require introducing concepts and constructs that were not clearly discernible in that situation (when we consider it in isolation) but that become clear when we consider the commonalities between that situation and other, more or less similar, (fragments of) situations.

practical disciplines, that are traditional in the established branches of engineering." The all-too-familiar term "software crisis" was introduced at that conference. The very useful discussions at the conference were related to the state of affairs in that area, including reasons for this crisis and ways to solve it. Most—if not all—ideas, concepts, and observations presented at that conference and at its follow-up in 1969 are still valid.

The ideas and concepts presented at the 1968 software engineering conference and earlier, in papers by Dijkstra, Hoare, and others published in the early to mid-1960s, ought to be reused rather than continually reinvented. These concepts provide an excellent framework for assessing the fashionable "novelties."[4] We are not there yet. We have encountered many successes and failures,[5] but in general it is difficult to declare that our present-day software engineering activities are always, or even most of the time, based on the same kind of foundations as established engineering activities are. In this context, we observe that the well-known need to *distinguish early between the essential and the ephemeral* is required not only for modeling of existing systems. This need was considered mandatory for an IT project success by Niklaus Wirth—one of the pioneers of computing system design—in his Turing Award lecture [W1985].

This book does not analyze the reasons of such a state of affairs. Rather, it deals with the most important issue in engineering, information management, and business transformation projects—the issue of *specifications* essential for understanding both the existing situation and the artefacts (whether existing or to-be-created) that may change this situation. For building or changing a system, a specification is the document defining the subject matter of the *contract* between the customer and the system builder (or changer). Engineering projects cannot succeed without specifications. Even if a project is very simple, its specifications exist in the minds of the project participant(s) including the customer. If different project participants have different specifications in their minds, then such a project may fail; the deliverable—if any—differs from the intended specification of that deliverable.

As one of the consequences, it may be extremely counterproductive to use in our projects any technologies that were not clearly and explicitly specified (or those technologies the realization of which does not satisfy their specification). We will see later that an IT system specification is composed of a business speci-

---

4. "Every novelty in knowledge is assessed in the light of some background knowledge that is not being questioned during the evaluation process." [B1990c] Not all apparent breakthroughs in software engineering have been assessed in this manner.

5. As many as 80% of IT projects cost more than they return [S2001a].

fication and a technology infrastructure[6] specification; and obviously, if the specification of one of the components is unclear, then the specification—and thus the realization—of the composite is likewise unclear.

Finally, specifications are essential for decision making of any kind—strategic, tactical, or operational.[7] Strategic business decisions made without adequate specifications, for example, based on a "few beautiful graphics that were laughably called a business plan" [L2001], often lead to spectacular failures. When strategic decisions are not being executed and the reasons are unclear, you must look at how these decisions are supposed to be realized within the explicitly specified organizational infrastructure, that is, within the structures, systems, incentives, and operating principles that collectively constitute that infrastructure, in order to understand the problem.

Core Competencies

Business specifications are created by competent business modelers who work together with business subject matter experts (SMEs). But why should a business modeler be proficient as a Java (or C) programmer? The results of such requirements, which can be often seen in various kinds of help wanted advertisements, may be quite far from optimal. The reasons were given by Adam Smith a long time ago. "The greatest improvement in the productive powers of labour, and the greater part of the skill, dexterity, and judgment with which it is any where directed, or applied, seem to have been the effects of the division of labour." [S1776].

Adam Smith probably reused some of these ideas from his Professor Francis Hutcheson's *System of Moral Philosophy*:

> "Nay 'tis well known that the produce of the labours of any given number, twenty for instance, in providing the necessaries or conveniences of life, shall be much greater by assigning to one a certain sort of work of one kind in which he will soon acquire skill and dexterity, and to another assigning work of a different kind, than if

---

6. This includes "middleware." The term was introduced by d'Agapayeff around 1968 [SE1969]. More recently, the explosion of middleware, that is, the abundance of superficially different but conceptually similar middleware systems in need of considerable consolidation, was discussed in the eloquent paper by Michael Stonebraker [S2002].

7. The distinctions and similarities between corporate strategy and tactics in the context of resource allocation were precisely described, for example, by Dines Bjørner [B2000a].

each one of the twenty were obliged to employ himself by turns in all the different sorts of labour requisite for his subsistence without sufficient dexterity in any. In the former method each procures a great quantity of goods of one kind, and can exchange a part of it for such goods obtained by the labours of others as he shall stand in need of. [...] Thus all are supplied by means of barter with the works of complete artists. In the other method scarce any one could be dexterous and skilful in any one sort of labour." [H1755]

We all want to be skillful—competent—in what we are doing. Therefore, we need to concentrate on our strengths and delegate everything else to others. Business modeling and Java programming are different kinds of work, and employment by turns in these different sorts of labor—still often promoted in various environments—has been, and is, unproductive.

At the same time, some basic knowledge is very useful, or perhaps essential, for many kinds of human endeavor. This knowledge is common to and is the foundation of many competencies. It is not fixed, and in most cases it is not about specific facts. In most modern-day environments, this knowledge is "what remains after you forget what you learned in university" (E.W. Dijkstra). It certainly includes the understanding and use of abstraction and precision—the core competencies of a successful professional. The specific competencies of different professionals are different due to division of labor. The foundations for their cooperation are in the core competencies; and when these competencies are articulated and used explicitly, the cooperation (for example, among business subject matter experts, modelers, and IT specialists) is much easier. In order to discover and use the core competencies, we should not be reluctant to go back to first principles.

Education

The approach to education in computing science and information management should be the same as in other areas of human endeavor. Unfortunately, this often has not been the case: tools and "skills" have been taught rather than concepts, resulting in a training, rather than an educational, process. The problem was recognized and articulated long ago: "...it is clearly wrong to teach undergraduates the state of the art; one should teach them things which will still be valid in 20 years time: the fundamental concepts and underlying principles. Anything else is dishonest." (Strachey, [SE1970]). David Parnas at the International Conference on Software Engineering in 2001 proposed a 30-year test: the material to be taught to students ought to have been valid 30 years ago and ought to be valid 30 years from now. We will leave it to the readers to determine whether the material taught to them—or by them—could pass this test.

On a more general note, the same approach should be used at the earlier stages of education. *The Spectator* expressed quite emphatically [H2001] that "[n]o one who leaves education now will find themselves with the scaffolding of understanding which would enable them to acquire another language with less effort; not many, it seems, are able to write their own language in any manner other than warbling their native woodnotes wild. Without that knowledge, which once was systematic and not anecdotal, which was abstract and not what our educators so fatuously call 'practical,' children are crippled. An education that drills children in the structure of a language will produce adults who are able to teach themselves how to send emails in an hour, or to speak an unfamiliar language in three months.[8] One that aims only to teach them to learn how to surf the Web is going to produce an ignorant underclass." Observe the explicit use of *abstraction* in this excerpt.

Consider in this context the two prerequisites of a good programmer formulated by Dijkstra decades ago: first, an exceptionally good mastery of one's native language; and second, mathematical maturity (which is not the same as specific knowledge). Clearly, the same prerequisites apply to a good modeler and to a successful decision maker. And when you educate, "you have to teach a grasp of method, a sense of quality and style. Sometimes you are successful." (Dijkstra, [SE1970]). As Dijkstra observed many times, developing the intellectual discipline to keep things sufficiently *simple* in the environment of unlimited technological opportunities is a formidable educational challenge. Presumably, the technological specifics should be abstracted out, while the underlying concepts should be made explicit and taught.

The educational and training concerns should be clearly separated: in many situations, the teaching of computing science or the teaching of modeling have emphasized training (the idiosyncrasies of the currently fashionable tools and buzzwords) rather than education (concepts and approaches). This results in failure of projects, in human frustration, and in continuous search for and reliance on various miraculous "breakthroughs."

This book emphasizes the educational concerns.

---

8. Or, should we add, programmers able to use an unfamiliar programming language (or a CASE tool) in a few of weeks.

The Need for Understanding: Abstraction, Precision, Explicitness

How do we achieve understanding essential for decision making? We should concentrate on the essential, we should be precise when doing so, and we should explicitly state what we mean—no more and no less.

Abstraction—the suppression of irrelevant details—is the only way for humans to achieve understanding of complex systems. Abstraction helps us to capture the essential and to make decisions demonstrably based on that essential. And abstraction works in everyday life [WD1996]. Harry Beck, the author of the abstract map of the London Underground created in 1933 (www.thetube.com/content/tubemap) was told that the *abstract shape* of that map would be too strange and incomprehensible for the ordinary user[9] of the Underground network. The evidence provided by billions of successful ordinary users of the London Underground shows that, contrariwise, this "instantly clear and comprehensible chart ... became an essential guide to London," as noted on the London Underground Web site (www.thetube.com).

We use abstraction all the time, so the usage of modeling as a kind of abstraction is only natural. As Friedrich Hayek observed, "from time to time it is probably necessary to detach one's self from the technicalities of the argument and to ask quite naively what it is all about" [H1937]. A specification of an IT system only by means of its code is certainly precise but not abstract and therefore cannot be understood. (Such kinds of specifications are sometimes called "write-only." A write-only specification, if it is precise, may be of some use for its author, but it is useless for everyone else.) Of course, abstraction is essential not only in modeling of existing businesses and IT systems, but also in specifying new ones.

Abstraction by itself is necessary but not sufficient for understanding. An abstract, but imprecise, model may mean almost anything at all, and therefore is useless for decision making. The "few beautiful graphics that were laughably called a business plan" [L2001] for dot-coms did not qualify as a business plan (or as any kind of a useful model, for that matter) precisely because they represented abstract but very imprecise models: the meaning of these graphics was

---

9.   Similarly, in computing science and related areas of human endeavor, the severe intellectual limitations of such fictitious morons as the "casual user" still have a great paralyzing power [D2000].

never clearly defined. Such models may be used only to make decisions based on hype and enthusiasm, as opposed to the fundamentals of the business.

A model should provide abstract and precise answers to all relevant questions about the modeled world. These answers demonstrate understanding of the modeled world and its environment, and lead to successful decision making. A useful model may be understood only if all statements of that model have *precise meanings,* that is, only if it is possible for each statement to determine whether or not it is valid. Statements like "this line between these two boxes formally identifies the relationship between the customer and the supplier" are anything but precise.

Even an abstract and precise model may not be sufficient for understanding. A model in which important facts and assumptions are not included because "everyone knows them" is inadequate because in most cases these "obvious" facts are understood differently by different stakeholders and because not all stakeholders are aware of these facts. Assuming that "they will figure it out" is a totally inadequate mechanism for dealing with such implicit information: a model should be understandable without the experts being around to explain it. All important facts should be *explicitly* included in the model.

In the same manner as E.F. Codd provided an abstract, precise, and explicit definition of the relational data model [C1970], as opposed to the then existing navigational data models formulated in terms of realization and therefore too complex, all kinds of specifications ought to be abstract, precise, and explicit, as opposed to some existing specifications formulated in terms of realization, or otherwise semiotically polluted [P2000], and therefore too complex. Codd's definition of a relational data model was based on a small number of simple concepts well-known from mathematics, and was centered around the stable properties of the domain of relational data rather than around navigation within that domain. Business specifications described in this book have similar properties.

Essentially, our specifications must be *elegant* to ensure that they are written and read with pleasure. After all, specifications are our tools; as in programming, "the tool should be charming, it should be elegant, it should be worthy of our love. This is no joke, I am terribly serious about this. ... The greatest virtues a program can show: Elegance and Beauty." [D1963]. As an important consequence, beautiful specifications are easier to change.

The following sections describe abstraction, precision, and explicitness in more detail. Abstraction and structuring mechanisms are emphasized because they have often been underestimated, especially in various IT contexts.

Abstraction: The Way to Put Management in Control

Abstraction (suppression of irrelevant detail) is essential for any kind of human understanding and therefore for decision making. In the specific context of large IT system design and development, J.I. Schwartz noted in 1969 that "control is needed by managers, so that they don't begin a task before the initial specification is clear" [SE1970]. Clarity may be obtained only by using abstraction.

As C.A.R. Hoare observed at the same conference, if for some task you don't know what you have to do, "you can start out with the hypothesis that it will take a great number of people. Following down this slippery slope of reasoning, as soon as you have a very large number of people you have a very large management problem" [SE1970]. In this situation, management is not and probably cannot be in control; i.e., management cannot make justifiable decisions with the objective to improve the well-being of the owners of the enterprise.

Abstraction leads to elegant and very useful insights in all areas of human endeavor. When the irrelevant details have been eliminated and only the essentials remain, the number of potential blind alleys is drastically reduced. (For example, the essential properties of a thing cannot be changed without changing the thing.) At the same time, commonalities between seemingly different areas (often using quite different languages) may become apparent. Generalizations based on the essential properties of specific situations become formulated. The "Aha!" is being distilled.

Abstraction is indispensable for establishing that rapport between individuals that is "a very significant factor in arriving at agreed upon specifications from which one can proceed to build a programming system... It is quite evident you cannot have an effective software engineering facility when you lack rapport" (J.D. Aron, [SE1970], in the context of the Apollo project). This observation is valid not only in the context of programming systems. The rapport between people may be achieved only if some characteristics of people and things are by mutual (implicit or explicit) agreement considered to be irrelevant[10] and thus ignored; the remaining characteristics will provide for a fruitful communication between the participants. Indeed, "[w]e get acquainted with another culture in the same manner as with another person: at our first meeting we look for commonalities in order for an acquaintance to become possible, and later we look

---

10.   Determining these characteristics is often not trivial.

for differences in order for the acquaintance to become interesting" (Averintsev's metaphor as described in [G2000]). It is instructive to observe that what was ignored as accidental when the communication was established becomes essential for the communication to become and remain interesting. At the same time, the essentials that made the communication possible remain as the fundamental context, when the communication participants concentrate on whatever at a higher abstraction level was considered to be accidental. For an important example of communication difficulties in the programming environment, of substantial interest to management at various levels, consider the infamous buffer overflows that have led to expensive and even dangerous consequences for too many IT users. A plausible explanation of such blindingly obvious violations of good programming practice (corresponding to violations of the most basic safeguards found in professional engineering) was presented in [N2002]: the programming culture of disciplined programming emphasizing the correctness concern differs from the programming culture emphasizing the efficiency concern in which it is imperative for "your dancing pigs [not to] dance slower than the other guy's."

The commonalities between cultures describe the essential *structure* of the subject matter of the cultures (for example, businesses). And the differences describe the specific *nature* of each culture.[11] Following the discoveries made in present-day mathematics,[12] we note that the structures of the *essential fragments* of apparently very different domains are often the same because the relationships between the individuals specified in these domains are of the same kind. We describe and use these relationships throughout the book.

Codifying corporate strategy

> "In the mathematics I can report no deficience, except that it be that men do not sufficiently understand the excellent use of the pure mathematics, in that they do remedy and cure many defects in the wit and faculties intellectual. For if the wit be too dull, they

---

11. For readers who may at this point wonder how this observation may be expressed in RM-ODP we propose to consider these structures as templates which are instantiated in each of the cultures using the culture-specific natures as actual parameters.

12. See, for example, [D1998]. This kind of mathematics may be called "structuralist mathematics" (Dusko Pavlovic). As F.L. Bauer noted in 1968, "what is needed is not classical mathematics but mathematics. Systems should be built in levels and modules, which form a mathematical structure." [SE1969] The foundations underlying all kinds of our specifications are in very good agreement with these considerations.

sharpen it; if too wandering, they fix it; if too inherent in the sense, they abstract it."

Roger Bacon (1214?-1294?)

In any domain, when we make important decisions we want to understand precisely what exists, where it is, and what it does [RM-ODP2]. A business specification of the domain defines exactly that.

In business modeling, we need to be able to discover and make explicit the structures[13] inherent in the business but often hidden within a huge amount of detail. In addition, we need to be able to discover how reasoning about these structures may lead to improving various properties of the business. And, of course, we need to be able to define precisely the corporate strategy, i.e., what properties are of interest and what "improving" means! In order to do that, we need to be able to reuse as much as we can, starting with well-defined fundamental constructs. Definitions of these constructs often come from mathematics (or philosophy) and can be translated from mathematical terms into terms more familiar to the stakeholders. Although the elucidation and explicit specification of concepts and structures described here may have happened relatively recently, the concepts and structures themselves have been around for centuries and perhaps millennia, and have been mentioned with varying degrees of explicitness and precision for quite a while.

In business modeling, when we use, discover, and formulate business laws and business rules, we can follow the founders of economics. And in economics (a science of complex phenomena, according to Hayek), specifications and discussions of the essential structures may be found in classical works by Adam Smith and Francis Hutcheson, and in more recent works by von Mises, Hayek, and others. All these structures are abstractions; that is, they are obtained by suppressing irrelevant details. Specification of corporate business structures within their environment is essential for reasoning about corporate strategy and tactics.

With respect to logical reasoning (which goes back to Aristotle), we note the remark by von Mises [M1949]: "Logical thinking and real life are not two separate orbits. Logic is for man the only means to master the problems of reality." Alternatives to logical reasoning—such as handwaving, reliance on those who "get it," or on business plans described by means of flashy presentations using box-and-line diagrams—often leads to business failures exemplified by many

---

13.   The structure of a system is "the set of all the relations among its components, particularly those that hold the system together" (M. Bunge) [B1999].

"dot-coms". As noted by Paul Strassman [S2001c], knowledge about a company's business environment and its competitive position is the most valuable insight for strategic decision making by executive management; 65 percent of the profit performance of corporations can be attributed to this knowledge.

As noted above, modeling is an area in which mathematical maturity is of great importance. Mathematical maturity is not the same as specific mathematical knowledge because mathematics in general is "the art and science of effective[14] reasoning." In other words, mathematics promotes simplification rather than sophistication; by using abstraction, mathematics elucidates the essentials instead of creating a language barrier. Mathematics emphasizes the *structure*—i.e., the relations among various objects—to a much greater extent than the properties of the objects themselves. As a result, we speak about the fundamental unity of all mathematics. In understanding and modeling a business, as in mathematics, we emphasize the structure—i.e., the relations among various business things[15]—to a much greater extent than the properties of the specific business things themselves. And as in mathematics, we can see a fundamental unity of the same kind in the basic concepts of all kinds of specifications. In this manner, the writers and readers of business, technological infrastructure, and IT system specifications use *the same basic concepts and constructs* and are able to communicate in precise and explicit terms.

Abstraction makes things simpler and makes understanding much easier. Concepts are understood much better than technicalities, and important results are essentially simple. Modeling experience suggests that business stakeholders (non-experts in modeling or mathematics) understand and use conceptual material very well.

As a result, we may speak about the profound commonalities among apparently different kinds of business. More specifically, we may speak about the commonalities between the "old" and the "new" economy or about discovering and reusing business laws (structural and behavioral) common to all businesses. In this manner, by using abstraction—suppression of irrelevant details—we break

---

14. *Efficient* is not the same as *effective*. Tom DeMarco in his invited talk at OOPSLA 2001 noted that becoming ever more efficient in whatever we have been doing makes change almost impossible. "An organization that can only accelerate is like a car that can speed but not steer. In the short run it makes a lot of progress in whatever direction it happened to be going, but in the long run it's just another road wreck." Being *more effective* rather than doing the same thing more efficiently requires some slack for us to think rather than to do. Thinking requires using abstraction to focus on important business issues.

15. We consider any concrete or abstract thing of interest.

through the traditional and not too helpful partitions separating different kinds of business.

The structuring of any system (business, IT, and so on) is where relationships, especially a small number of generic relationships encountered in all business, and other, specifications, come into play. The three kinds of generic relationships encountered everywhere and widely used in this book are *composition*, *subtyping*, and *reference*.

Concepts, like concrete things, do not exist in isolation: only a system of interrelated concepts makes it possible to be precise and explicit when the corporate strategy is discussed. We can bridge the communications gap between different people and departments when everyone can use the same well-defined— and small!—conceptual framework. And thus it becomes possible to make decisions based on reasoning about explicitly presented facts and structures within that framework rather than based on handwaving and eloquence. The fallacy of the latter kind of decision making was clearly visible in the failure of some "dotcoms" created, supported, and even valuated by those who "got it" as opposed to those who "didn't get it" [W2000].

Creating and maintaining elegant systems of concepts requires a considerable effort. Bypassing this effort is "about as appropriate for the software engineer ... as it is for the civil engineer to try to avoid expensive heavy earth-moving equipment, relying instead upon armies of men with baskets" (R.M. Needham, [SE1970]). Unfortunately, some important aspects of the current state of software engineering, especially the ones associated with "engineering" as a profession, can still be characterized by this quote. This is unacceptable. Producing and using demonstrably correct specifications as a foundation for making strategic decisions leads to success both in traditional businesses and in software engineering with further, and easier (due to reuse), success in traditional businesses.

Prerequisites for Decision Making

When we want to make reasonable decisions and justify these decisions to ourselves, our partners, customers, and other stakeholders, we need to base our decisions on the essentials of the information we have or can obtain while ignoring the accidentals. Choosing what is essential is often viewpoint-dependent. In other words, we need to apply *abstraction* in order to concentrate on the essentials, and *precision* in order to demonstrably "know what we are talking about." Thus, we act as scientists developing a theory of the business we are dealing with and validating this theory with the business stakeholders [CHJ1986].

These approaches have been around in traditional business and engineering for a long time. There has not been and cannot be any step-by-step guide showing how to create elegant specifications and how to use them in decision making. At the same time, important general guidelines exist.

Consider the Laws of the Problem Domain

> The helmsman used to stand by with tears in his eyes; he knew it was all wrong, but alas! Rule 42 of the Code, "No one shall speak to the Man at the Helm," had been completed by the Bellman himself with the words "and the Man at the Helm shall speak to no one." So remonstrance was impossible, and no steering could be done till the next varnishing day. During these bewildering intervals the ship usually sailed backwards.
> *Lewis Carroll, The Hunting of the Snark [C1876]*

Before solving a problem, we need to be able to understand what the problem is about. This approach is used in other areas of human endeavor, but not always in information management. Many of us have heard about solutions in search of problems. And many have heard about universal solutions apparently applicable to any problem of some—not always well-defined—type.

Before trying to solve a business problem by means of an IT solution, we need to understand the business context (i.e., the business laws, as well as explicit and implicit rules) and the specifics of the particular problem. Usually, this is the most difficult aspect of the job. The business context defines the properties of the business (things, relationships, and actions[16]) in the same manner as laws of nature define the properties of nature. In the context of IT system development, the need for "concept formulation at the beginning" was explicitly mentioned at least as early as 1969 by J.D. Aron from IBM Federal Systems Division [SE1970]. In order to be understood, the business problem should be explicitly formulated in terms of these essential properties of the business.

Understanding of a business problem may be compared with a "business diagnosis" (ICSE 2001 talk by J. Ning from Accenture). When we use this metaphor, we may recall that in medicine the normal characteristics of a human body—both static and dynamic—are supposed to be well known before dealing

---

16. An action is defined in RM-ODP as something that happens. von Mises [M1949] defines an action as the exchange of one state of affairs for another state of affairs. Either of these definitions may be used.

with its "abnormal" characteristics. This includes the determination of "normality" of the characteristics.

After we understand the business and the specific problem in the context of that business, we may see that a computer-based solution is not even needed: manual changes in business processes may help the business stakeholders to understand better the current business objectives and to achieve them. At the same time, in many situations, IT (computing support) may help the business to achieve its existing objectives or may provide for new business opportunities that may become or change, after approval by business decision makers, the current business objectives. In either case, the IT artefacts must be understood by the business decision makers and specified from the business viewpoint. This approach does not—and should not—differ from applying any technology in a business. For example, if we want to "get from here to there" we need to know some aspects of the map (which will show the relationships between Here and There[17]) and some aspects of the technology—the transportation mechanisms available to us.

Understanding and precise specification of the (laws of the) appropriate domains[18] is the essential prerequisite for understanding both the business and the IT artefacts,[19] and in particular, for trying to formulate any requirements for computing support. In other words, both the business problem and its solution could be understood only in the context of their business and solution domains since the laws of these domains ought to be satisfied all the time. This is as it should be: in more established branches of engineering, for example, we consider the laws of nature (specified, e.g., in physics) as a natural conceptual framework for dealing with engineering problems and artefacts. In software engineering, we ought to apply the same approach.

---

17. Different maps will probably show different relationships.
18. We shall refer to a generally non-software-related universe of discourse as the domain. There are at least six good reasons ... to describe this domain: (i) ... to ... understand what goes on in the domain ... (ii) ... to teach—educate ordinary people or train new staff—in how the domain 'works' and possibly ought to work ... (iii) ... to "re-engineer" how that domain is to work ... (iv) ... to develop computing & communications support for actions of and in the domain ... (v) ... to separate the ... concerns [of the domain and requirements] (vi) ... to obtain certification that a domain ... operates according to publicly verifiable rules & regulations" [B2000c]. Clearly, most of these good reasons apply to a software-related domain.
19. We have to distinguish between the existing (perhaps generic) IT artefacts and those IT artifacts that are created specifically to solve the business problem at hand.

Of course, there are differences between traditional and software engineering. Because laws underlying software engineering are relatively new, they may be less familiar than those underlying traditional engineering; some of these new laws have not been formulated yet. And because software engineering is applicable in many very different business areas, we ought to be able to find out how to specify in a uniform manner the laws of these business areas. Fortunately, mathematics, being the art and science of effective reasoning, helps us to do just that. Thus, we will see that specifications of very different businesses areas (including the businesses of software engineering) have much in common.

Some models of various application domains and their fragments are (publicly or otherwise) available, so in software engineering—of which business modeling is an essential part—it is often necessary to create new models or at least to evaluate and change models created by others, rather than merely to apply such models.

Requirements "Always Change" ... or Do They?

Business processes often change: such changes may lead to a competitive advantage for the business, or may simply be perceived as necessary for the business to survive. Similarly, decisions about using computer-based IT systems to automate certain business processes may also change (for example, due to perceived opportunities). At the same time, the basics of a business domain often remain the same for centuries if not for millennia: we successfully used banking and financial texts published in the early twentieth century (or earlier—for example, fragments from Adam Smith's *Wealth of Nations*) in order to understand and specify the corresponding business domains. The changes due to "modernity" were minimal and were mostly additions or refinements of the existing classical models.

It is interesting to note that in literature and art, modernity is an attempt to derive the eternal from the transitory. In the words of Baudelaire, "Modernity is the transitory, the fleeting, the contingent, one half of Art, whose other half is the eternal and immutable" [P2001a]. In our terminology, *invariants*—properties of things and relationships that remain true no matter what processes have been or will be performed—provide for the description of this immutable. This terminology has also been used by some scholars of humanities. For example, linguistic invariants provided the foundation of many deep discoveries by Roman Jakobson. For another example, the interesting book by Zholkovsky [Z1999] is about the discovery of a small number of invariants in the life and literary work of

Zoshchenko; these invariants help in understanding the seemingly very different kinds of Zoshchenko's creative work.

The invariants that define the business domain are a very good and stable foundation for a specification.[20] We do not want to start in the middle, that is, with a possible solution, or even with a specific problem; *we start with the stable (that is, invariant) basics* and proceed from there. In other words, we use abstraction to concentrate on the essential and ignore the transitory. The transitory cannot be understood without the basics. In particular, the interrelated concepts used in describing this transitory are defined by (and in) the basics.

The invariants are the "laws of the domain," and we use them in the same manner as laws of nature are used in more traditional engineering. And the basic laws of a domain—unlike the transitory[21]—are usually simple and elegant, as are the basic laws of nature. These laws of the domain constrain and govern all actions that happen in that domain; specifically, human participants of the domain use the invariants in planning their actions to improve their future conditions. In this manner, the stable structure of a business domain provides an excellent reusable foundation for creating and reasoning about all kinds of potentially volatile—but not frighteningly volatile—requirements for business processes and systems.

The invariants that define the basic structure of a business domain also may change. However, such changes happen much more seldom than changes in the transitory characteristics of the domain (sometimes called "business needs") or changes in behavior (business processes) governed by these invariants. In addition, business specifications based on the invariants have delivered an unusually high degree of robustness [KA1997]; almost all changes have been local. The structure of the business domain usually remains stable, while the changes of the contents often are about permission of prohibition of certain products or services, introducing of a product or service into new contexts, deregulation leading to competition where none previously existed, and so on. The general properties (but, of course, not the specifics) of many of these changes can often be antici-

---

20.   The perceptual psychologist James Gibson [G1979] observed that "an agent bombarded with signals from all directions, an agent swimming in a sea of information, . . . perceives *invariants* in this information-loaded environment."

21.   "While the computation of the square root of a floating decimal number remained the same in Pittsburgh, Los Angeles, and New York, the computation of gross-to-net pay obviously did not remain the same even in two installations in the same city" [H1957].

pated, and appropriate abstraction leads to substantially greater stability of specifications.

Strive for Simplicity and Elegance

> Association with ugliness blunts the instinct for beauty, and warps the intellect if long continued, whereas association with beauty sharpens instinct and allows the intellect to develop without hindrance. Beauty thus being hygienic, art should come into everything, and the architect, like every other worker, should make his work beautiful.
>
> *H. Kempton-Dyson, Design, in [S1904]*

The stable foundations often ought to be discovered and distilled from the complex world around us. These discoveries are the only way to master the complexity and abstract out the irrelevant details.

Unmastered complexity can creep in various ways. "Too much stuff" is probably the most familiar[22] and the most dangerous. A specification with too much unstructured stuff in it is a write-only specification, even if most names used in it are perceived to be very familiar to its possible users. Most of us have seen such specifications materialize in boxes full of precise information; if we want to ask a question, the answer is probably there, but impossible to find. Decision makers and others who have seen only such specifications may become convinced that all specifications are not worth their time and effort. Some practitioners may, as a result, strive for "quick and dirty" work with often disastrous consequences.

As E.W. Dijkstra noticed some time ago, "I get extremely suspicious when the engineer justifies adhoccery by an appeal to the presumed law of nature, summarized by 'quick and dirty,' for from my experience and from my understanding I feel that 'quick and elegant' is a much more likely combination" [D1969]. This adhoccery is often realized by following the appropriate buzzwords and starting from scratch without paying much (or any) attention to the basics of the discipline. Contrariwise, quick and elegant specifications help enormously in the collective work of business experts, modelers, and IT experts. (Most specifications shown in this book are generalized fragments of real-life business specifications.)

---

22. "The inclusion of extraneous detail proves a hardship to both man and machine," as noted by J.A. Friedman in [SE1970].

In business and IT system specifications, too much stuff is often realized as overuse of a huge number of detailed facts possibly including application-specific or technology-specific artefacts invented for the benefit of the initiated. Such a specification may be precise and even may be claimed to be complete, but who can read it? If we want to drive from New Jersey to California and we can use only very detailed road maps (e.g., having the scale of one mile to one inch) plus a "data dictionary" such as an alphabetized list of towns, rivers, and counties, we are in a very difficult situation; based on these complete and precise specifications, we cannot even figure out that we have to drive west! In addition, some specifications introduce new terminology invented for an apparently new area, while in fact many existing concepts could have been reused. We often see proponents of reuse who propose first of all to create a set of new and therefore better reusable constructs.

According to Ronald Posner [P2000], semiotic pollution harms our intellectual environment in the same manner as physical pollution harms our physical environment. Information overload often leads to our intellectual incapacitation: we are overwhelmed by complexity. "The most effective way of avoiding unmastered complexity is not to introduce that complexity in the first place" [D2000]. After such complexity has been introduced into a system, it is usually too late: only trivial changes can be "reliably" made to that system unless a complete rewrite is accomplished. Even changes considered to be trivial (i.e., apparently local) may lead to grave consequences if the locality assumption, often unstated, will appear to be mistaken. Some of these grave consequences were described as front page news. And similar problems have been well-known in traditional environmental pollution.

A system with unmastered complexity is far from elegant; "in the design of sophisticated digital systems, elegance is not a dispensable luxury but a matter of life and death, being a major factor that decides between success and failure" [D2000]. The same is true about any system. And Paul Erdös, one of the greatest mathematicians of the twentieth century, put forward the idea that the Creator has a Book in which all of the most elegant proofs are written [S2001].

In the same manner as many basic business concepts (e.g., those described in Adam Smith's *Wealth of Nations* or in the United States Uniform Commercial Code) are neutral with respect to a specific business, many basic IT concepts are neutral with respect to a specific technology (and of course, to a specific methodology or toolset). This approach has been used by E.F. Codd, the founding father of the simple and elegant relational data model, as opposed to navigational models that "burdened application programmers with numerous concepts that were irrelevant to their data retrieval and manipulation tasks, forcing them to think and code at a needlessly low level of structural detail" [C1982]. More generally, this approach has been used in excellent programming texts (such as [D1976, D1982]) that teach programming concepts rather than a specific programming language. It leads to simplicity and understandability, and it is not new. As an example, the concept of Occam's razor was formulated long ago and has been successfully used for centuries. The same approach has been successfully applied to humanities. Johann Joachim Winckelmann, an eighteenth-century German aesthetician, noted that it was easy to use lots of means to produce insignificant works while it was difficult to create real masterpieces—beautiful works (of art) with simple means. These observations were made in a very interesting paper on Web design simplicity [K2000a].

Using mathematics helps in avoiding too much stuff for any system. Yuri Lotman, one of the founders of semiotics, noted that mathematics is "a method of scientific thought, and a methodological basis for the discovery of the most general regularities of life" [L1964]. Observe that Lotman considered the main difficulty in using mathematical methods in literary studies to be "in the fact that the basic concepts of literary science have not yet been formulated." As an IT-related example, Jim Davies and Jim Woodcock from the University of Oxford presented at the Oxford-Microsoft Symposium in Honour of Sir Tony Hoare (in 1999) an extraordinarily successful project of a smart card (for electronic commerce) for a very large U.K. bank—the first U.K. system to gain the Level 6 security rating that was considered unattainable by the industry. Formal specification, design and implementation (with proof) were successfully used in the project. The emphasis was on simplicity: it made the specification "blindingly obvious," so that the specifiers could convince a bank manager that the specification was correct. The presenters stressed that their most interesting examples were characterized by *eureka* moments. The mathematics required for the specification, refinement, and proof was completed on time and under budget, and there was no problem of "using Greek letters"!

Some authors (E.W. Dijkstra, J.W. Smith [SE1969]) advise to use not more than several lines (or a paragraph) in order to explain something specific, be it in mathematics or specifications. This approach perfectly corresponds to presenting the main characteristics of a language used to express a specification on the back of the proverbial envelope. We try to follow these recommendations throughout the book.

Simplicity should never be at the expense of generality. Discovering commonalities in areas perceived to be somewhat or substantially different leads to generalization and simplification (by virtue of suppressing irrelevant details), and thus to better understanding. As a result, effective recurring templates may be discovered or distilled and specified for reuse. The simple, general, and powerful concept of a contract described, for example, by Francis Hutcheson [H1755] and by the U.S. Uniform Commercial Code—as a composite in the composition of parties, subject matter, and consideration—represents a well-known example used in a variety of contexts.

Elegant Representation

We have to communicate our specifications, i.e., to represent them in a language or languages understandable to the users of these specifications.[23] There are many specification languages, in the same manner as there are many programming languages. A programming language may be ugly, but at the very least it has to be precise because it includes instructions to an inanimate object (a computing system). A specification language may be ugly and also (independently) may be imprecise because it may be used only by humans. Box-and-line diagrams,[24] slide shows, narratives, and so on are familiar examples. This book does not promote a "best" specification language, but rather describes some criteria that make a language good.

A good specification language should first be simple and elegant. It should not add its own complexity to the intrinsic complexity of the problem. "All knowledge of one's programming language can conveniently be formulated on a

---

23. Different languages may be used for different audiences. A short and nice overview of representation mechanisms (including "a little semiotic theory") is provided in [S2001b]. A more foundational approach explicitly based on semiotics and preservation of essential aspects of specification semantics in its representations is shown in the papers by Joseph Goguen, see, for example, [G1999]. These foundational approaches help a lot, it is clear that "applying (relatively) precise principles in a (relatively) precise way can eliminate, or at least greatly reduce, the subjective, personal, and political considerations that so often dominate discussions of syntax." [GF1999] We may also recall the definition of a language provided by Mel'chuk in the 1980s—a many-to-many mapping between an infinite set of meanings and an infinite set of texts.

24. A very harsh criticism of such diagrams was provided by A.J. Perlis in 1968: he noted that some people "use phrases like 'communicate across modules by going up and then down'— all of the vague administratese which in a sense must cover up a native and total incompetence." [SE1969]

single sheet of paper and can be gotten across the limelight in about twenty minutes lecturing.... [O]nly then real difficulties of understanding and solving real problems can be dealt with; that activity requires the ability to think effectively more than anything else" [D1976a]. Thus, again we encounter the need for a well-defined elegant structure. The same approach applies to languages used for non-executable programs, i.e., for specifications considered in this book.

A good specification language should be precise. In other words, the semantics of its concepts and constructs and the relationships between them should be explicitly and unambiguously defined. Thus, if diagrams are used, then they should not be pictures of anything; rather, all elements of these diagrams should represent mathematical objects. (As a counter-example, consider a line between two boxes that intends to represent a relationship graphically; the semantics of such a representation is not clear; different lines that look the same often denote different semantics; and in most cases, a relationship has more than two participants.) Of course, we do not need to repeat the definition of a construct every time we use it; once defined, the construct may be abbreviated (named) and reused. We reuse such constructs, from very basic to very specific, in this book.

A good specification language should permit the specifier to say what is meant without any language-imposed restrictions: it should permit an easy mapping from the structure of the problem to the structure of its representation. This is a very important characteristic of any notation: to quote E.W. Dijkstra, "the tools we are trying to use and the language or notation we are using to express or record our thoughts are the major factors determining what we can think or express at all" [D1972]. The specifiers should be able to, and should be encouraged to, say what they mean rather than something quite different.[25] For example, if the specifier means to say that there exist several independent subtyping hierarchies for the same supertype, then the specifier should say precisely this, and the specification language should be able to express this directly and explicitly, rather than prohibiting such an expression "because you cannot do that in [insert your favorite programming language]." For another example, if the specifier means to say that a composite in a composition has three components of different types, then the specifier should say precisely that, and the specification

---

25.   This problem was observed in programming a relatively long time ago. ". . . The way in which people are taught to program is abominable. They are over and over again taught to make puns; to do shifts instead of multiplying when they mean multiplying; to multiply when they mean shifts; to confuse bit patterns and numbers and generally to say one thing when they actually mean something quite different" (C. Strachey [SE1970]).

language should be able to express that directly and explicitly, rather than prohibiting such an expression and imposing instead three binary compositions that collectively have a very different semantics.

Basic Structuring Constructs

Let us look at a couple of small examples that will lead us to the basic structuring constructs used in specifications.

An Example: Two Simple Relationships

> "...grammar is substantially the same in all languages, although it may vary accidentally."
>
> *Roger Bacon (1214?-1294?)*

The diagram[26] at the top of page 25 demonstrates that a project participant should be exactly one of an employee or a consultant, and at the same time, should be at least one of technical, managerial, or clerical (some managerial employees may also be technical, for example). We see that things are shown as named rectangles, and relationships are shown as named triangles with lines connecting the triangle with the participants of the relationships. The essential properties of the relationship are shown in the triangle.

So far so good. We observe that a specific technical project participant has all the properties of a project participant and some additional properties specific to a technical, but not to a managerial or a clerical, project participant (unless, of course, that technical project participant is also a managerial or a clerical one).

We also observe that the *shapes* (relationships) of the situation shown in the diagram above are repeated in many other situations. And we observe that putting that many words in a triangle is "too much;" the same words are repeated again and again in many triangles. So we decide to abstract and abbreviate.

Both relationships shown above are *subtyping* relationships: *an instance of a subtype has all the properties of its supertype and some additional, subtype-specific, properties*. The kinds of these two subtyping relationships are somewhat different; the subtypes in the "employee-consultant" relationship are exhaustive, so that an instance cannot satisfy the properties of both subtypes at the same

---

26.   Many thanks go to Steve Wolfe with whom this kind of representation was extensively discussed.

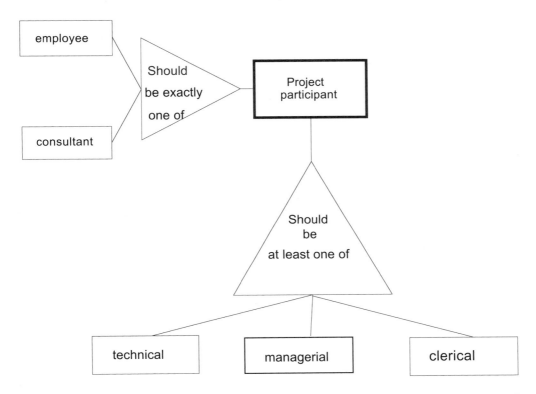

time (an employee cannot be a consultant within the same project); but the sub-types in the "technical-managerial-clerical" relationship are overlapping, so that an instance can (but does not have to) have properties of two or even three of the subtypes at the same time. And finally, we observe that these two subtyping relationships themselves are different because they use different criteria for sub-typing: employment status and job classification, correspondingly. We may, if we wish (or if the customer wishes), attach the subtyping criteria as names (labels) of these relationships.[27] The semantics of our very small business fragment obvi-ously requires us to show two, rather than one (or five!) subtyping relationships.

The abbreviations that we use are determined by the language used and by its (graphical) representation. This book uses UML™—the Unified Modeling Lan-guage. It is a standard adopted by the Object Management Group and widely

---

27.   We will not overuse relationship names because in larger diagrams this may lead to over-crowding. At the same time, in some cases relationship names are very useful, and essential to distinguish between several relationships of the same kind between the same elements.

used in the IT industry; there are hundreds of books describing UML. However, the complete language as it currently exists is huge and may be considered over-whelming by business people. We will use only a small subset (see Appendix A) essential to represent the semantics of our specifications. Here is the same speci-fication in UML, where a triangle without a name is used to abbreviate the sub-typing relationship.

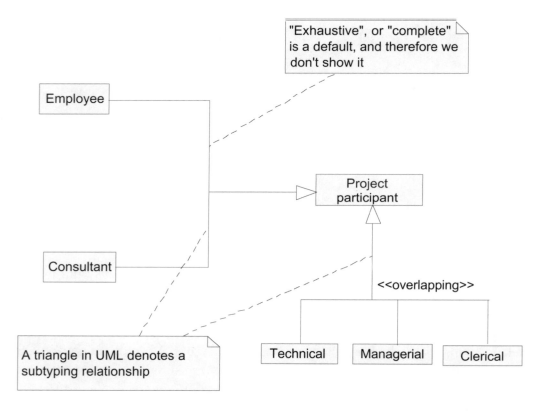

As shown in this figure, the distinction between the overlapping and non-overlapping subtyping relationships is shown by means of using the "stereo-type"[28] «overlapping» where needed; the non-overlapping is the default for sub-typing and is not shown. Similarly, the exhaustiveness of the subtyping relationships, that is, the property that all subtypes are enumerated (and there

---

28.   A UML stereotype for relationships represents a relationship type, that is, a predicate charac-
      terizing properties of the relationship.

are no other subtypes) is not explicitly shown because it is the default property. Thus, the default characteristics, encountered much more often than non-default ones, are precisely specified, but are not shown at all in the representations, leading to more concise diagrams.

From Specifics to Explicit Models

While examples often introduce a large amount of details, the underlying essentials are usually rather simple. Discovering these essentials may not be easy. By abstracting, that is, by suppressing the irrelevant details, we can determine and formulate the important commonalities between concepts and constructs from apparently different business or technological areas. The same approach is used when we have an incompletely specified problem; we consider a class of problems and thus concentrate on the essential similarities between the elements of this class.[29] In other words, we generalize, that is, we concentrate on the supertype rather than on its multiple and various subtypes. In this manner, abstract concepts have been discovered and reused, and abstraction is the ultimate in understanding and reusability (Mac an Airchinnigh). By using abstraction, we may discover, understand, and specify the basic structure of a business domain or its fragment.

Sometimes we have to pay a price for doing so. When we generalize, we often introduce concepts and terminology absent in the specific situations. These concepts and terminology may be new and unfamiliar to the experts in a particular subject area. In some cases, the experts do not even have a term for the concept ("yes, we know about it, but we don't have a name for it"). The explicit formulation of the abstract concepts, together with consistent and explicit usage of their names, may be unconventional, but becomes very convenient for clarity in understanding and reasoning. In this manner, *reasoning is reduced to a doable amount* [D1976a]. Time and effort may be required to get used to such an approach, but it certainly pays off.

As an example, consider the discovery of numbers and their positional representation: in ordinary arithmetic, we calculate, i.e., manipulate uninterpreted formulae. We do not justify the manipulations by referring to the perceived properties of things, such as apples or dollars, denoted by their symbols. "Hilbert the formalist showed that such interpretation was superfluous because which manip-

---

29.   When we have a completely specified problem taken in isolation we have to find out the generalization of this problem in order to distinguish the essential from the accidental.

ulations were permissible could be defined in terms of the symbols themselves"
[D2000]. Similarly (and more generally), Bunge observed that "interesting problems of interpretation of contemporary scientific theories can be tackled almost
like calculations, without resorting to arguments from analogy or authority"
[B1990b].

As another example, consider one of the main topics of this book: the com-
monality of concepts and constructs used in business, IT system, and technological
specifications. Some of these essential basic concepts, such as invariant, type, or
template, as well as the basic structure of such relationships as composition and
subtyping, are described in RM-ODP. Similarly, and on a more foundational level,
commonly used concepts and structures have been discovered and precisely
defined in mathematics, notably in category theory. Although these concepts may
have been perceived as second-degree abstractions, they have in fact been successfully taught to high school students [LS1997], and have helped in successful
elucidation of important specification properties, specifically in showing how to
put seemingly very different things together. It was shown that change of notation
(that is, a mapping between sign systems) and refinement should preserve essential structures. In particular, the quality of metaphors including user interfaces is
determined by the degree to which structures are preserved [G1999].

We should not forget, of course, that a concept—like a specific thing or an
action—does not exist in isolation. A single concept by itself may be valuable but
often is insufficient. To quote Lawvere, one of the founding fathers of modern category theory, "comparing reality with existing concepts does not alone suffice to produce the level of understanding required to change the world; a capacity for
constructing flexible yet reliable *systems* of concepts is needed to guide the process."

Discovering and describing a system of simple and elegant concepts is difficult. Understanding and using such a system is much easier, just by virtue of its
simplicity and elegance. A system of such RM-ODP concepts as type, class, template, invariant, composition, and so on, successfully has been introduced to and
used by business experts in various areas including those traditionally considered
to be quite far from mathematics. Even in a business area where specific business
patterns have not yet been discovered, it is always possible to use these fundamental concepts as a basis for modeling and eventual discovery of more specific
patterns. This solid foundation will never let you down.

From Lines Between Boxes to a Precise Specification

Let us consider another example that will demonstrate two additional kinds of relationships. These two kinds of relationships, together with the subtyping relationship shown above, are the basic structuring constructs encountered in all kinds of specifications.

In an insurance environment, an application for some kind of insurance is to be "underwritten," i.e., assessed by an underwriter taking into account the information in the application and other information available about the specific applicant and situation. The underwriter either accepts the application (which implies creation of an insurance contract between the applicant and the insurance company with the subject matter described in the application), or rejects it (which implies either conducting additional negotiations between the applicant and insurance company, or terminating the *specific* relationship among the applicant, the insurance company, and the application). An application for insurance creates a "case folder" into which the application and additional information will be put. In turn, the case folder is "assigned to" an underwriter.

It may seem that the following UML diagram would be a faithful representation of the most important aspects of this situation:

However, this diagram shows almost no semantics. Its creators assume that "everyone knows what 'assigned to' means." This meaning might be somehow invented, named "business rules," and realized by the IT developers to be then forever hidden in the code. The information about this specific small fragment of the insurance business domain is not presented in the diagram; rather, it is still in the head of (for example) the underwriter. Nevertheless, the diagram above may be perceived as a specification, while in fact it is not.

In order to prevent such misperceptions, among other things, the language used to represent specifications should enforce appropriate representations. In other words, it should not permit semantic-free elements to be considered as valid expressions in that language. Similarly, as noted by C.A.R. Hoare, a programming language is distinguished not so much by what it empowers a programmer to express, but rather by what it prevents him from expressing.

A precise specification ought to explain (in any representation, whether graphical or textual) the meaning of 'assigned to' and may look like this in UML:

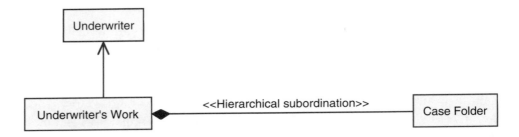

This diagram expresses the following. First, some characteristics of the Underwriter's Work are determined by the characteristics of the Underwriter (shown by the *reference* relationship from the Underwriter's Work to the Underwriter). Second—more important—a Case Folder is a component of an Underwriter's Work; the Underwriter's Work must exist in order for a Case Folder to exist (shown by the *composition*[30]-subordination relationship between the Underwriter's Work and the Case Folder); and the composition-subordination is hierarchical, so that a Case Folder may be a part of the Underwriter s Work of only one Underwriter (shown also by the black diamond rather than by a white one).[31] This diagram, by virtue of using the composition relationship, shows a very important fact—that there are some properties of the Underwriter's Work determined collectively by the properties of its Case Folders. The modeling process participants may want to discuss the specifics of these properties and, for example, may be interested in the maximum amount of Case Folders included in the Underwriter's Work; presumably this amount is determined not so much by the number but by the complexity of the Case Folders.

---

30. For UML experts, the semantics of the existing definitions of composition and aggregation in UML 1.4 is not always clear. These definitions do not refer to any property determination. There are many papers about the "real" meaning of these UML terms. So, instead of trying to participate in such discussions (also known as discussions about "the black and white diamonds"), we just reuse the definition of composition that the rest of the world—philosophers [B1999], information technologists [RM-ODP 2] and others—have been successfully using for a long time. And even in a chemist's window, we read "prescriptions compounded' [C1915]!

31. In order to make the specifications more readable, we improved this representation. We will not demand the reader to remember the semantic differences between the white and the black diamond. By default, the composition is not hierarchical. However, if a composition is hierarchical, we explicitly say so with words in our diagrams. Technically, these words represent (a part of) the name of a UML stereotype. The stereotype «Hierarchical subordination» describes the specific properties of the subtype of the composition relationship.

From Details to Clear Big Pictures

> "...And yet it was a very clever pudding to invent."
> "What did you mean it to be made of?" Alice asked, hoping to cheer him up, for the poor Knight seemed quite low-spirited about it.
> "It began with blotting paper," the Knight answered with a groan.
> "That wouldn't be very nice, I'm afraid—"
> "Not very nice alone," he interrupted, quite eagerly: "but you've no idea what a difference it makes mixing it with other things such as gunpowder and sealing-wax. ..."
> *Lewis Carroll, Through the Looking Glass [C1872]*

Discovering similarities between individuals and reasoning in terms of these similarities is not the only way to simplify and understand complex systems. We often want to suppress the details about parts of the whole and concentrate only on the whole itself. As in the roadmap example, when we need to get from here to there, we want to have a clear big picture of where we are in the context of what is around, and where we can (or have to) go. Of course, we cannot directly obtain such a picture from a set of very detailed roadmaps; we need to compose that picture from its components. In order to do that, we choose the appropriate components and combine them in a particular way. This combination includes ignoring the details that are of no interest for the business of looking at the whole. And because different businesses are interested in different aspects of the whole, different compositions of the same whole concentrate on (and ignore) different collective properties of the parts.

A traveling customer of a bank can easily obtain a non-collateralized loan to buy goods or services, even in a foreign country, just by using a credit card. In this manner, the world banking system is at the service of such a customer, and the details of the credit card (such as its issuer, the country of issuance, the currency of issuance, and so on), as well as of the business that provides such a loan, are of no importance. Moreover, the same customer may, by using an ATM (and usually paying a small fee), demand repayment of a part of the customer's loan to the bank (in accordance with the contractual terms of the customer's account). Again, the world banking system is at the service of such a customer, and the details of the account (such as its issuer, the country of issuance, the currency of issuance, and so on), as well as of the business (usually a bank) that accomplishes such a repayment, are of no importance. In this manner, by virtue of entering into contracts with a specific bank, the customer appears to use the world banking system as a counterparty in various transactions, without going into any detail whatsoever about that system and its structure.

As another interesting example, consider the "fast save" functionality of a popular word processor. On the one hand, the composite result of multiple executions of "fast save" appears to be the same as the composite result of multiple executions of ordinary "save" operations. Therefore, it seems that, at a certain abstraction level, it does not matter whether the "save" is fast or not, and in fact it may be preferable to use "fast save" because it is faster. On the other hand, at a lower abstraction level, a "fast save" saves only the changes to a file that become components of the file. Information about the existence and contents of the components at this lower abstraction level may become visible to the reader of the file *at a higher level* who accesses that file using simple software tools different from the word processor. Because some document authors may not want to make the complete history of updates (including deletions) to their documents available to readers (because of possible serious undesirable consequences), an explicit—and very simple—information model of document components and processing of their versions would help in understanding and making decisions about using the appropriate kind of "save."

As still another example, consider the portfolio approach to investments—be they a collection of retirement investments or a collection of IT project investments [S2001a]. In either situation, we deal with a composition of investments with different risks and rewards. By considering the investments as components of a portfolio rather than each investment in isolation, we can optimize the desirable properties of the composite in this composition (e.g., stabilize the risk), as well as determine the commonalities between some or all components, rather than concentrate on trying to deal only with the specifics of each component.[32] The same approach is used for calculating the properties (including risk characteristics) of and making decisions about a position of a customer (having a single strategy or several strategies) or of a trader in financial instrument trading.

Or consider a book (or another document) with many small errors. Although each of these errors may be of little consequence when considered in isolation, their "cumulative effect is to destroy a knowledgeable reader's confidence in the author's standards of accuracy" [R2001]. The cumulative effect here

---

32.   In order to make justified decisions, debuzzwordification with respect to (some of) the specifics is often necessary.

is, of course, the property of the composite determined by the properties of the components and by the way these components are combined.

Different ways to choose and compose parts result in different kinds of clear big pictures of the same whole. In our roadmap example, we may be interested in the political subdivisions of the parts and the whole, or in the existence of multiple interesting parts between here and there (where "interesting parts" and "between" may be defined in various ways), or simply in the minimal time needed to cover the distance. Different compositions will be used to specify whatever we are interested in. In all cases, we are constrained (or encouraged) by the rules of traveling from here to there using a chosen transportation mechanism. Similarly, a clear big picture is obtained from its details by using the (generic and specific) rules of composition and by satisfying the general business rules of the domain of which that composition is itself a part.

Three Basic Kinds of Relationships

We have used three basic kinds of structuring constructs or relationships: subtyping, composition, and reference. Let's summarize what each of these kinds of relationships *means*. The complete definitions of these kinds of relationships are provided in Appendix B.

A *subtyping* relationship is between a supertype and its subtype(s). An instance of a subtype has all the properties of its supertype and some additional, subtype-specific properties.

A *composition* relationship is between a composite and its components (in other words, between the "whole" and its "parts"). Some properties of the composite are determined by properties of its components and by the way these components are combined.

A *reference* relationship is between reference and maintained instances. Some properties of the maintained instance are determined by properties of its reference instance.

Each of these kinds of relationships—*business patterns*—may be specialized (we have seen, for example, overlapping and non-overlapping subtyping relationships, as well as different kinds of composition), and the complete definitions of these specializations are also presented in Appendix B. At the same time, we observe that the three kinds of relationships discussed here are *generic*, that is, they are used everywhere, in all kinds of specifications. Various versions of their definitions have been known for millennia and have been formulated in terms of *properties* of their participants. The definitions used in this book are essentially the same as in international standards—the Reference Model of Open Distributed Processing (RM-ODP) and the General Relationship Model (GRM).

Using and Overusing Examples

> When a number of drawings are made after one pattern, though they may all miss it in some respects, yet they will all resemble it more than they resemble one another; the general character of the pattern will run through them all; the most singular and odd will be those which are most wide of it; and though very few will copy it exactly, yet the most accurate delineations will bear a greater resemblance to the most careless, than the careless ones will bear to one another.
>
> *Adam Smith, The Theory of Moral Sentiments [S1759]*

We used examples to explain the concepts of subtyping, reference, and composition relationships. Of course, this approach is not new at all. Lewis Carroll in his *Alice* books (and elsewhere) used many examples in explaining important mathematical and logical concepts to children. These examples were crisp, clear, and representative of the concepts illustrated there.

As a familiar example[33] of business patterns (both basic and more specific), consider Lewis Carroll's Court of Justice [C1865].

> The King and Queen of Hearts were seated on their throne when they arrived, with a great crowd assembled about them—all sorts of little birds and beasts, as well as the whole pack of cards: the Knave was standing before them, in chains, with a soldier on each side to guard him; and near the King was the White Rabbit, with a trumpet in one hand, and a scroll of parchment in the other. In the very middle of the court was a table, with a large dish of tarts upon it ...
>
> Alice had never been in a court of justice before, but she had read about them in books, and she was quite pleased to find that she knew the name of nearly everything there, "That's the judge," she said to herself, "because of his great wig." ...
>
> "And that's the jury box," thought Alice; "and those twelve creatures" (she was obliged to say "creatures," you see, because some of them were animals, and some were birds,) "I suppose they are the jurors."

---

33.   This example was partially developed in collaboration with Ian Simmonds.

We see here how and why (the business pattern of) *subtyping* was used when Alice had to use the term *creatures* (Carroll does not introduce the name of the *subtyping* concept, but clearly introduces the concept itself) and also how the business pattern of a *court* was used in a very explicit manner. Indeed, Alice had read about that pattern in books (because she knew the name of nearly everything there, she successfully recognized the *structure* of the pattern and its formal parameters), and the rather unusual actualization of parameters needed to instantiate the pattern presented no problems whatsoever for Alice!

Here is a fragment of this business specification represented in UML (extended with precise specifications of generic relationships, see Appendices A and B): We will not go into the details here; just note that «assembly» denotes a composition in which components must exist in order for their composite to be able to exist.

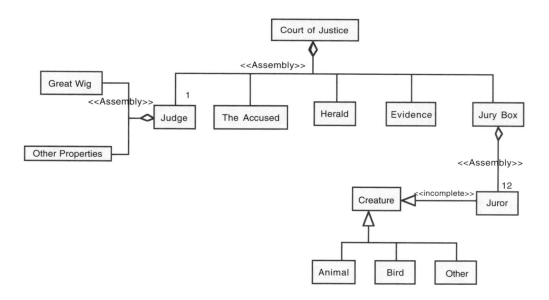

Thus, a (somewhat) unusual example may be considered as a good choice of a representative one. Such a choice encourages thinking, and explicit reasoning about the example and the underlying concepts helps to infer these concepts, anticipate changes and determine the commonalities between various situations. As a result, we root out general underlying concepts (and assumptions). We see an abundance of such beautiful unusual examples in Carroll's books.

At the same time, *the example above is not a specification of subtyping or composition, and neither is it a specification of a court of justice*. It is a specification of a *very particular* court of justice described in the fragment of Lewis Carroll's *Alice in Wonderland*. Nevertheless, a general specification may be inferred—and then validated!—from a *set* of suitably chosen representative examples. We should take into account that any example presents much more specific information than necessary for a specification and thus makes it much more difficult to separate the essential from the accidental. This characterizes the difference between the Aristotelian approach [BETA1992, KR1994] and a prototypical approach. The former provides for the intension of the (predicate of the) specification; the latter provides for a probably incomplete extension of the (predicate of the) specification. When we use the former, we can always find out whether a fact corresponds to the specification;[34] when we use the latter, we often cannot do that.[35] In other words, replacing a specification with an example, or with a set of examples, makes treatment of any facts not directly dealt with by these examples substantially more difficult: the user of examples has to guess.

Business Rules: Precision vs. Handwaving

> Alice carefully released the brush, and did her best to get the hair into order. "Come, you look rather better now!" she said, after altering most of the pins. 'But really you should have a lady's maid!
>
> "I'm sure I'll take you with pleasure!" the Queen said. "Twopence a week, and jam every other day."
>
> Alice couldn't help laughing, as she said, "I don't want you to hire *me*—and I don't care for jam."
>
> "It's very good jam," said the Queen.
>
> "Well, I don't want any to-*day*, at any rate."
>
> "You couldn't have it if you *did* want it," the Queen said. "The rule is, jam to-morrow and jam yesterday—but never jam to-day."
>
> *Lewis Carroll, Through the Looking Glass [C1872]*

The success (or otherwise) of a business system is determined by the handling, that is, discovery, specification, management, and realization, of "business rules." We will start with a definition of a *business rule*.

---

34.   "It is objectively determinable whether or not a phenomenon has a certain property" [BETA1992].

35.   "It may not be objectively decidable whether or not a phenomenon has a property of the intension." [BETA1992] lists "rock music," "intelligence," and "food" as examples of concepts described using this approach.

Most importantly, we want to be able to determine whether a specific business rule does or does not hold. Thus, we can say that a business rule is a *proposition* about business things, actions applied to them, and relationships between these things and actions. "Proposition" is a technical term defined in RM-ODP as an observable fact or state of affairs involving one or more entities of which *it is possible to assert or deny* that it holds for those entities [RM-ODP2]. Essentially the same definition of proposition is used in mathematics (e.g., in [GS1993]) and in logic (e.g., "A Proposition is, a perfecte sentence spoken by the Indicatiue mode, signifying either a true thyng, or a false," in T. Wilson *Logike* [1580]). A proposition, in Karl Popper's terminology, offers an opportunity for refutation.

Thus, a narrative (a story) is usually not a proposition and, therefore, not a business rule (although it may include propositions). A collection of examples is also not a proposition, nor is a prototype. In these cases, we may "figure out" a proposition or several propositions (and, therefore, a business rule or rules) from this information. Different readers of the information may "figure out" somewhat different propositions. In order to handle this unpleasant situation, we need to make the proposition(s) explicit.

We always encounter propositions in our life and in our work. They may be very specific (such as "the balance of the checking account number 64642136423784 in Bank XVCHAHJ is equal to USD 24,984.32 as of 1/1/2001" or "the fee for maintaining a checking account with a minimum balance per month less than USD 2,000.00 in Bank XVCHAHJ equals USD 7.50 per month"), more generic but still business-specific (such as "an account is a composite in a composition of owners [an owner is a subtype of a party], indicative information [composed of the kind of account, currency, etc.], initial balance, and transaction entries"), or very generic (such as "a subtyping is a relationship between a supertype and at least one subtype such that an instance of a subtype has all the properties of its supertype and may have some additional [subtype-specific] properties"). The last proposition always holds, while the first three may or may not hold.

The structure of a proposition, and thus of a business rule, is more important than its specific content. For example, the structure of all business rules about bank fees determined by account balances is the same (or similar), although the content is clearly different. Similarly, the structure of all business rules about discounts, commissions, and the like—in appropriate contexts—is the same (or similar), although the specific content is different. Moreover, the structure of a business rule is usually stable (defined by its invariant), while the specifics may change often or not so often.

A good specification of an action is also a proposition. However, a caveat is in order: to understand such a specification (and to be able to determine whether it does or does not hold), we need to make explicit the specification of the business domain in the context of which the action happens. As in programming, it is desirable to define data before using it. The business domain specification includes the most important business rules—the invariants of the domain.

We may be told that for simple action specifications we do not need an explicit domain specification because "everyone knows what it means." This statement is incorrect because when we write or read an action specification, we always refer—either explicitly or in our mind—to the specification of the[36] context of this action, i.e., to the appropriate domain specification, and we want to assure that the domain specification is understood in the same manner by all stakeholders for various action specifications used in the context of that domain. This assurance is possible only when the domain specification is *explicit*, i.e., when the context is rendered as text [S1999]. This may not be easy, because some things in a business are not explicit. Some business communications, in particular, may not even be considered as meaningful by some participants. For example, a wave of the hand signifying the acceptance of an offer in contractual negotiations may not be perceived as meaningful information by a participant or observer who is not "in the know."

Successful business modelers always articulate the need for articulation: the contexts of all actions, the elements of business communications, and the nature of their composition are essential for understanding the actions and business communications, and must be discovered[37] and formulated by the collective efforts of the modelers and SMEs.

---

36. There may be several contexts, for example, determined by several viewpoints.
37. In some situations, it may be decided that certain elements or their compositions should better remain unspecified, for example, because they are used only by humans in a process that cannot or should not be made completely predictable. This is, of course, acceptable provided that such decisions are explicit, and the pre- and postconditions of the process are also explicit, although possibly non-deterministic ("one of the following happens ..."). Lotman [L1990] observed that the non-determinism of historical processes may be explained in a similar manner.

Challengeable Well-Defined Statements

A precise and explicit specification in which everything has been articulated still must be validated by the SMEs. This is easy because such a specification is composed of challengeable well-defined statements (propositions, see above), so that the SME who thinks that some of these statements are wrong just points to these statements and explains what specifically is wrong. In other words, a draft of a precise specification does not need to be correct; in fact, a specification can be considered as a question: "Is this a correct and complete model of your business; and if not, what needs to be changed?" Clearly, an answer to this question is possible only when the specification is precise.

As an example, the simple specification below shows the investments that an individual investor has with a financial institution. These investments are composed of accounts of various kinds. These accounts have common properties shown in their supertype, "account." The existence of a cash account is a prerequisite for any other account shown here, and some properties of these other accounts are determined by the properties of the cash account. Each customer must have at least one cash account (and may have more than one), but may have at most one margin account and at most one short sales account, provided that a margin account exists. Other accounts are also possible. All previous statements in this paragraph are well-defined and can be challenged by the business SMEs. Some of these statements may be considered incorrect by the SMEs (for example, it may happen that a short sales account may exist even if a margin account does not exist for this customer), while some statements may be considered incomplete (for example, some important types of accounts with their specifics may be missing).

This approach of *precision over correctness* is not restricted to business specifications. It is championed in a much more general philosophical setting by Bunge's insistence not to put the cart of truth before the horse of meaning [B1990b]. The SME's rejection of a fragment of a specification based on the incorrectness of that fragment is a good symptom of modeling success: it means that the SMEs understood the specification and *were able to point to errors*. The alternative is much worse: continuous apparent acceptance of specifications by the SMEs may be a symptom of "glazing over" due to excessive complexity or vagueness of those specifications so that it was impossible to point to specific errors. Although the SMEs may agree with the specific stories and examples, they are unable to agree or disagree with the generalizations of these stories and

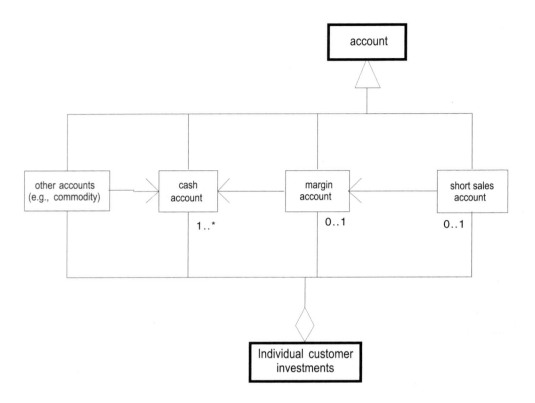

examples that remain implicit and exist only in the heads of the analysts and others who make these possibly wrong or mutually inconsistent generalizations.

Let us recall in this context that Peter Naur proposed in 1968 [SE1969] to use the work of Christopher Alexander long before it became fashionable to refer to it as a source of ideas about attacking the software design problem. Naur justified his choice by the fact that Alexander was concerned with the design of large heterogeneous constructions. Indeed, Alexander emphasized in *The Timeless Way of Building* that "...a pattern defines an invariant field which captures all the possible solutions to the problem given, in the stated range of contexts... the task of finding, or discovering, such an invariant field is immensely hard... anyone who takes the trouble to consider it carefully can understand it... these statements can be challenged because they are precise" [A1979]. In business modeling, discovering invariants is hard, but it does not have to be immensely hard because we can, and do, reuse various existing business patterns defined by their invariants. Other than that, Alexander's approach is valid and has been used extensively in business modeling, specifically when the stakeholders (especially the SMEs), as suggested by Alexander, consider carefully, challenge, and validate the business specifications.

Contrariwise, warm and fuzzy feelings represented in stories are not definitions. As Wittgenstein observed in his *Tractatus*, "The silent adjustments to understand colloquial language are enormously complicated" [W1933]. This is an excellent explanation of failures caused by statements like "Everyone knows what XXX means," or "They [the developers] will figure it out."

Common Explicit Modeling Concepts

> "Well, now that we have seen each other," said the Unicorn, "if you'll believe in me, I'll believe in you. Is that a bargain?"
> "Yes, if you like," said Alice.
> *Lewis Carroll, Through the Looking Glass [C1872]*

We often hear (and sometimes speak) about the apparently insurmountable communication gap between business subject matter experts (SMEs) and information technologists; or about the equally apparently insurmountable gap between (business and) IT specifiers and IT implementors. In 1969, the significance and extent of the communication gap between different participants in the computing science and software engineering professions was the most important discussion topic at the second (Rome) Software Engineering conference [SE1970].

To try to bridge this communication gap if it exists, the parties need to speak *semantically* the same language, i.e., to share the same concepts.[38] In some cases, the perceived gap exists just because the parties use different terminology to express essentially the same ideas. In other cases, however, the concepts are, or appear to be, semantically different.

Common specification concepts have been around for a long time. Most basic ones come from mathematics. Different specification areas—such as various business and IT system specifications—may have used systems of differently

---

38. As I.P. Sharp noted in [SE1970], "a lot of what we construe as being theory and practice is in fact architecture and engineering; you can have theoretical and practical architects; you can have theoretical and practical engineers. [...] And if you examine why [good software] is good, you will probably find that the designer, who may or may not have been the implementor as well, fully understood what he wanted to do and he created the shape." Architecture is a specification of a system (to be) created for human use; and we want such a system to be elegant, as observed by Ruskin in 1849: "Architecture is the art which so disposes and adorns the edifices raised by man... that the sight of them contributes to his mental health, power, and pleasure."

named concepts to express the same semantic structures. At the same time, some concepts used in specifications have not been explicitly formulated. The "true nature" (Dieudonné) of these concepts may have been understood and formulated only relatively recently. In the same manner as classical mathematics explicates and formulates such concepts used in science and engineering, "conceptual mathematics" (Lawvere/Schanuel) explicates and formulates at least some concepts used in understanding and specifying (the shape of) large systems. In either case, we are not dealing with collections of *isolated* concepts; we use systems of *interrelated* concepts instead. More pragmatically, many of these concepts and the relationships between them have been defined in RM-ODP, and we describe and use them throughout the book. This usage permits us to discover generalizations and drastic simplifications: we may and do use the same general approach in different areas instead of being intellectually drowned in a sea of numerous special cases.

The most important concepts here are those that deal with structuring—organizing intellectually—a large amount of information. Specifications that describe various systems are written for humans, so understandability by humans is the objective of such structuring of specifications. It permits us to avoid the "too much stuff" syndrome that has been among the most important reasons of IT system failures.

We use specifications to understand and describe the *semantics* of existing systems, of future state(s) of such systems, or of new (planned) systems.

"Semantics" Means "Meaning"

We should separate the semantics of a subject matter from its representation. In fact, having more than one representation helps; as Gasparov noted in [G2000], in order to understand a subject matter, its description must be translated into another language. We are using in this book both a stylized (also known as "regimented") English and a graphical representation; experience suggests that both representations are needed and useful in demonstrating a business specification to its customers. Moreover, when a graphical representation is described as a stylized English narrative, the semantics of that graphical representation may become clearer as a result of such translation, and errors in that representation may be discovered and corrected. Finally, not everything can or should be conveniently represented graphically; and there may, of course, be various, more or less convenient, graphical representations (they existed before UML and will exist after).

Thus, when an analyst discusses with the SME the business fragments of interest, the resulting specification re-represents the semantics of the subject matter from the business-specific language of the SME (which could be understood only if the defaults of the writer and of the reader are the same) into a neutral and much more explicit specification language. Often this specification language is a mix of graphical and stylized English representations such that each representation element (and specifically each graphical representation element) has clear and explicitly defined semantics. The same approach should be used with respect to the English narrative: all terms should be well-defined. This is possible, and the English text of RM-ODP is a good example: each term is either defined in the standard itself or is considered to be defined as in "normal English usage." The source of the latter is the Oxford English Dictionary.

Precise Is Not the Same as *Detailed*

Intellectual discipline requires precision and explicitness. The details—such as the specific individuals participating in a structure—are abstracted out; but the essential—such as the properties of that structure—ought to be formulated in such a crisp manner that it could be understood without ambiguity. This formulation may require sometimes rather substantial effort. And here we see the difference between being able to write a specification and being able to read it. Writing a specification is usually more difficult than reading, but the writer's effort pays off by creating a specification understandable to a large(r) audience. To quote E.W. Dijkstra, "[i]f your text is going to be studied by 60 people and by pondering almost an hour about a turn of phrase that saves your average reader more than a minute, your hour has been well-spent. ... There is only one respectable way of improving your text, viz. by being as clear as possible." [D1986]. It is well-known that a shorter—and crisper—text is more difficult to write than a lengthier one with the same semantics. Clearly, the reader also ought to put some effort in reading and understanding the text!

RM-ODP widely used throughout this book is a good example of a crisp and short text written in carefully phrased stylized English. The foundations of RM-ODP describe the basic concepts and constructs used to specify any system. These foundations are only 18 pages long and require some effort for their reading and understanding. At the same time, the effort to write the foundations took several calendar years of work by a distributed team of world-class experts.

The Algol60 Report is a perhaps less well-known example of an excellent crisp and short text describing in a formal and semi-formal—but rigorous—manner the syntax and semantics of a powerful and elegant programming language.

The rigorous semantics of Algol60 is written in stylized English. E.W. Dijkstra noted in his Turing Award Lecture that few documents as short as this have had an equally profound influence on the computing community.

Papers by C.A.R. Hoare—such as *Software—barrier or frontier?* [H1999]— are an excellent example of presenting the essence of non-trivial IT concepts to a broad audience of non-specialists in this subject matter, including business managers. These short and crisp papers ignore details (that may, for example, change from one buzzword to another) and emphasize the semantics of the invariant properties of software in various contexts.

A clear and crisp business specification may demonstrate the essence— without any details whatsoever—of a business domain in a very small number (five or less) of understandable and elegant diagrams. Such a precise specification demonstrably serves as a conceptual framework for discussions by business decision makers (including discussions at the board level). Some of these discussions may lead to decisions about business process change. Some examples from finance include specification and execution of complex contracts like initial public offerings [K1999], mortgage-based securities, handling of a customer's equity margin account with an emphasis on margin calls, and support of a single-strategy-based customer's position. Some business transformation examples from the publishing industry were presented in [TS1999]. (Of course, when required, the fragments of interest of the high-level business domain specification become refined and discussed in the same manner. The examples from finance referred to above have themselves been obtained by appropriate refinements of business information models similar to the one shown in [K2001].)

As a final example, we may again consider Dijkstra's approach of calculating, i.e., manipulating uninterpreted formulae when reasoning about specifications and programs. This manipulating deals explicitly with the structure of the formulae while consciously ignoring the nature of the specific contents. Using the formal laws of operations on these structures leads to a substantial intellectual economy. It successfully scales up, thus letting us keep sophisticated systems under control [D1997]. We all learned this in elementary school when we were taught that the laws governing operations on numbers are the same for the numbers of apples and the numbers of oranges. We later learned that the same laws apply not only to operations on natural numbers but to operations on other kinds of numbers, and to operations on objects other than numbers. And we have also learned that the same laws—invariants—determine the stable properties of analogous structures no matter what elements participate as members of these structures. This approach helps us to concentrate on the essential, rather than on a huge amount of accidental details, when we look at various problems and their proposed solutions.

Tacit Assumptions and "Evident Truths"

> "I mean, what *is* an un-birthday present?"
>
> "A present given when it isn't your birthday, of course."
>
> Alice considered a little. "I like birthday presents best," she said at last.
>
> "You don't know what youre talking about!" cried Humpty Dumpty. "How many days are there in a year?"
>
> "Three hundred and sixty-five," said Alice.
>
> "And how many birthdays have you?"
>
> "One."
>
> "And if you take one from three hundred and sixty-five, what remains?"
>
> [...]
>
> "[A]nd that shows that there are three hundred and sixty-four days when you might get un-birthday presents—"
>
> "Certainly," said Alice.
>
> "And only one for birthday presents, you know. There's glory for you!"
>
> *Lewis Carroll, Through the Looking Glass [C1872]*

Having a well-structured, explicitly available system of concepts and constructs is not sufficient for writing good specifications. We also need to articulate the tacit assumptions, i.e., make explicit the facts that "everyone knows." Different people may know and articulate different data about facts,[39] i.e., they may have different and mutually inconsistent viewpoints about the facts, and unless the contents of their viewpoints are made explicit, this will not be determined or discussed. To make the contents explicit, we ask questions in terms of the system of concepts and constructs that we introduce and use. For example, when we discover business rules, we may determine that some of them are written and some are unwritten; and also that some of them are due to legal obligations while some are due to customary behavior within a specific business context [KS1997]. Some of these rules may be missed because they are considered "obvious," "assumptions that everyone knows," "never explicitly mentioned," and so on. At the same time, these rules are often of essence, for example, in contract negotiation, especially in establishment and persistence of long-term business agreements. Unfortunately, "in what passes for high-level

---

39.   Even the same person can use the same name in the same sentence to denote (substantially or somewhat) different things. This happens because the specific contexts in different parts of the same sentence may be different, and may, of course, not be explicitly formulated.

discourse, insistence on the obvious can be made to sound trivial and therefore not worth saying" [B2000]. We should avoid this expensive fallacy in our modeling work (and elsewhere).

Tacit assumptions are worse than unformulated hypotheses: in most cases, there is only one such hypothesis (and it is either correct or not), while inconsistent tacit assumptions about the same fact used by different people cannot be correct at the same time. In addition, the tacit assumptions left out of a specification must be figured out—i.e., made explicit—by those who will realize the relevant fragments of the specification, often IT developers who are not (and should not be) subject matter experts. This is a recipe for failure also known as "business rules defined by developers." More generally, the meaning to the person who realizes the specification is often not the same as the meaning to the person who wrote that specification [S2001].

Ignorance—real or perceived—of the subject matter helps in making the tacit assumptions explicit. As early as 1969, P. Burkinshaw urged this: "Get some intelligent ignoramus to read through your documentation; [...] he will find many 'holes' where essential information has been omitted. Unfortunately intelligent people don't stay ignorant too long, so ignorance becomes a rather precious resource. [SE1970].[40] This essential information often is about the basics of the business domain; and when the information is omitted—often because it is perceived to be clear to everyone—disasters may happen. Therefore, the "intelligent ignoramus" ought to be the most active participant in the specification process from the beginning rather than act just as a(n afterthought) validator or tester of existing specifications.[41] Good business analysts fulfill this role from day one (or zero) of a project.

---

40.   See also [B2001].
41.   It is very instructive to explain this using the approach of the Tartu school of cultural semiotics as described by Sonesson [S1999]. Something which is a text in the culture of the sender (SMEs in our example) becomes a non-text or a "deformed text" in the culture of the receiver (analysts or developers in our example) because the "codes" (i.e., the schemes of interpretation)—and more generally, the pools of knowledge including norms—of the sender and receiver overlap only in part. This non-text or deformed text is gradually transformed into a text in the culture of the receiver when the "code" of the sender becomes gradually reconstructed and when new meaning is often generated. Such reconstruction in our example may happen either during modeling meetings in which representatives of both cultures participate, or later. The former is much more successful than the latter. This explanation abstracts from the existence of somewhat different cultures in the sender communities and in the receiver communities as well as from the (possibly) less than explicit formulation of the texts by the senders.

Tacit assumptions may be hidden in a huge amount of information that is supposed to be deep and therefore important. To quote George Orwell, "[w]e have sunk to such a depth that the restatement of the obvious has become the first duty of intelligent men." Discovering and elucidating such obvious assumptions—the background knowledge that is supposed to be shared among the stakeholders—usually leads to better understanding and modeling of the structure underlying the huge amount of detail and is of extreme importance. Different viewpoints of different stakeholders determine their tacit assumptions and the perceived need to elucidate these assumptions. The modeler, together with the stakeholders, discovers, articulates and composes the (possibly inconsistent) tacit assumptions into an explicit model appropriate for the context(s). Various viewpoint specifics are then formulated in terms of this explicit model. More details about composition are provided below, in Chapter 2.

Some "evident truths" are not beneficial. We can follow the lead of mathematics where the abandonment of the concept of "evident truths" sometimes led to very important and far-reaching results. However, before a decision whether to abandon an "evident truth" can be made, that truth must be explicitly formulated, i.e., the tacit assumptions about it must be made explicit. This should happen not only in mathematics but also in science, engineering, business, and information management.

When we evaluate and sometimes abandon "evident truths" in information management, we often return to basics. In other words, we reuse excellent existing ideas that have been around for a long time, but either have been forgotten (and perhaps reinvented under different names) or have been considered too obvious to be mentioned or too abstract (as the map of the London Underground). These "too abstract" ideas have been successfully presented to and used by business SMEs and decision makers (for examples referring to the experience in large financial firms, see [KA1999, BK1999, G2001]) on the one hand, and by high school students [LS1997] on the other hand.

Rejecting an approach, or an idea, just for the reason that "nobody does it that way" is extremely counterproductive. Certainly, some new approaches do not lead to success, but the reasons for rejection ought to be more specific. In software engineering, as noted by David Parnas in his talk at ICSE 2001, relying on currently fashionable software engineering ideas and advanced technology often implies looking for magic tools that will (supposedly) help to deal with the horrible legacy that they keep creating. We need to do much better than that.

Specifying Problems and Solutions

Before a solution is created and elaborated, its problem—or, better, a class of similar problems—must exist (and be understood). This may or may not happen; we all know about solutions in search of problems. At the same time, it may happen that (technological) artefacts provide excellent opportunities to be used in solutions[42] of problems that were not even looked at when these artefacts were designed and developed. In fact, the technological artefacts collectively comprise a virtual machine on top of which a convenient solution of a problem may be built.

For better understanding by all participants in information management work, the same basic concepts and constructs may and should be used to express the semantics of both problems and solutions. Although the viewpoints of business SMEs, decision makers, analysts, IT managers, developers, and other participants are quite different, these viewpoints can be described using the same foundations—in the same manner that very different viewpoints of scientists, engineers, and technologists have been described using subsets of the same set of mathematical foundations, in the same manner that different database views use the same data modeling foundations, and in the same manner that the substantially different Five Basic Viewpoints of RM-ODP are described using the same set of RM-ODP foundations. The same foundations make it possible and even fairly simple to bridge the communication gaps between different participants in information management work, and more specifically, between business and IT experts.

Using the same concepts and constructs in business and IT frames of reference avoids various solution-related specifics when dealing with a (business) problem. In particular, we do not discuss problems of a traditional business[43] in terms of objects exchanging messages, or in terms of responsibility-driven design; these concepts are not known, and *need not be known*, to business SMEs and, therefore, cannot be shared by business and anything else.

---

42. E.W. Dijkstra observed in 1961 that "in the last instance, a machine serves one of its highest purposes when its activities significantly contribute to our comfort" [D1961].

43. As opposed, for example, to the business of legacy OO design and development governed by the classical object model [OODBTG1991]. As William Kent noted [K1979], the way we ar viewing things should not be dictated by the simplistic tools we have at our disposal.

Where to Start and Why: Business Domains

Making business decisions (including decisions about automation or otherwise of some business processes) requires, first and foremost, an understanding of the business problem to be solved. Many, and varied, business problems ought to be solved in running a business. These problems are often determined by the business environment that is never fixed. It appears that everything in business changes, and that "the only constant is change." But is it true? Clearly, many properties of business things, relationships, and actions change with time, and competitive advantage is obtained by means of advantageous changes. At the same time, some fundamental properties of a business have remained the same for a long time.

When we create or read business requirements, we always refer—implicitly or explicitly—to the appropriate fragments of the business domain. We use the nomenclature of the domain that refers to the things, relationships, and actions of that domain, and we need to assure that all stakeholders have the same understanding of the domain. To do that, all stakeholders must be able to refer to the same clear and explicit specification of the business domain, in the same manner that, for example, the parties to a contract refer to that contract (and possibly to contextual documents) in cases of doubt or disagreement. Thus, in the same manner as we rely on an explicit contract when we want to improve our future conditions[44] by opening a bank account or buying an annuity, we also rely on an explicit business domain specification when we want to discuss how an IT system (or a different arrangement of business processes) can improve some properties of that business. Most importantly, we must rely on the *basic structure* of the business domain. Unfortunately, in some circles this reliance may be considered unfashionable, and other approaches and buzzwords may be promoted.

As in modern economics, "[p]rominent, distinguished practitioners seem often to find it difficult to resist the vagaries and winds of fashion, even when they are ephemeral or blow them off course" [B2000]. Submitting to these vagaries may lead to serious failures, both in economics and in other areas of human endeavor. And as in economics, submitting to the vagaries of fashion in information management is made possible by the disregard of reality. For example, an analyst hired as a consultant by a large insurance company initiated several sessions with the business people of that company—as opposed to their IT surro-

---

44.   All human actions are so directed, see [M1949].

gates—and determined that for a long time the IT departments communicated only with the IT surrogates of the business SMEs who were supposed to know the business better than these business SMEs. An outsider who ignored the fashionable was needed for the return to reality that was eventually highly praised by both the business and the IT departments.

In some cases, we encounter fashionable proposals to define a new information management system with, and rely on, stories, scenarios, and the like that are supposed to characterize that system. (These proposals often also make an implicit, or even explicit, condescending suggestion that business experts cannot understand the precision required for other approaches; apparently, "only IT experts can do that.") Such proposals are plainly wrong. They make a very unlikely assumption that the business terminology used *and implied* in the stories—as well as the structure of these stories—is understood uniformly and correctly by all stakeholders, from business managers to developers. Even if this were the case, an IT system based on these approaches is brittle and often cannot be changed when circumstances warrant, for example, when security-related considerations—which often have been in the domain for a long time—should be introduced in a more vigorous manner. This may lead to serious problems, including potential for loss of human life.

A business domain specification defines things and the relationships between them. We specify the invariant properties of those things and relationships, that is, those properties that remain the same no matter what is being done to these things and relationships.[45] In this manner, we abstract out the differences among specific processes, steps, requirements, and so on, and retain only the commonalities. The resulting specification is simpler and easier to understand than a specification based on process details that were different yesterday and that may change tomorrow. At a more detailed abstraction level, we recognize that invariants themselves are not frozen and may change (the RM-ODP concept of epoch may be used to specify that; see below), and we structure our specifications accordingly. Further, we specify business operations (also known as processes and their steps, or tasks in a workflow, and known in RM-ODP as actions) and relationships in which those operations, together with things, participate.

These are the foundations of any business specification. They let us avoid polluting the specification with "too much stuff" such as IT-specific constructs

---

45. Except perhaps during the time intervals while the things and relationships are being acted upon.

(data flow diagrams, objects exchanging messages, responsibilities, screen shots, database records, and so on). They also let us avoid anthropomorphism: for example, in business an account never sends a message to a transaction, or vice versa. And they let us avoid premature decisions: for example, the semantics of an operation is defined by its pre- and postconditions, and we do not have to choose the owner[46] of that operation.

On Communicating a Model

> The Bellman himself they all praised to the skies—
>   Such a carriage, such ease and such grace!
> Such solemnity, too! One could see he was wise,
>   The moment one looked in his face!
>
> He had bought a large map representing the sea,
>   Without the least vestige of land:
> And the crew were much pleased when they found it to be
>   A map they could all understand.
>
> "What's the good of Mercator's North Poles and Equators,
>   Tropics, Zones, and Meridian Lines?"
> So the Bellman would cry: and the crew would reply
>   "They are merely conventional signs!"
>
> "Other maps are such shapes, with their islands and capes!
>   But we've got our brave Captain to thank:"
> (So the crew would protest) "that he's bought us the best—
>   A perfect and absolute blank!"
>
> This was charming, no doubt; but they shortly found out
>   That the Captain they trusted so well
> Had only one notion for crossing the ocean,
>   And that was to tingle his bell
>   *Lewis Carroll, The Hunting of the Snark [C1876]*

A model must be communicated to and discussed with the recipients of that model. This requires some shared foundations, that is, some commonalities between the writer of a model and its readers, commonalities that are essential to

---

46. If this fragment of our business specification will be realized by an OO IT system then—for that system—it will be necessary to determine or create objects—owners of operations, and perhaps more important, owners of invariants.

establish a communication. To quote Joseph Goguen [G2001], "speech is carefully crafted to match the needs and capabilities of recipients, taking account of such varied factors as shared background information, shared values, linguistic competence, attention span, shared past history, and much more." This clearly applies to any kind of speech including business models.

Two kinds of commonalities are essential for communication. First, the syntactic ones—a model has to be readable by its recipients. Therefore, the languages used to represent a model should be as clear and simple as possible: the complexity of a language should never be added to the (intrinsic) complexity of the subject matter. Second, the semantic ones—the meaning of the concepts and constructs used in a model should be understood by the model's recipients.

Business models are used by very different recipients including business SMEs, analysts, decision makers, IT experts, testers, and so on. The amount of background *business-specific* knowledge that these recipients implicitly share is rather limited, and different stakeholders often perceive this knowledge in different and mutually inconsistent ways. Therefore the background business-specific knowledge—the basics of the business domain—should be explicitly included in business models. The same considerations apply to the specifications of technological infrastructure—the virtual machine on top of which various IT solutions have been, or will be, built. At the same time, the shared background *generic* knowledge needed to understand business and other specifications is small and can be explained without serious problems.

A systematic presentation of these foundations follows. You have already encountered most of them in this chapter.

Chapter 2

The Basics of Modeling

A Few Concepts and Structuring Rules

I refer throughout the book to different kinds of specifications. These specifications have to "work together," i.e., have to be mutually consistent. They have to be composed, refined, generalized, and so on. It would be extremely difficult or even impossible to reason about several specifications based on different conceptual foundations; such reasoning would require us to translate (or interpret) the conceptual foundations of one specification into those of another, and still another.

Fortunately, we do not have to speak different languages. The conceptual foundations of all our specifications are the same, are few in number, and are rather simple. I describe them in this book. These foundations are the mental aids available to the specifiers and to all kinds of specification users. They are used to structure and master complexity inevitable in any non-trivial system.

Most conceptual foundations have been standardized in the ISO Reference Model of Open Distributed Processing (RM-ODP) [RM-ODP2]. This standard did not invent concepts and constructs; on the contrary, the authors of the standard chose the most relevant and important ones that have existed (in mathematics, philosophy, and software engineering) for a long time and provided for precise definitions of those concepts and the relationships between them in the context of system specifications. The term *system* in this context is not restricted to an IT system, but—as RM-ODP prescribes—can be applied more generally to refer to *"something of interest as a whole or as comprised of parts."* This is how the term "system" is used in this book.

A system does not exist in isolation; it exists in the context of other systems. Moreover, various systems have substantial commonalities, so we do not start from scratch when we try to understand a system. The importance of such recurrence of abstract patterns formulated in a theory—which may be "a particular way of fitting together statements about the relations between the individual elements"—and instantiated by means of actualization of parameters has been emphasized in the context of complex systems "of life, mind, and society" by F.A. Hayek [H1964]. Various examples shown in this book and elsewhere demonstrate how this approach may be effectively applied for better understanding of different areas of human endeavor.

An Aside: On Using the Term "Architecture"

Some people prefer to use the term "architecture" in the context of specifying and creating various systems. Various derivatives of this term, such as job titles like "systems architect," are also widely used. This book avoids such usage because, in accordance with the definition from the Oxford English Dictionary (OED), the term "architecture" applies only to something created rather than to something that already exists; architecture is "the art or science of building or constructing edifices of any kind for human use." There indeed exists an important analogy between a traditional architect, such as described by Vitruvius, Christopher Alexander, and many others, and an IT systems architect. At the same time, in business modeling we deal with systems that more often than not already exist, so the OED definition does not apply.

However, the definition of "architecture" from RM-ODP is not restricted to new systems; it applies to all kinds of modeling. Architecture is characterized there as "a set of rules to define the structure of a system and the interrelationships between its parts." This definition may also be used to understand what business rules are!

The Basic Stuff:
Things, Relationships, and Actions

A specification describes things, the relationships between them, and actions applied to these things and relationships. We never specify "everything" about the "real world": rather, we discover and select the (concrete or abstract) things, relationships, and actions that are of interest.

RM-ODP uses *objects* to model things of interest (these things are also named "entities"). Of course, an object itself may be such a thing of interest and, therefore, may also be modeled. An object is defined as a model of an entity characterized by its state or by its behavior, and it is the specifier's (and the specification users') choice which of these approaches to emphasize. These choices are not mutually exclusive: a specification may, and most specifications do, describe both state and behavior.

We are usually not interested in a specific state.[47] Rather, we are interested in certain *properties* of that state, and more often, in properties common to several similar states or in certain properties of the collective state of several objects (the state of a system is an abstraction of the collective state of its components). Some of these state properties are *invariant*, i.e., remain true no matter what actions the object(s) participate in.[48] These invariant properties are of special importance. The specification of a business domain is based on the invariant properties of the collections of objects—models of the entities of that domain. *These invariants are the laws of the domain.* We may recall Bunge's observation that laws are patterns satisfied by facts: an invariant of a collection of objects is satisfied by facts, that is, by observable[49] states of that collection of objects. For a simple example of an invariant, a consideration of a contract may be either a financial consideration, or another consideration such as goodwill. Thus, in any observable state of a contract instance (a fact), the specifics of the consideration will satisfy that invariant.

Most invariants of a business domain are not discovered from scratch. These invariants often are specific instantiations of invariants of the business patterns (such as "composition," "contract," "trade," "financial derivative," "foreign exchange option," and so on) reused in the specification of that domain (such as the business domain of financial derivatives). Similarly, the invariants of a technological domain often are specific instantiations of invariants of the technology

---

47. Of course, in some situations, such as criminal investigations or testing, we may study specific states.

48. Invariants may also change (for example, a person may cease to be employed, or the objective of an enterprise may change). We may deal with such changes—when they are of interest—by using the concept of an epoch.

49. Actions should preserve invariants, but within an action an invariant may be violated, to be restored before the action completes. Therefore checking the correctness of an invariant by an observation of a state within an action does not make a lot of sense and may not succeed.

patterns (such as "composition," "B-tree," "relational DBMS," and so on) reused in the specification of that domain. Of course, some basic patterns—such as "invariant," "persistence," or "composition"—are the same for all domains. (Interesting specifications, like any interesting texts, enrich the collection of patterns we use.)

Invariant properties of a collection of individuals—things, relationships, or actions—define the relationship(s) between those individuals. RM-ODP defines important generic relationships (composition and subtyping) and provides a foundation for defining the structural and behavioral properties of any relationship. In addition, more details about relationships are provided in another ISO standard—the General Relationship Model (GRM). We will reuse concepts and constructs from both standards as needed.

Behavior is defined in RM-ODP as a collection of actions with a set of constraints on when they may occur. And an action is defined in a very simple manner—as "something that happens." Clearly, an action considered elementary at some abstraction level may be decomposed into a collection of actions at another abstraction level. For example, the action of contract negotiation may be decomposed into an offer and a reaction to that offer. The constraints on when actions may occur may be defined, for example, by means of pre- and postconditions of a single action (this definition is very familiar from programming and is used in the same effective manner in any specification), as well as by means of the relationships between those actions. Specifically, relationships are preferable when we define processes as composites in totally or partially ordered compositions of their steps, while pre- and postconditions are preferable when we define a single business action such as "deposit of cash to a checking account."

When we concentrate on a single action, we are interested not so much in the invariants of the domain that the action must preserve, but more specifically, in the *action invariant*, that is, in the specific invariant that the action itself must preserve. The action invariant is usually much simpler than the invariants of the domain. In this manner, we reduce the amount of information relevant for analyzing the action. Similarly, the "frame problem" in artificial intelligence is the problem of representing what remains unchanged as a result of an action.

We are often interested in the history of some system. This history is recorded in a trace that is defined in RM-ODP in the context of interactions of an object as "a record of an object's interactions, from its initial state to some other state." An interaction is just an action that takes place with the participation of the object's environment. Here, participation of the environment simply implies that the actions are observable. Because a system at some abstraction level may be considered as an object representing that system, this definition of a trace works for any system. As most other RM-ODP definitions, it was not invented by the authors of RM-ODP. The same approach to defining a system's history is used in philosophy: "the sequence of states (of the system) traversed in a given interval of time is the systems history in that interval" [D1990].

We sometimes use terms such as "operation," "step" (or "task"), and "process" as synonyms of the term "action." This corresponds to ordinary business usage. Note, however, that in the context of the computational viewpoint of RM-ODP, "operation" is a technical term denoting a specific subtype of an action (close to the concept of a message as defined in the message-oriented object model); I describe this specific usage when I discuss the computational viewpoint.

Actions, like things and relationships, do not exist in isolation. On the one hand, we describe relationships between actions, for example, processes composed of steps. On the other hand, when we look at an action defined by means of its pre- and postconditions, we observe that these assertions refer to things. Similarly, when we discover relationships between actions, we observe that things are used in some of these relationships at least for reference purposes. Sometimes we may want to abstract out some or all of the relationships referring to things. Thus, every action is associated with at least one object, in accordance with RM-ODP.

Finally, we observe that various secondary concepts, such as processes and behavior, are built upon the primary concepts described here and used in all specifications. Thus, a small number of basic concepts and structuring rules are the building blocks of clear and understandable specifications in various areas of human endeavor.

Systems, Behavior, and Interconnections: The Basic Concepts of Engineering

The approach described above and used throughout this book for software engineering (including business modeling) is very close to the one described by a modern-day mathematician, Joseph Goguen, when he discussed engineering in general: "The most general concepts of engineering might be system, behavior, and interconnection, formalized in such a way as to include hierarchical whole-part relationships. Systems were taken to be diagrams in a category, behaviors were given by their limits, and interconnections were given by colimits of diagrams; some very general laws about interconnection and behavior hold in this setting" [G1998]. It is clear that our approach is based on a solid mathematical foundation, and that it is very close to what traditional engineers have been doing for a long time, possibly without an explicit specification of the foundations of their subject matter.

The fundamental insights we get from the mathematical concepts, some of which only now are becoming explicit, demonstrate how we can organize our thoughts, how we can understand things and structures better, how we can find commonalities between different constructs possibly from very different disciplines (and be sure that what we have found are indeed essential commonalities), and how we can be explicit about these commonalities and reuse them. The variety of examples used in this book shows that the same general constructs—like laws of nature—are instantiated in quite different contexts, often in a similar manner. This is as it should be; mathematics has been around for millennia and has been successfully used to enhance, and often to make possible, our understanding. Structures of various kinds, such as relationships, provide very good examples. These structures often have been rediscovered in various contexts, both traditional and "modern" ones; for example, in the context of searching the Web, Gary Flake noticed that keywords (that is, the site content) are not as effective as relationships among sites [I2002a].

The Shape of Structuring Rules: Structure Over Content

The concepts and constructs used to describe and reason about relationships are not determined by the individuals participating in these relationships. Specifically, the structure ("shape") of relationships between things is the same as the structure of relationships between actions (sometimes also known as relationships between the steps within a process). Therefore, for an even more specific example of using UML, the same relationship concepts represent relationships between objects and relationships between actions (some of these actions may also be known as "use cases"). Using the same concepts implies the possibility of using the same (graphical) representations, so we may use the same kind of UML diagrams, i.e., the UML "class diagrams." In doing so, we observe that compositions of actions often tend to be at least partially ordered, but this is also true about some compositions of objects. Thus, Occam's razor is again reused: we do not need to introduce extra concepts (or constructs or graphical representations) to explain *essentially* the same structures.[50]

---

50.   At the same time, it may be possible and perhaps even desirable to use different context-specific names for the same concepts. Often, such specific names are requested by (or already familiar to) the users of a particular context.

Consider, for example, the process of contract negotiation. As described in RM-ODP, it is an example of a particular kind of establishing behavior (that is, behavior by which a given contract is put in place) in which information is exchanged in the process of reaching a common view of permitted future behavior. As described (independently and more specifically) in the U.S. Uniform Commercial Code, it includes an offer, a possible counteroffer, and an acceptance.[51] A somewhat more detailed specification may be represented in UML as follows:

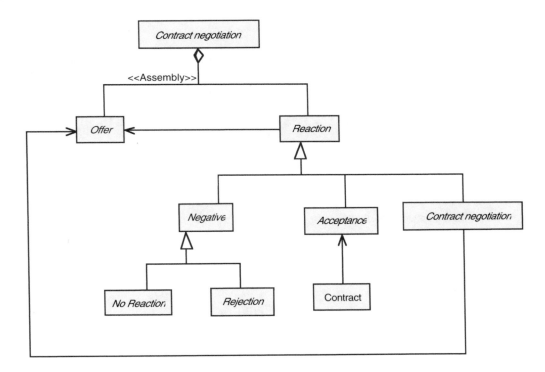

Here we see that a contract negotiation is decomposed into an offer followed by a reaction to that offer. (The offer includes the components of the proposed contract, that is, parties, subject matter, and consideration; see below.) Properties of the reaction are determined by properties of the offer, and this—as well as the ordering of the components of contract negotiation—is shown by the reference relationship between the two. Further, the reaction is subtyped into (i.e., can be one of) negative, acceptance, and contract negotiation. In the first case, the

---

51. Any party can initiate the negotiation. This specification abstracts these details out.

negative reaction (further subtyped into no reaction and rejection) leads to the end of contract negotiation, so that there is no meeting of minds (of the parties) and no contract. In the second case (and only in the second case), the offer is agreed upon and becomes a contract; this is shown by the reference relationship from contract to acceptance. Finally, in the third case, a new contract negotiation happens, properties of which are determined in part by properties of the offer, and this leads to any of the three subtypes of reaction already discussed.

Observe that the diagram includes actions (or steps), things, and the relationships between them. It is very desirable to represent actions and steps in a manner visually somewhat different from things because they have different types. I used *italics* for the names in the action boxes for this purpose.

How Not to Get Lost:
Abstraction Viewpoints and Levels

When in mathematics we use a theorem, we refer to the theorem itself rather than to a specific (one of many) proof of that theorem. Similarly, in programming when we use a procedure, we refer to the specification of what the procedure does rather than to the particular realization of that procedure. And similarly, in a business specification when we use a business pattern, we refer to that pattern itself rather than to the specifics of the realization of that pattern. We do that in order to concentrate on what we think to be essential in the current context (and to suppress the details that may be relevant in other contexts but not in the current one). In other words, we use abstraction as defined in RM-ODP: we suppress irrelevant details to enhance understanding.

Consider a simple example. The U.S. Uniform Commercial Code (UCC) implies that a contract is a composite in the composition-assembly[52] of several (two or more) parties, subject matter, and consideration.[53] In a market economy, parties in a (possible) contractual relationship are symmetric, and this differs from a hegemonic relationship between parties when a director acts freely while wards act only in choosing subordination [M1949]. Thus, at a high abstraction level of the UCC, we do not name the parties; we merely observe that there should be several of them. The subject matter of a contract may, in particular,

---

52. Recall that a composition is an assembly when the existence of the composite implies that its components already exist.

53. The same conclusions can be easily inferred from earlier sources, such as Hutcheson [H1755].

prescribe certain actions in a certain order, and this may include the establishing of other contracts. We may also say that the contract itself as well as parties, subject matter, and consideration are placeholders—formal parameters—to be actualized when we will consider specific contracts, i.e., when we will instantiate the business pattern of a contract with specific parties (e.g., a specific buyer and specific seller), specific subject matter (e.g., a specific financial product), and specific consideration (e.g., fees).

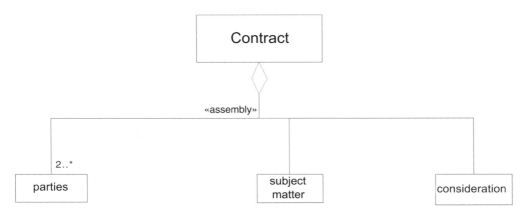

At a more detailed abstraction level, for example, in defining a real estate purchase-and-sale contract, we refine the business pattern of a contract (that is, we transform the business pattern into a more detailed one) and, specifically, refine appropriate parameters. In doing so, no details about the consideration may need to be provided, but we distinguish between parties (the buyer and the seller), and we provide information about the subject matter (the real property, the procedure of transferring the real property, and so on; this often includes the establishment of a contract for a mortgage loan with the specific real property as a collateral for the loan).

At a still more detailed abstraction level, many additional details may be provided (such as a mortgage contract that defines a secured loan to the buyer); these details do not matter at the topmost level of the real estate contract.[54] Sim-

---

54. For example, if a contractual agreement about the mortgage loan could not be reached with a certain financial institution, such an agreement (perhaps on different conditions) could be reached with another party. This change may not matter at the top level of the real estate contract (provided, of course, that other constraints specified in that contract—such as deadlines specified as components of the procedure of transferring the real property—have been satisfied). This decision about a mortgage contract is of the same kind as a locally independent design decision in programming a module.

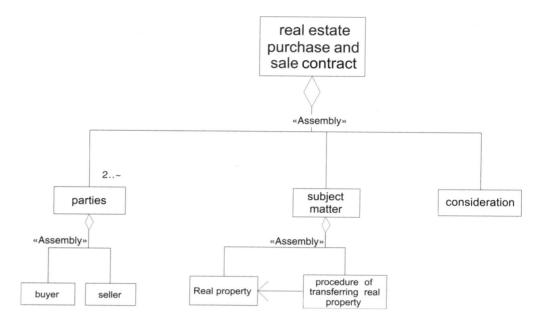

ilarly, and from a different viewpoint, a title search and title insurance contract are provided to ensure the legal status of the real estate ownership. Other contracts may also be necessary. When all these contracts are presented together in a single folder, with all their details, the total amount of information is very substantial, and the contractual parties may get lost in that information, *so that someone else (an "expert") makes decisions for them.* When, however, the information is appropriately structured, the parties can easily understand it and make such decisions as they see fit to improve their future conditions. As discussed earlier, abstraction puts decision makers in control!

The (top-level) business domain specification here is rather simple, so that the buyer, the seller, and other parties of a real estate purchase-and-sale contract usually have the same understanding of that specification. However, in this example, as in other business situations, an explicit and properly structured business domain specification is essential in the inevitable cases of misunderstanding (including questions) and disagreements between the parties.

We often encounter serious difficulties in abstracting out the substance from a semiotically polluted [P2000] environment. The amount of pollution may be very high, and the criteria for separating the essential from its semiotically polluted environment may not always be clear or even explicit. Semiotic pollution results in complexity due to the amount and variety of extraneous material. For example, we all have encountered and probably signed multiple-page contracts with only several non-contiguous sentences representing relevant information; and we complained about the difficulties of extracting these relevant sentences. The same kind of problems exist in using instructions for completing tax returns, using certain software products, and so on. Some of us have encountered and possibly even tried to work with very semiotically polluted specifications stored on long shelves ("shelfware") or in large boxes. Semiotic pollution can be, and has been, successfully avoided: compare the complete specification of a life insurance annuity in [M1835] on 30 small pages with a current substantially larger specification of the same kind of a financial product.

The problems of semiotic pollution can be understood and solved only by separation of concerns. First and foremost, avoiding semiotic pollution is much easier than cleaning up (as in dealing with more traditional pollution!). But if the information was already polluted, then it has to be *structured* in accordance with explicitly specified concerns before it can be understood.

Appropriate structuring of information requires using abstraction viewpoints and levels.

Viewpoints

Different users of a system, or the same user at different times, consider different characteristics of that system. We do that in order to understand the specific characteristics in which we are interested. Of course, we do not forget about the context of these characteristics, but we do not want to pay too much attention to that context because we cannot understand too many characteristics at the same time. In other words, we are using a specific *viewpoint*, i.e., "a form of abstraction achieved using a selected set of architectural concepts and structuring rules, in order to focus on particular concerns within a system" [RM-ODP2].

Viewpoints are used for human understanding.

There can be any number of viewpoints. As rather generic examples, we may consider a business viewpoint and an IT viewpoint of a financial system; or, within a business viewpoint, the economic, legal, and accounting viewpoints; or, within any of these viewpoints, the Five Basic RM-ODP Viewpoints (i.e., the enterprise, information, computational, engineering, and technology viewpoints described in more detail below).

This book presents some examples of using the Five Basic RM-ODP Viewpoints to specify various systems, with an emphasis on financial systems. In particular, we demonstrate how a banking clearing house as defined in the 19th century can be easily specified in this manner. Similarly, we describe a trader, such as an e-commerce antiquarian book exchange. Similarly, the same viewpoints can be used for an IT system specification and for a technological infrastructure specification, such as for a relational DBMS.

But the most important constructs used in a specification are *not* the Five Basic Viewpoints. When RM-ODP defines these viewpoints, it explicitly states that each viewpoint's language uses the foundational concepts and structuring rules together with refinements and additional viewpoint-specific concepts that are, in turn, defined using these foundational concepts and rules. The same approach is certainly applicable to any other viewpoint. Therefore, we emphasize the most basic concepts and constructs used in any specification.

We do not use a viewpoint in order to provide a more detailed specification; abstraction levels are used for that. Different viewpoints are based on different concepts of interest and (business) rules that govern the collections of these concepts. Thus, a viewpoint may be visualized as a projection of a specification that includes only characteristics formulated in terms of the viewpoint-specific concepts and rules, while all other characteristics are suppressed. As an example, we do not include any IT-specific characteristics of a system (such as information about screens, databases, character string lengths, objects exchanging messages, and so on) into its business viewpoint specification.

Within a business, we may discover—when we articulate the approaches of various stakeholders—that different business organizations (cooperating, competing, or otherwise interacting with each other) hold and support different and sometimes inconsistent viewpoints. It may or may not be possible to consolidate these viewpoints [S2000], and in the latter case, it is clearly impossible to provide for an automated IT system that would help. But everything need not be automated: human decision (based on expertise that is too expensive or impossible to automate) has been and will continue to be fundamental in any business. Humans will continue to be responsible and will make decisions leading to success even in the context of inconsistent viewpoints.

As an example of viewpoint usage, consider a document specified from three viewpoints: content, logical layout, and physical presentation.[55] From the content viewpoint, we are interested in a document as a composite in a compo-

---

55.   The main ideas of this approach were presented in [KC1996]. More recently, they were successfully used by Thomas Kudrass in his assessment [K2001a] of problems related to the semantics of using XML.

sition of ideas and concepts (decomposed, in turn, into descriptions, justifications and examples). These content elements should be structured in a way that enhances the understanding of the document. From the logical layout viewpoint, we are interested in a document as a composite in a composition of logical fragments such as prose components (e.g., chapters, sections, subsections, list items), figures, tables, notes, as well as overview components such as tables of content, indices, and so on. From the physical presentation viewpoint, we are interested in a document as a composite in a composition of pages with lines consisting of characters of different fonts, styles, and sizes, as well as of pictures produced in a specific manner, etc.; all these fragments are arranged on pages of specific sizes in specific ways. This arrangement is different for paper and electronic documents (and perhaps very different for documents that use sound, movies, etc.). A simplified representation of this model may look as follows.

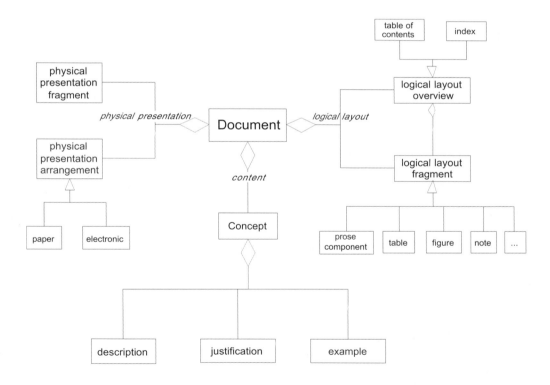

We observe that a single content component does not necessarily correspond to a single logical layout component, and neither of these components must correspond to a single physical presentation component. For example, different aspects of the same concept may be treated in different and not necessarily contiguous subsections, and the same subsection may discuss different concepts (therefore a document may have several indices in addition to a table of contents). Merging these viewpoints, especially in electronic documents, often leads to consequences contrary to the intents of the document owners; we have seen various Web pages with excellent physical presentation and little useful content.

Levels

A program has to be precise and explicit because it instructs inanimate things, that is, computers. At the same time, a specification is for human understanding, and a good specification—in order to avoid miracles—should be as precise as a program; it should provide precision without programming.[56] The most important difference between a precise (traditional) program and a precise specification is *understandability*. A precise business specification should be understandable by the stakeholders including the SMEs of that business, while a program realizing (fragments of) a specification has a different purpose—to be executed on a computer—and, therefore, does not have to be understood by a SME. The amount of detail in a program is usually much larger than the amount of detail in a specification. Different kinds of businesses, such as the business of banking, the business of an information management project, or the business of portals, have quite different viewpoints, so that a SME of one of the businesses may need to understand only some characteristics of a business specification of a different business. These essential characteristics of a business specification usually are about the wholes (composites) without referring to the details of their parts (components), and about the supertypes without referring to the details of their subtypes. Such descriptions are crucial for understanding and for decision making.

Detailed monolithic specifications are difficult or sometimes impossible to understand, even if they are based on familiar concepts and constructs. (Here's a well-known example in a traditional business context: at the end of the 1990s, it was impossible to determine whether certain HMOs—US health maintenance organizations—violated Medicare rules because the specification of those rules was about 45,000 pages long.)

Proper *structuring* is essential for understanding, and we focus either on higher-level (less detailed) specifications within a chosen viewpoint, or, within a

---

56.   This expression is due to Anthony Hall.

more detailed specification, on specific viewpoints that restrict the amount of information we consider at the same time. In order to understand 45,000-page rule books, we clearly need to structure them using several *abstraction levels*. In doing so, we observe that an element, that is, a thing, action, or relationship, at a higher abstraction level can be decomposed into elements at lower abstraction levels. In accordance with the RM-ODP definitions, "fixing a given level of abstraction may involve identifying which elements are *atomic*," while an atomic element at a given level of abstraction cannot be subdivided at that level of abstraction. And information system developers work in the same manner. They are the SMEs for the code they write and reason about, and the structuring mechanisms described here have been known and used by good programmers for decades.

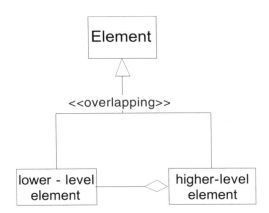

The subtyping shown in the figure is overlapping because the same element may, in one composition instance, be considered as a composite (that is, non-atomic) element at a lower abstraction level, and in another composition instance, be considered as one of the component (that is, atomic) elements at a higher abstraction level. For example, when we decompose a process into its steps, we observe that at a higher abstraction level each step is considered as atomic, while at a lower abstraction level a chosen step becomes a composite (and so we may want to name it a process) and, in turn, is decomposed into its own steps. And when we concentrate on a specification at a higher abstraction level, we abstract away (do not look at) elements at lower abstraction levels. This business pattern has been successfully reused in many different contexts.

The same approach to "our inability to do much" (E.W. Dijkstra) is used in specifying information systems and in realizing them. Of course, using a higher abstraction level does not mean being vague, because being precise is not the same as being detailed (a road map having the scale of 100 miles to the inch is as precise as the one having the scale of 1 mile to the inch). For our specifications to be useful, we have to be precise when we specify at any chosen abstraction level.

As an example, consider preservation of an ordinary invariant. An invariant to be preserved at some abstraction level can be violated within (but not outside of) actions at that abstraction level. Therefore, if this invariant is violated within such an action, it must be restored immediately before the action is finished. In turn, actions at lower abstraction levels must preserve invariants of those levels that may not be relevant (and not even visible) at higher abstraction levels. For example, the concept of an underwriter is usually unknown at the level of the atomic action "application for credit," but is very important at lower abstraction levels where this action is not atomic.

We use composition and generalization when we create specifications at higher abstraction levels from those at lower abstraction levels; we use decomposition and specialization when we refine higher-level specifications into more detailed ones at lower abstraction levels.

The Structure of a Composition

Things can be combined to form a composite thing. Similarly, actions may be combined to form a composite action (sometimes we call such an action a "behavior" or a "process"). Similarly, contracts may be combined to form a composite contract (for example, a contract between a privileged bank customer and a bank is a composite in a composition of several contracts such that the total amount of the customer's deposits and loans is greater than a certain predetermined amount).

The *structure* of a composition is the same no matter which individuals (components) are collected in order to yield a composite individual. We often consider the composite individual at a different abstraction level from the level of its components. For example, a contract is a composite in a composition of several parties, a subject matter, and a consideration. We may consider contracts independently of their components in that composition; for example, a real estate agent (or a potential customer of such an agent) may define "hot" locations as those in which the number of real estate purchase-and-sale contracts per year was greater than some predefined number such as 500, and here the specifics of each such contract are of no interest. At the same time, some fragment of a specification should include both the composite and its components of that composition, in the same manner as some fragments (viewpoints) of a specification should include the relationships between different abstraction levels of that specification.

Composition always implies *property determination*: some properties of the composite are determined by the properties of its components and by the way these components are combined. These properties of the composite are called *emergent* properties. It follows that a change in the properties of components (this includes adding or deleting a component as well as changing the properties of an existing component) may imply a change in some emergent properties of the composite. At the same time, the characterization of emergent properties is based, first and foremost, on the structure of the composition rather than on the specifics of the components.

The previous paragraph describes both the property determination invariant of a composition and the way of its preservation. These concerns should be separated because the invariant itself does not determine how it should be preserved. In most cases, we use the upward view[57] to preserve the invariant, as described above. In some cases, however, we use the downward (rival) view in which the behavior of a composite determines the behavior of its components.

Examples of Composition

You have seen many composition examples throughout this book. Some additional interesting examples of composition are presented below. These examples often show only the essentials of the composition relationship under consideration. It is hoped that they can be used as food for thought.

Division of Labor

Division of labor is the base of our civilization [H1945]. To quote Adam Smith's *Wealth of Nations*:

> The greatest improvement in the productive powers of labour, and the greater part of the skill, dexterity, and judgment with which it is anywhere directed, or applied, seem to have been the effects of the division of labour. [...] The division of labour, however, so far as it can be introduced, occasions, in every art, a proportionable

---

57. This term was proposed by Mario Bunge, although he did not refer to the concept of a composition invariant.

increase of the productive powers of labour. The separation of different trades and employments from one another seems to have
taken place in consequence of this advantage. [...] It is the great
multiplication of the productions of all the different arts, in consequence of the division of labour, which occasions, in a well-governed society, that universal opulence which extends itself to the
lowest ranks of the people. [...] [The division of labour] is the necessary, though very slow and gradual consequence of a certain
propensity in human nature which has in view no such extensive
utility; the propensity to truck, barter, and exchange one thing for
another. [S1776]

Adam Smith was a student of Francis Hutcheson, who described the essentials and objectives of division of labor in his text *A System of Moral Philosophy*
published in 1755:

... we may employ the surplus as matter of beneficience, or of
barter for goods of different kinds which we may need. Otherways
each one would be obliged to practise all sorts of mechanick art
by turns, without attaining dexterity in any; which would be a publick detriment [H1755].

In this important example, different emergent properties of the composite
(such as the universal opulence of a well-governed society[58]) can be inferred
from the properties of its components (different trades and employments and the
people—*individual decision makers*—specializing in these) and the way they are
combined (the "invisible hand" characterizing a market economy and its internal
structure constrained by regulations). The components must be discovered and
their properties must be explicitly formulated. In order to succeed, among other
things, it is necessary to apply abstraction and separation of concerns essential
for understanding and solving any problem. As a result, it is possible for each
person and each enterprise in the society to concentrate on his or its core competencies, sell the products and services resulting from these core competencies,
and buy everything else.

Much more is known about the emergent properties of the composite in the
context of this example. Specifically, "liberty itself is an emergent property"
[F1990], as well as, for example, such properties as unemployment rate, eco-

---

58.   In a less ideal situation, as Mario Bunge observed, it is possible to construct the exact con-
       cepts of global well-being of an economy (that is, closeness to optimal working), and, by
       analogy, global health of an organism.

nomic growth, growth of science and technology, and so on. Also, in accordance with Hayek's observations, prices constitute an essential emergent property that makes possible the functioning of a market economy and that embodies more information than each participant of a market economy directly has. The insight about the invisible hand is an excellent example of explaining not an individual event but rather the appearance of a specific pattern [H1964], in this case, specifying a set of emergent properties. The misfortunes of the pricing mechanism, as noted by Hayek, are that it is not the product of human design and that the individuals guided by it usually do not know why they are made to do what they do. Thus, while the prices themselves are the emergent properties of the composite, the pricing mechanism is the way the components of a market are combined. In this context, we recall that, in accordance with von Mises, the selective process of the market "is actuated by the composite effort of all members of the market economy" [M1949]; this refines the invisible hand concept.

As a specialization of this example, we may look at division of labor in software engineering. In the same manner as in society in general, it takes some time for various software engineering professions to crystallize. Nevertheless, software engineering as an area of human endeavor is sufficiently mature to have distinguishable "sorts of mechanick arts" in which it is possible to attain dexterity. Most importantly, E.W. Dijkstra noted decades ago the necessity to make a clear separation between the concern of specifying a problem—"what it does"—and the concerns of specifying and implementing its solution—"how it works." Different software engineering professions specialize in practicing the art of "what" and the art of "how." Information management projects in which most participants "practise all sorts of arts by turns" are likely to result in inferior deliverables or even fail altogether leading, as predicted by Hutcheson, to a "publick detriment."

At the same time, different areas of human endeavor have important commonalities that are often underestimated or at best reinvented. As early as 1605, Bacon noted that "[a]mongst so many great foundations of colleges in Europe, I find strange that they are all dedicated to professions, and none left free to Arts and Sciences at large." Similarly, and more specifically, all kinds of business specifications have a common foundation based on fundamental concepts from mathematics and philosophy. And similarly, all kinds of software engineering— including business modeling—have lots in common, as demonstrated, for example, by Dijkstra, Bjørner, Parnas, and many others. These common foundations are the most important concepts to be taught to software engineers. The essentials of most foundations can and should be presented to business stakeholders in an appropriate manner, to be used in reading and understanding various specifications. Most of these essentials are overviewed in this book.

Document

We have seen earlier how three viewpoints on a document—based on content, logical layout, and physical presentation—are defined using, at the top level, three composition relationships. Let us now consider three important emergent properties of a document, namely, its table of contents, index, and abstract.

Handling the table of contents is easy: it may be created and changed automatically based on clearly delineated logical layout fragments (mostly such prose components as chapters, sections, and so on), together with criteria for inclusion of the title of a specific class of such components into the table of contents.

Handling the index is more difficult. It requires human intervention to determine which terms to include in index and which occurrences of these terms deserve to be included. To avoid a semiotically polluted index, only the most important (which includes the most interesting) occurrences of terms should be included in the index. Moreover, some items in the index may have a hierarchical or some other type of structure. Also, some concepts may be included in the index under more than one name. This only scratches the surface of considerations important in creating a good index. Therefore, indexing (and changing an existing index) is mostly a human job, which certainly can and should be helped by an automated system.

Handling the abstract of a document, if it is to be useful, should be done only manually. It requires a careful consideration of the content viewpoint. Understanding the essential semantics of a substantial document and representing the semantics as a crisp and very short text is a highly non-trivial modeling job.

This example shows that values of some emergent properties can be determined only by humans, using various, often unspecified, valuation criteria. (Valuation is described in more detail below, as an example in the section "How to Treat Environments.")

Bank Account

A bank account is a composite in a composition of account owner(s), initial information, and transactions. In this composition, transactions cannot be deleted or changed. A bank account is also an instantiation of a loan contract, so it is a composite in a composition of parties (owners and the bank), subject matter (the characteristics of the account) and consideration. Indeed, the account owners loan their money to the bank while the bank, in consideration for using the money, handles the parties' transactions, may pay interest, and so on. Thus, depending upon the viewpoint, a bank account is decomposed using two different compositions—from the contractual viewpoint and from the accounting viewpoint. Adding a transaction may change the values of the emergent properties of the account; it usually changes the account balance and may change the account type (e.g., "overdrawn," "VIP," "suspicious" when a transaction is with a suspicious party, and so on). These changes of emergent property values are automatic.

Saleable Unit

A saleable unit,[59] that is, a product or service sold by a business entrepreneur (person or company), is a composite in a composition of generic properties and differentiators. This decomposition is of critical importance in deciding which kinds of saleable units should be created and developed by the business and which should be subcontracted. This decision must satisfy the explicitly specified purpose of the business.

Generally, a business that is not specialized in producing and selling commodity products and services can subcontract such products and services to other businesses and add its own value (the differentiators) by appropriately composing the relevant commoditized saleable units. This composition need not be trivial; for example, the business of a trader is of this kind. Any business provides unique differentiators by means of the properties of saleable units that it delivers. These properties may include pricing if the saleable units are commoditized, or such characteristics as existing or perceived uniqueness within some context. A business that produces non-commoditized saleable units may differentiate itself either by creating a differentiating simple saleable unit or by composing saleable units in a differentiating manner.

At the same time, market conditions are not frozen, and a business usually cannot succeed by continuing to produce the same saleable units all the time. The decomposition of a saleable unit into generic properties and differentiators is determined not only by the saleable unit itself but also by the context, that is, by market conditions including competing saleable units, and is *context-dependent*

---

59.   Substantial fragments of this example were discussed with Jason Matthews and Mike Guttman.

even if the composite—the saleable unit itself—remains unchanged. In most cases, the context is time-dependent, but it can also be determined by regulatory and other characteristics. For example, the market conditions may change in such a manner that the formerly differentiating properties of the saleable units will become generic because competitors will start producing saleable units with similar properties. An important change in market conditions must be recognized and clearly requires a reconsideration of business strategy. An example of applying this approach for a successful strategy change in a publishing industry business was presented in [TS1999].

Retail Trade

Retail trading has been considered so obvious in the modern society that its importance has often not been appreciated. However, if we look at two examples from different contexts, we will see how vital retail trade is for well-being of an economy. Both examples are within the context of market economy.

On the one hand, Peter Bauer observed that retail trade during the last 100 years played a very substantial role in transforming many of the Third World regions from largely subsistence economies to largely exchange economies [B2000e]. Retail trade in these regions has been characterized by a large number of small-scale actions (and participants in these actions). The actions include selling to the ultimate consumers in small amounts at frequent intervals, leading to many levels of physical distribution of consumer goods (including transport, breaking of bulk, storage, and so on). As Bauer notes, if consumers could not buy the goods in the small quantities (such as ten matches or one cigarette), they would not be able to consume these goods at all. This consumer product affordability is a very important emergent property of the composite economy. Consumer product affordability leads to increases in consumption, which, in turn, lead to increases in investment and capital formation essential to increase the consumption. This leads to a model of an economy in which, in addition to producers such as farmers, many intermediate levels of traders (including intermediaries who break bulk and store it) as components of that economy have a substantial, essential role. Most of these traders are self-employed because these trades are labor-intensive rather than capital-intensive. And, as Bauer observes, the trader often also provides credit to his customers leading to "bulk-breaking in the financial market," so the same person fulfills both the trader role and the credit provider role. Of course, the multiplicity of levels of trading (and credit) intermediaries is explained by the invisible hand of the market: any redundant intermediary level can be bypassed provided that it is cheaper to bypass it than to use its services.

On the other hand, and in a similar manner, modern-day application service providers (ASPs) have the potential to deliver expensive enterprise software for predictable and affordable fees [N2001]. In this manner small- and medium-scale businesses that could not afford the price of a full license (and, of course, the cost of an IT maintenance team) could use the software they consider appropriate for their businesses. Moreover, even for large businesses, this approach may become an important step toward escaping the inefficiencies inherent in today's customer-based IT, which, in the words of Paul Strassman, became "a do-it-yourself cottage mode of production and medieval guild mentality." The structure of the ASP business model is the same as above; as an emergent property, it permits buying services in small quantities by all businesses, including those businesses that would otherwise be unable to afford these services at all. Of course, this example is not on such a large scale as the previous one, but the similarity of objectives (avoiding the do-it-yourself subsistence mode of production and concentrating on the core competencies of the producer), composition structures, and emergent property in these very different contexts is striking.

More Composition Examples

Checks and balances in a government with separation of powers provide an excellent example of demonstrating that the way the components—such as the legislative, executive, and judicial branches of the U.S. government—are combined is essential for determining the emergent properties of the composite. The most important of these properties is limiting of the wrongful use of government power. Clearly, the values of various emergent properties of the composite—the government—in this example are determined only by humans. In doing so, explicit dealing with feature interactions due to inconsistent properties of components is a rule rather than an exception.

A **performance of a symphony** is, from one viewpoint, a composite in an ordered composition of performances of movements of the symphony; from another viewpoint, is a composite in a composition of performances of each participating musician. The way the components are combined is defined in either of these compositions by the author of the symphony and by the conductor. The same approach ("Music is not just notes; it is the way the notes are combined.") was mentioned, in the context of the beauty and brilliance of mixing of ideas, by

Daniel H. Ullman [U1999] in his review of *Proofs from THE BOOK* [AZ2001]—a collection of elegant mathematical proofs.

Semiosis, as per Charles Saunders Peirce, "is an action, or influence, which is, or involves, a cooperation of three subjects, such as a sign, its object, and its interpretant, this tri-relative influence not being in any way resolvable between pairs ... If this triple relation is not of a degenerate species, the sign is related to its object only in consequence of a mental association, and depends upon habit. [P1931]. The concept of an interpretant is very close to the concept of a context within which a text is being considered. It is very instructive to observe the impossibility of representing a non-binary composition relationship as a collection of binary ones. This is as it should be: here and elsewhere, the invariant of composition refers to the composite and all its components in that composition.

An eloquent example of property determination was provided by C.A.R. Hoare who noted that "**engineering** would be essentially trivial if a fast and economical product could be assembled from two components, one of which was fast and the other one economical" [HJ1998].

Finally, Oliver Goldsmith in *The Vicar of Wakefield*, published in 1766, used **pudding** as an example of the importance of the way the components of a composition were combined: "In the composition of a pudding, it was her judgement that mixed the ingredients."

A "Whole" and a "Part"

> The perennial Western malady, the revolt of the individual against the species...
>
> *August Comte, quoted by Friedrich A. Hayek*

Each part contributes to the emergent properties of the whole in the composition. The specifics of this contribution cannot always be explicitly expressed, especially taking into account that the result of the contribution is determined by the collective properties of parts and the actions in which these parts participate. The parts do not exist in isolation; the parts contribute to the properties of the whole in the context of the contributions of the other parts. For example, individual (often spontaneous) contributions of participants in the market economy leading to unforeseen emergent results are essential for the development of our society. In the process of contract negotiation, these participants mutually adjust their activities. With the increased importance of knowledge-based properties of the economy, the contribution of each knowledge worker becomes especially important, because a knowledge worker owns specific knowledge as the means of production and can directly exchange it in the marketplace ("as an entrepreneur" as opposed to "as an employee," because a large knowledge-based enterprise is not intrinsically superior to a small one). Of course, knowledge workers have existed for a long time, but their number was sometimes very small, and they often (but not always) might have been near to the top of the pyramids of not-too-pleasant societies. Currently, the number of knowledge workers has substantially increased, and they start to become the main contributors to the economy [D2001].

As another example, in Book One, Chapter VI "Of the Component Parts of the Price of Commodities" of the *Wealth of Nations* [S1776], Adam Smith describes the three components of the price of every commodity: "the whole price still resolves itself either immediately or ultimately into the same three parts of rent, labour, and profit." Adam Smith carefully distinguishes between these parts, for example, by demonstrating that "the profits of stock constitute a component part altogether different from the wages of labour, and regulated by quite different principles," while noting that "labour measures the value not only of that part of price which resolves itself into labour, but of that which resolves itself into rent, and of that which resolves itself into profit." Further, the same considerations apply to the society as a whole: "As the price or exchangeable value of every particular commodity, taken separately, resolves itself into some one or other or all of those three parts; so that of all the commodities which compose the whole annual produce of the labour of every country, taken complexly, must resolve itself into the same three parts, and be parcelled out among different inhabitants of the country, either as the wages of their labour, the profits of their stock, or the rent of their land."

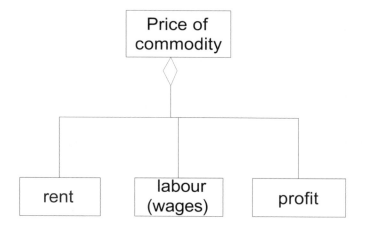

Both in Adam Smith's times and in more modern times, "when those three different sorts of revenue belong to different persons, they are readily distinguished; but when they belong to the same, they are sometimes confounded with one another, at least in common language." The explicit reference to common (that is, colloquial) language in this context suggests the need to be more careful and explicit in analysis than that language permits.[60] To illustrate this situation, Adam Smith uses, among others, an example of "a gardener who cultivates his own garden with his own hands, unites in his own person the three different characters of landlord, farmer, and labourer. His produce, therefore, should pay him the rent of the first, the profit of the second, and the wages of the third. The whole, however, is commonly considered as the earnings of his labour. Both rent and profit are, in this case, confounded with wages." Exactly the same considerations apply to the modern-day example of a self-employed consultant. Adam Smith demonstrated how the business pattern of the price of commodity was discovered from numerous dissimilar examples, and how it could be applied even in situations where two or three of these components were "confounded with one another." Further, this business pattern is used in *The Wealth of Nations*, for example, to explain the mechanism of establishing and supporting market prices. This is an excellent presentation of the work of a business modeler.

Ways to Choose and Combine Parts

When we combine parts in a composition to determine the properties of the whole, we may not be interested in all parts, and we choose only some, but not "all," properties of the parts. Our choices are determined by the viewpoints of the modeler and the model users, and specifically by the context in which we consider the composition. A business specification itself is a composition of various viewpoints of its stakeholders, and the modeler together with the stakeholders collectively choose which of these viewpoints are relevant, what in the relevant viewpoints should be combined into the (composite) specification rather than abstracted out because it is "out of scope," and how the relevant fragments of the relevant viewpoints should be combined into the (more abstract) business specification.

---

60.   In a more modern setting, Bunge observed that ordinary language expressions are just "handy abbreviations of long conjunctions of prepositions" that should be investigated "if one wishes to dig up causal connections and thus find out what kind of objects can be related by such connections." Many business domain models consisting of such objects and relationships between them have been carefully discovered by modelers working together with business SMEs. You have seen some of these models in this book.

In the context of the definition of a contract as a composite in the composition of several parties, subject matter, and consideration, are we always interested in the specifics of the parties? Let's look at a possible specification of a real estate purchase-and-sale contract.

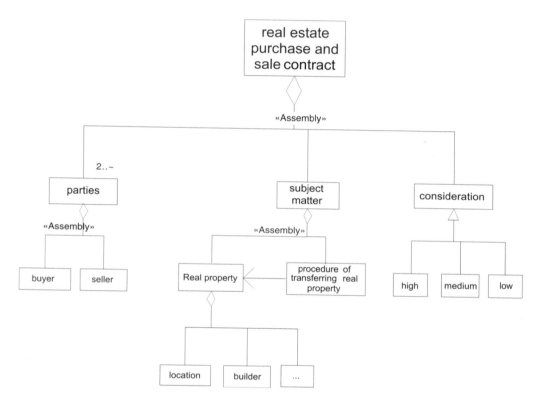

When real estate agents consider whether a location is "hot," they do not care about parties of the real estate purchase-and-sale contracts but rather care only about the number of contracts per location per some time. Another viewpoint would consider only such contracts for which the seller was the builder of the same property (the buyer and the other specific properties of the seller being of no importance). Still another would consider only such contracts for which the consideration would be "high" (for marketing purposes). Parties are at a different abstraction level in many of these cases, i.e., abstracted out.

Similarly, it may be possible to suggest that at a higher abstraction level we do not care that a contract's subject matter is composed of clauses. But this is also determined by the (modeler or model user) viewpoint. Some clauses of a real estate purchase-and-sale contract in a particular location may require the buyer to do some specific inspections (for lead paint, radon, etc.). Realtors may not particularly like these locations. The other components of these contracts may be of no importance (abstracted out) in such a viewpoint.

Feature Interactions

The determination of emergent properties of a composite in a composition is not always straightforward. As we know, these properties are determined by the properties of components and by the way the components are combined. It may happen that the properties of components are inconsistent within the context of the composition. This situation is called "feature interaction" because it was reasoned about in telecommunications, in the context of telephone service features such as call forwarding, call waiting, and so on. Feature interaction may happen when a new component is added to an existing composition, and especially when this new component is of a type different from the existing and known types of components of this composition. This also happens when a system is introduced into a community different from the original community (or communities) of which that system was a participant, and when the invariants of the original and new communities are inconsistent.

Of course, feature interactions happen in areas other than telecommunications. A typical technical report on the interaction of two widely used software tools says: "The crash problem seems to be an incompatibility between XXX's default activation keys of Command and Option and YYY's reserved use of the Option key to 'Print One Copy.' A workaround is to select different activation keys for faxing, so that YYY's keys won't conflict with XXX's." Clearly, the XXX and YYY products were specified independently of each other.

In business specifications, when we combine viewpoints of different parties, we often observe that these viewpoints are inconsistent (such observation may not be trivial because a common set of concepts is necessary in order to compare these viewpoints). As an example, feature interaction happens when several enterprises are merged. Composing the information systems used by these enterprises is usually a lengthy and error-prone process, as exemplified by a (too typical) quote from *U.S. Banker*: "Wheels within wheels, within wheels. That's the best description of what it takes to merge two electronic bill presentment and payment companies" [B2001]. (Compare this metaphor with the epicycle metaphor used below to describe exceptions and exceptions within exceptions. Clearly, simple and elegant specifications provide enormous help in formulating and solving these problems.)

In order to solve a feature interaction problem, we need first to determine that such a problem exists. In other words, both the relevant properties of each component and the clash of components' semantics should be made explicit. Unfortunately, the semantics of some existing components is "in the code," and they are used before being explicitly specified, leading to serious problems independent of whether feature interaction will ever exist. After determining the component semantics, a decision maker (usually a SME) should become aware of the feature interaction problem. The decision maker will make an informed decision that will usually specify which properties of the inconsistent components should be changed (as in the software example above), overridden by properties of "more important" (for those properties) components, or handled by people in a subjective manner determined by the relevant (often time-dependent) context. In some cases, the offending component(s) may be deleted from the composition.

In this manner, the text describing the component semantics (that is, the component models) demonstrably influences the possible changes of its context (that is, changes of the business domain in which these mutually inconsistent components are combined). This is an example of the change of a context caused by the creation of an important text in that context or in other, possibly unforeseen contexts. (The component models, of course, may have been created in some other context.)

The same approach has been used in database view updates. An attempt to update a specific view may lead to introducing information inconsistent with database constraints specified for some other view, even though the new state of that specific view will remain internally consistent.

Determining and Optimizing the Properties of the "Whole"

In many business situations, it is not possible to provide an algorithm for determination of emergent properties of a composite in a composition. This is due to the need to take into account the individual contributions of the components and the often non-trivial relationships between these components. Similarly, it may not be possible to determine which component contributes to the specific property of the composite. As Mario Bunge noted, "... a mapping from the state space of the total system into the cartesian product of the state spaces of its subsystems holds only for systems the subsystems of which are only very weakly linked together. If the couplings are strong—as in an atomic nucleus, a binary star, a living cell, a brain, or a business firm other than a conglomerate—such a decomposition is impossible" [B1990a].

At the same time, in some important business situations, algorithms that determine the emergent properties of the composite in a composition exist and have been successfully used. Many familiar examples of a composite's property determination—such as in group insurance or in a clearing house—are "social inventions" [ON1947], i.e., neither "mechanical" inventions nor discoveries in natural science. Some social inventions (such as a chain store) may be facilitated by technology but many are technology-neutral. For example, group insurance or clearing houses have existed for a long time and have been realized by different technologies.

The objective of group insurance is to reduce the combined risk of an insurer by means of underwriting the type that determines a "group," i.e., a collection of individuals of that type, rather than underwriting each of these individuals separately. The type is defined in such a manner that the average risk of the insurer in insuring a group participant based only on its type is (supposed to be) less than the risk of that insurer in insuring a participant based on properties of that participant more specific than that type. Smaller risk of the insurer may lead to smaller premiums paid by the group participants. In this technology-neutral example, the group is composed of participants of the same type, and the insurability of the composite is considered to be (statistically) better than the total insurability of components considered in isolation.

The objective of a clearing house is to reduce cash movement in a settlement of claims and counterclaims of parties by mutual cancellation. The composite cash movement is substantially smaller than the sum of the cash movements necessary for each of the claims and counterclaims separately. The concept of a clearing house is also technology-neutral: settlements in a banking clearing house and similar settlements of securities transactions were described in books published in the nineteenth century. Here again, we include in the composition only claims and counterclaims (and parties!) of prespecified types.

In many situations, the objective of an enterprise—or of a system in general—is to optimize the emergent properties of some composite. This optimization does not have to be achieved by means of optimizing relevant properties of all the parts of that composite in that composition. In fact, optimizing all such properties may be "trying to do too much" and thus counterproductive because customers who evaluate and compare commercial values (that is, the emergent properties of different products, services, or enterprises) have specific expectations inferred by the specific contexts, so they emphasize—and compare—only some, but not all, aspects of the emergent properties, while requiring all of these properties to be within the acceptance limits. The way the properties of the parts are combined to produce the emergent properties of the whole is determined, in part, by the context in which the properties of the whole are evaluated. The comparison of competing products and services provided by different enterprises should be based on the *composite commercial value* within a specific context rather than only on price, as is the case, for example, when the comparison service is provided by many Internet comparison sites (traders). This comparison is an evaluation by people governed by the properties of the context.

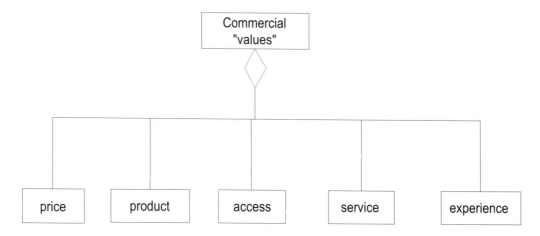

A clear, concise description of this situation is provided in the *Wall Street Journal* book review by Paula Throckmorton Zakaria [Z2001a].

Various kinds of "relationship accounts" in banks and other financial firms are an example of optimizing the customer's experience with that financial institution. While properties of the components of the relationship account separately may not be optimal in competing with properties of analogous components provided by other financial institutions, the combination of these components may lead to a customer's overall experience perceived as optimal by the customer. This experience may be realized by dedicated service representatives; convenience by concentrating many financial transactions, both short- and long-term, in one place; high-quality advice (financial and otherwise); and so on. Various kinds of such experience may be determined either by objective criteria (such as total amount of investments) or more subjective ones (such as customer's potential valuated by the financial institution's experts).

As we have discussed elsewhere, when we want to enhance the understanding of a complex system, we often concentrate on the abstraction level that describes a composite and its properties and ignores the components of this composite. When we do that, we encounter actions that result in a change of the value in some property or several properties of the composite but that, at the same time, are internal [RM-ODP2] to that composite, that is, take place without the participation of the environment of the composite. In other words, we observe only the result of an internal action but not its specifics (for example, a financial institution's response to a customer request for a loan underwriting, or the sudden disappearance of an existing component account from a relationship account monthly statement due to the change of the internal information systems of that financial institution). The internal actions of a composite may be refined as actions in which some components of that composite participate in a manner visible at the abstraction level of that composite.

Multiple Decompositions

In non-trivial models, we often look at the same thing from several viewpoints. Each of these viewpoints may describe a decomposition of that thing. These decompositions may be considered separately; at the same time, they are fragments of the same model and should be consistent.

We have already presented an example of decomposing a document from three different viewpoints—its content, logical layout, and physical presentation. Each of these viewpoints has its own, viewpoint-specific, components.

Let's consider another example—a small fragment of a business model of a customer's position, i.e., a customer's collection of financial instruments.[61] Holding financial instruments of only one kind is considered to be a bad strategic approach, in particular, because of risk exposure. Different kinds of financial instruments may decrease this exposure: for example, an appropriate combination of an underlying asset together with call and put options[62] on that underlying asset may make the position "neutral" with respect to changes in the price of that underlying asset. Some customers for various reasons prefer to remain "neutral," and the diagram below is a substantially simplified fragment of a position

---

61. This specification was extensively discussed with David Weiss.
62. An option gives its buyer the right, but not the obligation, to exercise, i.e., to buy (a call option) or sell (a put option) an underlying (asset) for a set price on or before a given date. (An option exercise may result in a financial settlement other than an exchange of assets.)

specification for such a customer. When the price of the underlying asset changes, the invariant of that position changes. As a result, the customer wanting to remain neutral may want to rebalance the position (based on some decision-making criteria), and to do so, he appropriately changes the quantity of call or put options having that underlying asset. (Of course, if such changes happen "too often," then fees paid for each transaction begin to accumulate and will need to be explicitly considered).

This specification shows two viewpoints. One viewpoint considers the instruments out of which the position is composed and demonstrates that the call and put options refer to the same (single) underlying asset. (Usually, the position of a customer is more complicated because a customer has several strategies.) Another viewpoint shows the properties of the position and the way these properties are calculated. Clearly, the considerations of this viewpoint may be applied to any position independently of the instruments of which that position is composed.

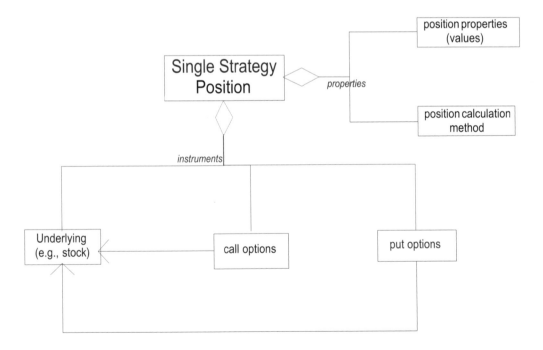

Different Kinds of Compositions

Mereology—the theory of parts and wholes—classifies different kinds of compositions. Various classification criteria may be used for this purpose, and many papers and books have been written on the topic. Charles Peirce [P1931], in particular, provides a long alphabetized list of various kinds of compositions. At the same time, according to Bunge [B1999], mereology does not involve the concepts of property and of change, although these concepts are certainly essential—and widely used throughout this book—in understanding and specifying compositions.

We will not delve into many details of composition classification here. Clearly, any such classification is determined by the criteria used in classifying the invariants that determine compositions. When required by modelers, these classifications of compositions are helpful because they prevent reinvention. At the same time, modeling experience suggests that existence dependency is an important characteristic used to classify composition (of course, it was also mentioned by Peirce).

To be more specific, it is often important to determine and specify whether the composite or the components can exist independently of the composition itself. Thus, we have four types of composition:

- the existence of a composite implies the existence of its components in that composition ("assembly"),
- the existence of a component implies the existence of its composite in that composition ("subordination"),
- the existence of a composite implies the existence of its components in that composition, and the existence of a component implies the existence of its composite in that composition ("list"),
- both the composite and its components may exist independently of each other ("package").

We will not include examples here, but will refer the reader to the compositions defined elsewhere in the book and in the reader's own specifications (see also Appendix B). The invariants that define each of these subtypes of composition clearly imply the multiplicities of the composite and components, thus making it unnecessary to overload specifications with extraneous, and often more difficult to comprehend, information of this kind. Moreover, the invariants that define each of these subtypes of composition imply the specifications of CRUD (Create-Read-Update-Delete) operations applied to the participants of a composition. A detailed specification of these operations is presented in [KR1994].

Note that, in some cases, this classification of compositions may not be of importance or even of interest to the specifiers and the users. In such cases, we use just the term "composition."

The Structure of Subtyping: How to Recognize, Treat and Structure Similarities

Montesquieu observed very justly, that in their classification of the citizens the great legislators of antiquity made the greatest display of their powers.

Edmund Burke [B1790]

Some properties of an individual may be the same as those of another individual. We often are interested in these common properties, and we may wish to collect together and reason about individuals with the same properties (for example, books about Lewis Carroll published in English in the nineteenth century). RM-ODP defines the concepts of a type, a class, and some derived concepts for this purpose. We will follow these definitions.

A type is a predicate that characterizes a collection of individuals. (A predicate is a function that has a Boolean, that is, a *true* or *false* result.) Thus, "a thing is of a certain type" has the same meaning as "the properties of a thing satisfy a certain predicate (of that type)," or the same meaning as "the properties of a thing satisfy a certain invariant (of that type)." Therefore we can ask a question "is this thing of that type?" and get a definite answer ("yes" or "no"). For example, such types as "person," "party," "employee," "full-time employee," "manager," "technical employee," and so on, have meanings well-defined[63] in particular legal contexts. Of course, not only things can have types: actions, relationships, contracts, epochs, and so on also have types. For example, an account withdrawal can have either the type "manual withdrawal" or the type "ATM withdrawal." The set of all individuals of a particular type is called a class (for example, "the class of all full-time employees" or "the class of all real estate purchase-and-sale contracts").

Thus, there are (too) many types. But we observe that not all predicates deserve to be used as types; we want to use only those predicates that describe individuals of interest to the modeler and model stakeholders. We also introduce some structuring rules into the world of types.

We define subtypes (and subclasses) in the same manner as subsets: a type is a subtype of some other type (its supertype) if all individuals of the former

---

63. These are well-defined as predicates—although the term "predicate" may not be used in these definitions

type are also individuals of the latter type. In other words, the set of individuals of the former type is a subset[64] of the set of individuals of the latter type. Therefore, an individual of a subtype has all the properties of its supertype and some other properties that distinguish the subtype both from other subtypes of its supertype and from the supertype itself.

For example, the type "manager" is a subtype of the type "employee," which is a subtype of the type "person." For another example, the type "real estate purchase-and-sale contract" is a subtype of the type "contract," which is a subtype of the type "composition." In finance, a debt instrument composed of an interest rate and a maturity or expiration date is subtyped into short-term, intermediate-term, and long-term instruments. Each of these instruments, by virtue of being a debt instrument, has all properties of the latter and therefore is also composed of an interest rate and a maturity or expiration date. This small example is shown in the diagram below.

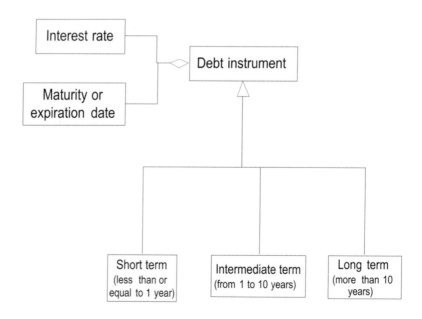

---

64.   The subset does not have to be proper, although in modeling practice we prefer to deal with such situations by introducing and using synonyms because any name, including a type name, can have synonyms.

In addition, we often use structured types, i.e., quote types within more complex types. For example, a contract is a structured type: it is a composite in a composition of several parties, subject matter, and consideration. This type specification quotes the types "composition," "party," "subject matter," and "consideration." (We may also say that the type "contractual composition" is a subtype of the type "composition," but this statement by itself provides less information than the information about a contract as a structured type.)

Multiple and Dynamic Typing

> "...It next will be right
> To describe each particular batch:
> Distinguishing those that have feathers, and bite,
> And those that have whiskers, and scratch.
>
> "For, although common Snarks do no manner of harm,
> Yet, I feel it my duty to say,
> Some are Boojums—" The Bellman broke off in alarm,
> For the Baker had fainted away.
> *Lewis Carroll, The Hunting of the Snark [C1876]*

So far so good. However, the situations in real life are complicated. Things (as well as actions and relationships) in the world are not grouped into a single frozen hierarchy. On the one hand, changes are inevitable, and in particular, individuals can change their types. On the other hand, different viewpoints demonstrate how properties of things relevant to a viewpoint holder can be abstracted out for better understanding. The two classifications of Snarks, above, represent a good example: the latter viewpoint, as Carroll demonstrates, is of greater consequence.

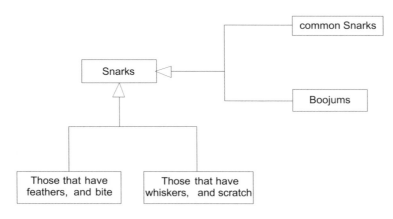

An individual can be of several types at the same time. An individual can acquire and lose types: for example, a person can become an employee and later cease being an employee. Such types are usually determined by the context of that individual, and we may also say that the individual acquires (or loses) the type that characterizes its role in that context (see also the subsection about multiple and dynamic contexts, below). There may be several subtyping hierarchies of the same type (each of these hierarchies uses its own "discriminator" to distinguish it from the others). For example, a project participant (as we have seen earlier) may be characterized in one subtyping hierarchy as being either technical, managerial, or clerical, and in another subtyping hierarchy as being either an employee or a consultant. Even within the same subtyping hierarchy, not all subtypes may be known (or be of interest); such a subtyping hierarchy consists of *non-exhaustive* types. And within the same subtyping hierarchy, an individual may have more than one type. For example, some employees are both technical and managerial; such a subtyping hierarchy consists of *overlapping* types. The predicate of a type—such as the definition of a "technical employee"—may change. New types may be introduced: for example, the type "party" was introduced as a supertype of a "person" and a "legal entity," or the type "homeowner" was introduced into some societal structures in which, previously, the government was the only (default) homeowner, so there was no perceived need to have a class with only one member.

For another example, when we need to classify a book using a library catalog as a classification scheme, we often encounter difficulties because most books can be classified using more than one classification mechanism. In other words, the content of the book (note how we ignore here all other considerations such as "first edition," "incunabula," "English," and so on) satisfies more than one predicate of interest—more than one type. Specifically, the *Alice* books by Lewis Carroll may be classified as (i.e., having the type of) "fairy tale," "book on elementary logic," "book on specifications," "nineteenth century Victorian literature," and so on.

For a final example, an Option is subtyped into an American (which can be exercised at any point in time before or at its expiration date), European (which can be exercised only at its expiration date), and Custom. Independently, an Option is subtyped into a Put (the right to sell during a fixed period) and Call (the right to buy during a fixed period). And also, an Option is subtyped into a Binary (for which the payout, often cash, is prespecified and happens if the Option finishes in the money) and Ramp (in which the payout amount is not so prespecified).

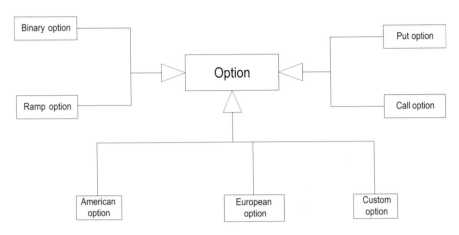

A specification of this kind (provided that each subtyping hierarchy is exhaustive[65]) demonstrates that an instance of an individual satisfying a super-type (such as an *option*) satisfies a type, or several types (if the hierarchy consists of overlapping types), in each of the subtyping hierarchies. As an example, we may look at an American ramp put option. Of course, we may consider only one of the subtyping hierarchies, and for each of its subtypes recall that the subtype satisfies all the properties of its supertype, including the subtyping into the other subtyping hierarchies. Therefore an American option satisfies the subtyping of an Option into the "binary-ramp" and the "put-call" subtyping hierarchies.

We may reformulate the previous paragraphs in terms of classes: an individual can be a member of several different classes (sets), and can become and cease being a member of (some of) these classes. Within the same subclassing hierarchy, some of the subclasses may have a non-empty intersection, and the union of all subclasses does not necessarily have to represent the "universe" of that hierarchy. (Nevertheless, it would be good modeling advice to try to determine all possible subtypes (subclasses) of a hierarchy, even if one of them will have to be named "other XXX" where "XXX" is the name of that hierarchy.)

A business model should represent the real-life facts of interest. Therefore, as noted earlier, there should be no restrictions on constructs used to represent specifications; for example, it should be possible—and easy!—to represent multiple and dynamic types, multiple subtyping hierarchies, and so on. Similarly, it

---

65.   If the subtyping hierarchy is not exhaustive then it may be always possible to add one or more subtypes with incompletely determined characteristics, such as "other XXX".

should be possible to represent multiple and dynamic compositions, multiple decompositions of the same composite, and so on.

Discovering and Specifying Common Properties

In accordance with the definition of a type, any predicate may be used as a type. In practice, however, we do not want to have an excessive amount of types: we want to include in our specifications only the information that is absolutely necessary for us and our stakeholders. Thus, the modeler together with the stakeholders ought to decide which characteristics of the modeled world are of interest for the particular viewpoint of the specification.

Some individuals are considered similar in accordance with the criteria of interest to the user. Similarity is in the eye of the beholder. The similarity criteria may be applicable only within a certain viewpoint. These similarities are determined by the applicability of the same predicate to all similar individuals; this predicate is their type. We may imagine a viewpoint in accordance with which these similarities (and therefore this type) are of no importance, and only the differences between various kinds of the (super)type matter. In such a viewpoint, the general concept may be of no interest, and therefore the specification of that viewpoint may be more complex. Generalization usually leads to simplification and better understanding.

When we generalize similar items, we discover and distill into the supertype definition only those properties that are common to all those items. These common properties cannot be overridden (that is, altered) in subtypes of that supertype because all instances of a subtype have to satisfy its supertype. Property overriding requires incremental modification, which is totally different. In fact, as defined in RM-ODP, an arbitrary change may be considered as an incremental modification if certain criteria and conventions so permit. I will not discuss such arbitrary changes here but will note that the concept of inheritance is interpreted in RM-ODP using incremental modification, so inheritance is not the same as subtyping.

At the same time, the commonalities between something and its incrementally modified versions often deserve to be discovered, made explicit, and formulated as a common supertype of all the versions.

In some cases, discovering common properties of individuals may be useful only for limited purposes. For example, the type "homeowner" may be applicable to various parties or collections of parties, and this applicability is of interest to financial institutions (in their role of lenders), property tax infrastructure, some politicians, and so on. However, the properties of an individual as a homeowner alone are not sufficient to instantiate that individual (because a person, a legal entity, or a composite in a composition of people or legal entities may be a homeowner). We need something else for this purpose.

Templates

When we want to be able to instantiate a specific individual from the specification of common properties of similar individuals, we use *templates*. A template is a specification of those common properties in sufficient detail [RM-ODP2] that an individual may be instantiated using this specification with some other information. This additional information usually represents parameters to be bound at instantiation time [RM-ODP2]. For example, as we have seen, instantiating the template of a contract (as a composite in a composition of several parties, subject matter, and consideration) includes the specification of appropriate actual parameters (also known as "arguments") corresponding to the formal parameters—the composite and components defined in the specification of the contract template. Clearly, the parameters need not be elementary, as anyone who instantiated a contract template can attest. A template may be a subtype of another template: for example, the general contract template is a supertype of various more specific contract templates, such as the template of a real estate purchase-and-sale contract or of an internet service provider contract. A template may impose restrictions on the types of actual parameters and on relationships between these parameters; for example, a real estate purchase-and-sale contract template in the U.S. may require the parties who are physical persons to have social security numbers.

We may rephrase statements in the previous paragraph by using roles. A role is a placeholder for an individual that exhibits the behavior identified by that role. To quote [RM-ODP2], "specification of a template as a composition of roles enables the instantiation process to be explained as the association of a specific component of the resultant composite ... with each role." When a template formulated in terms of roles is instantiated, specific instances (individuals) fulfill these roles. For example, a contract template specification may be formulated in terms of the roles of several parties, subject matter, and consideration (and, of course, the contract itself), while in a simple contract instantiation, a specific person and a specific bookstore fulfill the roles of parties, the purchase-and-sale of the first edition of *Human Action* by von Mises fulfills the role of subject matter, and $450 fulfill the role of consideration.

Business patterns discussed and used at length throughout this book are templates, so the terms "business pattern" and "template" are used interchangeably. When we reuse a business pattern—be it a generic or specific—we are instantiating a template; when we discover a business pattern by using abstraction, we discover and specify a template. A template defines a variety of structurally related instances, and a more general template defines a greater variety of such instances.

When a template is created or used, it is often desirable to look at its potential or actual flexibility. This flexibility is being realized (among other things) by means of an appropriate choice of parameters and their types. On the one hand, a more flexible template—such as the template of a composition—may be used in a greater variety of situations with very different actual parameters, but the actualization of these parameters (and sometimes even the determination that the template is appropriate!) may be non-trivial and may include handling a substantial amount of information. On the other hand, a less flexible template—such as a real estate purchase-and-sale contract for a single home in the state of New Jersey—could possibly be used almost "as is," with a rather trivial actualization of parameters, but in a smaller variety of situations.

Examples of Templates

You have seen many template examples throughout this book. Some interesting examples of templates are presented below. These examples often show only the essentials of the template under consideration. It is hoped, as in examples of composition, that these examples could be used as food for thought.

Division of Knowledge

According to Hayek [H1945], division of knowledge is of the same kind, and at least as important, as the more traditional division of labor. As Hayek observed, "[e]very individual has some advantage over all others because he possesses unique information of which beneficial use might be made only if the decisions depending on it are left to him. ... This dispersed knowledge is essentially dispersed, and cannot possibly be gathered together and conveyed to an authority charged with the task of deliberately creating order. ... Nobody can communicate to another all that he knows, because much of the information he can make use of he himself will elicit only in the process of making plans for action." Therefore, computer-based information management that may be supposed to combine and process all information essential for decision making cannot help here at all. Hayek stresses in his elegant paper that "the 'data' from which the economic calculus starts are never for the whole society 'given' to a single mind which could work out the implications and can never be so given" [H1945].

In other words, the *detailed* properties of the composite—the society—cannot be conveyed to a single individual member (human or [planning] organization) of that society, so decision making within the society, based both on globally available information and on the detailed information that is available only locally, should be distributed. At the same time, some *global* properties of the society, that is, some emergent properties of the composite, are essential for making effective local decisions in a market economy, and Hayek considers prices of goods and services (including labor) to be just such properties. By using prices, "only the most essential information is passed on and passed on only to those concerned." This is an excellent example of using abstraction.

Distributed decision making happens because of the complexity inherent in modern societies, and because many important aspects of the tacit knowledge of individuals can be discovered and formulated only when required within the appropriate context. Even locally, this tacit knowledge of different people may be inconsistent. Good business modelers know that tacit knowledge is discovered and formulated, and that inconsistencies are resolved collectively by the modelers and business SMEs within the context of the specific model. In this manner, a business specification appropriate for the context is composed of the suitable fragments including the articulated background knowledge of various SMEs. Precise specifications of some detailed aspects of human knowledge, that is, detailed models of those fragments of the world that are relevant within a specific context, clearly are prerequisite to determine what is available, what contradictions should be resolved, and what can be improved, for example, by using—or not using—information technology, within that local context some properties of which are not fixed and will change. Business decisions (for example, about agreeing to a specific contract) are made on the basis of these local, detailed, precise specifications. Due to the division of knowledge—which makes the process of intellectual progress possible—these detailed models will not and cannot be globally complete. Thus, *there is no template that could be used to predict particular economic phenomena* "because you would have to insert into the blanks of the formula so many particular data that you never know them all" (F. Hayek). The basics of the business models, the top-level global specifications of the domain and of its fragments, have been and will be stable for sufficiently large epochs (and, as we have seen, are necessary to understand the details!), while more detailed models, and especially process models, will inevitably change. Thus, it may be possible to predict the general structure and properties of economic phenomena, but not the specifics. This was also observed by von Mises in *Human Action*. This template of a society based on division of knowledge and distributed decision making is applicable to all complex societies, and the failure of economies that ignored the division of knowledge was not too surprising.

Corporations of the Future

Various templates ("models") of corporations of the future were overviewed by Peter Drucker in his elegant article [D2001]. Specifically, in most cases all activities of a traditional corporation have been parts only of that specific corporation, in order to lower transactional and communications costs. In contrast, some activities of a modern corporation—such as handling of financial accounting, human resources, maintenance, and so on—can be (and have become) parts of various other corporations and thus have become reusable. Successful reuse clearly requires the reusable components to be precisely and explicitly modeled. In a modern corporation, its activities are subtyped into those that are its core competencies and those that are not. Ideally, a modern corporation realizes only those activities that are its core competencies and subcontracts (on the marketplace) everything else.

Similarly, we may *reuse the structure* of these two simplified models of corporations to describe a traditional and a modern industry. In doing so, we use the same template with different actual parameters. A traditional industry is composed of industry-specific technologies, and this composition is *hierarchical* because the technologies pertain only to "their" specific industry, while a modern industry is composed of various technologies, and this composition is *non-hierarchical* because many technologies are not specific to that industry and thus are reused by various industries.

Thus, the value added by a modern corporation, or—similarly—by a modern industry is most often not in the specific components but rather in the determining of the appropriate components, classifying them in the appropriate manner (core competencies or not), and combining them in a specific way.

In this context, we especially note that a knowledge worker is the owner of knowledge, that is, of the means of production in the knowledge-based economy, and the private ownership of the means of production essential for the market economy becomes immediately obvious (and cannot be replaced with anything else) within a knowledge-based economy. A single knowledge worker is a subtype of a modern corporation. The instantiation of the templates of the division of knowledge, modern corporation, and knowledge worker collectively demonstrates an exemplary modern-day instantiation of the template of market economy well-known from the classical works of Adam Smith, Ludwig von Mises, F.A. Hayek, and others.

More Template Examples

Relationships (including generic relationships): these templates are probably most widely used in any specification. Various kinds of detail may be used in these templates, but mostly these templates describe the relationship structure. A relationship is defined by its invariant, which refers to the formal parameters— participants of that relationship. For example, when we define a subtyping relationship, the invariant refers to the supertype and its subtypes. Of course, we can define each specific relationship without using templates, pretending that it is unique; but such an approach is very counterproductive because it requires lots of reinvention of essentially the same relationship structures. Depending on the abstraction level, we may use and instantiate the template of a relationship, of a composition, of a composition-assembly, of a contract as a specific composition-assembly, of a simple financial contract, and so on.

Reference models (including domain reference models): these templates are used both by modelers (including business modelers) and by authors and promoters of large IT systems. When an IT system is promoted and sold as one helping to solve a business problem (such as automation of business processes in the human resource area), a business should not necessarily be commanded to change in order to satisfy *the* model already realized, or to be realized, by that IT system. Note that a reference model used as a template by a good modeler is usually explicit. If this model is well-structured then it can be instantiated even if the specifics of the domain to be modeled are somewhat different from the ones assumed by that model: the model can be generalized and the result can be instantiated with more complex actual parameters, or fragments of the model can be instantiated as "smaller" templates. At the same time, reference models used by large IT systems are often not well specified and may be very difficult or even impossible to customize.

Book contents and book instances: these templates, like any other, are determined by the properties of interest to the modeler and model user. We may consider a book template comprised of fixed contents (including the author, title, and text) and variable edition. This template is instantiated, for the same contents, by means of different specifics of the edition, such as "first edition," "hard cover edition," "electronic edition," "third, substantially revised, edition," and so on. These specifics may be modeled using different subtyping hierarchies (one dealing with book appearance, another dealing with semantic changes of and additions to the original text, and so on). If we are interested in a specific instance of a chosen edition, then we instantiate the template by providing the specifics of the instance of that edition; for example, each instance may have a different code in a library, or if the edition is a "limited numbered edition," then the identifier (such as the number) of the specific instance is attached to that instance when that instance is created. In some cases, the specific instance of an edition becomes a template itself: for example, a specific instance of a very rare book like [H1755] may be used as a template from which a modern publisher (Georg Olms Verlag) makes and sells instances. We may also consider different instantiations of "the same" contents, for example, translations into different languages; in this case, we may also be interested in the name of the translator. And of course, this template may include the semantic differences between the texts of different editions (for example, the author or the editor might improve the text).

Human actions, including discretionary and unpredictable ones, directed toward the improvement of future conditions (von Mises): templates of human actions are used in understanding and planning of our everyday life, including business life. They are essential both in traditional business and in e-business. It is well known that for a business to survive, a business model must exist and the human actions of that model must be able to demonstrate profit-making [E2001].

Generic compounds used as prototype drugs in the pharmaceutical industry: The discovery of commonalities between multiple related proteins and therefore the ability to design drugs inhibiting many kinases (proteins that rely signals from one part of a cell to another) at once, instead of handling a single disease at a time, is based on these templates. Instantiations of generic compounds are supposed to produce specific compounds targeting specific kinases as their role in diseases becomes clearer [L2001a].

Trade: A trade is a specific kind of contract between a financial institution and a party external to that institution. In accordance with the Uniform Commercial Code, a **contract** is (another template) composed of parties, subject matter, and consideration. In addition to contractual elements, a trade includes information that is not a part of the trade contract (such as trader and trade identifier, as well as risk information [e.g., for option trades] including mark-to-market price). The subject matter of a trade contract is a composition-assembly of a tradable (see below), legal terms of the trade, contractual prices, product (such as a spot, forward, future, option, etc.), and so on. A tradable is a composition-assembly of an underlying asset upon which the exercise of a trade is based (i.e., that may have to be delivered in a physical settlement) and a payment asset that specifies how that underlying asset is or will be paid for. The underlying asset may be a stock, while the payment asset may be USD; or the underlying asset may be USD, and the payment asset may be EUR. (Thus, a tradable is an instantiation of the template of a product bartered on the market, and currency may be, but does not have to be, used for barter.) The trade template is used by all kinds of financial institutions and various customers of such institutions.

Settlements: When a check written by a customer of one bank is presented by the recipient of that check for payment to another bank, the first bank's liability to the check writer in the amount of the check is cancelled, and the second bank's liability to the check recipient is recognized. This leads to the corresponding demand and payment between the two banks. More generally, "in a community where there were several banks, the transaction would not stand alone ... [a]t the end of a day's business, every bank ... would naturally make its settlement with every other, not by making mutual demands and mutual payments, but by offsetting of demands and the payment only of such balance as might then remain due from one or the other" [D1901]. In this manner, the total physical movement of money is minimized. This offsetting and payment is realized by a *clearing house* —an "institution for the settlement of claims and counterclaims by mutual cancellation" [M1949]. The settlement template is used not only in banking, but also, for example, in securities transactions where mutual demands to be offset (as a result of the need to settle a set of trades or their components) are of different types (different securities, currencies, commodities, and so on); note that in banking settlements, we also consider different currencies. Settlement can also decrease the real or perceived risk of the parties. As an example, consider the following specification from the Government Securities Clearing Corporation site: "GSCC interposes itself between the original trading parties and becomes the legal counterparty to all netted transactions in order to guarantee settlement. GSCC guarantees settlement of netted transactions, effective at the time netting results are made available to the participant" [GSCC].

Mathematical structures (e.g., sets, relations, order structures, groups, fields, as well as more general structures such as categories and institutions) that do not depend on the nature of elements—parameters of the templates of these structures: These templates[66] have been fruitfully applied in many areas of science (including computing science—consider the relational data model), engineering, and business. Some of these more general templates have been implicitly employed for centuries, but have become explicit only in the last century.

Musical scores: A score of a symphony, for example, indicates a set of roles collectively performed by musicians in a prescribed manner.

Metaphors as instantiations of metaforms: A metaform is a composite in a composition of a *signifier* referring to an abstract concept in terms of a concrete and widely known *signified* [D1999]. In a good metaphor (and a good metaform), the structures of the signifier and signified are similar. Joseph Goguen [G1999] provides a precise (category-theoretical) description of such similarity for metaphors based on an explicit specification of these structures. The composition of a metaform generates emergent properties of the composite—metaform (and its instantiations, metaphors)—which are often used in abstract concept formation. For example, a metaform may be composed of an abstract signifier *thinking*, conceptualized in terms of concrete signifieds associated with *seeing*; and the metaphors instantiated from this metaform include "those ideas are circular," "I don't see the point of your ideas," "I have a different point of view," and so on. Various graphical notations may also be considered as instantiations of this metaform. Clearly, metaforms may be composed into higher-level metaforms. At the same time, the concept of "widely known signified" is clearly context-dependent, and the cultural context for the successful usage of a higher-level metaform may be more restricted than for its lower-level components [D1999].

In essence, we can say that business patterns are templates used in business contexts where, of course, the term "business" is also context-dependent.

Parameters: Simple and Complex

In any kind of business, we reuse templates all the time. When a party (person or legal entity) opens a checking account in a financial institution, neither that party nor that bank (as a rule) invent the specifications of the contractual relationship, which includes that party, that financial institution, the chosen financial product, and consideration.

---

66. The specific formal systems used to represent these templates are not that important: they may be regarded as "vehicles of meaning, not its cargo" [T1999].

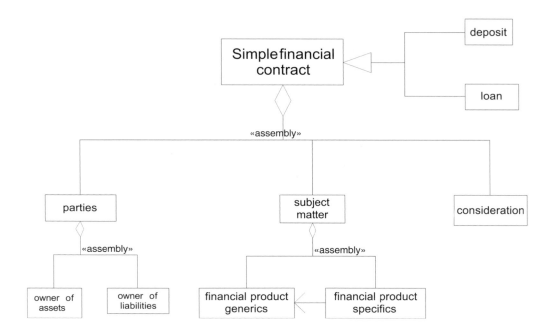

The diagram above demonstrates a high-level specification of such a simple financial contract based on [D1901] (additional details are presented in [K1999]). We see that a simple financial contract is either a deposit or a loan, depending upon the viewpoint: a mortgage (or a credit card) loan is at the same time a deposit of the financial institution's money to the customer, while a checking account is a loan of the customer's money to the financial institution. The parties of that contract include two owners: an owner of assets loans assets to the owner of liabilities. In the case of a checking account, the customer is the owner of assets and the financial institution (bank) is the owner of liabilities, while in the case of a mortgage loan, the financial institution is the owner of assets and the customer is the owner of liabilities. The subject matter of such a contract is composed of financial product generics and financial product specifics while properties of specifics are determined, in part, by properties of its generics. The financial product properties include, for example, characteristics of required and permitted cash flows. And finally, consideration includes various fees, interest payments, and so on. All compositions in this specification are assemblies because the components must exist in order for their composite to exist.

Thus, when a specific contractual relationship is negotiated between the parties, one of several available contract templates—each is a refinement of the simple financial contract shown above—is chosen (by mutual agreement between the parties) and the "slots" are filled in, that is, the relevant formal parameters are actualized. These parameters include the properties of the party (such as name and address), some properties of the financial product, i.e., of the checking account (such as the specifics of permitted usage of checks and of check processing, the specifics of permitted ATM usage, and so on), properties of consideration (such as the current interest rate, rules for changing that rate, fee structures within the constraints prescribed by the specification of the template of that account[67]), and possibly some other properties.

Further, when a financial institution decides to introduce a new kind of a financial product, such as an account, it most probably does not invent the template for this kind of account from scratch. Rather, the financial institution considers a template of a more general financial product (and possibly the corresponding consideration) such as a deposit or a loan and actualizes such formal parameters as the types and processing of business communications (checks, statements, customers instructions, and so on) and possibly the structure of consideration.[68] The result is a specification of a template of a new kind of account that will be instantiated for those parties who will want to open such a kind of account—i.e., enter into a corresponding contractual relationship—with that financial institution. This instantiation will include actualization of simple parameters.

Alternatively, a bank may introduce a totally (or relatively) new kind of a financial product or service such as "relationship banking" or "superspecial credit card." In this case, the novelty of the product means that there is no specific template that might be easily instantiated using a set of simple parameters with known types. The bank will need to start with a more general template (possibly of a financial contract for retail banking) and instantiate it using more complex actual parameters (such as "a composition of accounts" composed of checking, savings, retirement, and other accounts with the total balance exceeding a prespecified amount, and "a package of exceptional services" composed of "points," travel services, concierge services, and so on[69]).

Thus, novelty of something implies that a template for that thing with *simple* parameters does not exist or is not known and will have to be invented or discovered. (Of course, simplicity is in the eye of the beholder.)

---

67.   These constraints may determine the fees as a function of the balance of that account.
68.   For example, "points" or airline miles may be included in the consideration.
69.   It is of no importance here that most or all of these services are subcontracted to third parties.

In programming, a reusable component (template) library goes back at least to a subroutine library in the 1940s (and probably even earlier—to the works of Turing). In 1969, IBM representatives presented their support software in terms of a "programming parts warehouse," which presumably was more than a collection of subroutines.

The algorithm library from *Communications of the ACM* is another interesting example of using parameters when instantiating templates. This library includes several hundred algorithm specifications. Such an algorithm is a template that must be instantiated using appropriate actual parameters (in some cases, the algorithm could be used "as is"). In addition, often the template defined by the algorithm might have to be instantiated in a different programming language (many algorithms from *Communications of the ACM* have been written in Algol 60); thus, the representation mechanism of the template itself becomes a parameter. In order to instantiate the algorithm template in a different programming language, the algorithm specification first had to be generalized in such a manner as to get rid of language specifics;[70] after that, it could be possible to instantiate the specification (template) using a language (dialect) as a parameter. Clearly, this is a rather complicated parameter!

How to Treat Stable Properties: Invariants

The structure of most businesses has remained stable for centuries. For example, the essential properties of banking and services provided by a bank could be studied using texts published long ago [D1901]. The same considerations apply to other businesses such as insurance [H1755] or transportation. More generally, the same is true about the market economy as described by Adam Smith [S1776] and Francis Hutcheson [H1755]. Some specifics of business services might have changed, and different businesses differ when they compete in providing the same kinds of products or services, but the essentials—the basic laws of a business—remain stable.

These stable essentials of a business are specified using invariants, that is, properties that remain true at some abstraction level no matter what actions were, are, or will be accomplished at that abstraction level. An invariant may be

---

70. In this context, we determine what is, and what is not, specific to a language by comparing the fragments of the language in which the algorithm was originally represented with the required fragments of a language into which the algorithm will have to be translated.

violated only within such an action, and, in that case, it should be restored immediately before the termination of that action.

We have used invariants in all specification fragments of this book. Any business pattern from generic (such as composition) to business-specific (such as foreign exchange options) is defined using invariants. The stability of a specification structure means that there exists an invariant that defines the properties of that structure. The stability of an element of a specification structure means that there exists an invariant that defines the properties of that element. For example, the structure of a price of commodity collectively determined by its components—rent, labor, and profit—has remained stable for a long time; the invariant here is that the price of commodity is a composite in a composition-assembly of rent, labor, and profit. For another example, the properties of a person as a homeowner may remain stable for a long time even when other properties of that person change in a substantial manner; the invariant here is that a person has a type "homeowner." In either of these examples, the invariants may be refined.

When we say that structure is more important than content, we emphasize that the invariants that define the structure are more stable, that is, persist in a larger variety of contexts, than the invariants that define the elements of that structure.

We can understand and handle the volatile properties (and actions) only within the context of something stable—the invariant properties. Jeannette Wing provides an excellent example of an operational approach to be avoided: "'If you do this and then that and then this and then that, you end up in a good state...' This [...] process quickly gets out of control. The problem is related to understanding invariants." And, more generally, "learn to abstract: try not to think like a programmer" [W1996]. Some modelers pursue the operational approach under different names, and some better modelers properly complain that this approach (even though it may be fashionable) quickly gets out of control. Clearly, understanding and using invariants leads to good domain models that solve the control problem, as well as the problem of requirements that change all the time.

How to Treat Changes: Epochs

Invariants may change. For example, a party may be a homeowner within a specific time period; after the end of that period, the party may cease being a homeowner, and then, after a passage of some additional time period, the party may become a homeowner again. These properties of a party may be of interest, and in this situation we will say that the invariant "the party is a homeowner" was valid only during some periods of time. Such periods of time during which an individual has specific properties are called *epochs*. In the same manner as in dealing with types, we consider only those property changes that are of interest. Therefore, an individual may be within various epochs at the same time, depending upon the viewpoints used in modeling the properties of that individual and related individuals. For example, the existence of some important epochs of a company—such as that company being publicly or privately owned—may happen to be of no interest to some parties having contractual relationships with the company.

The knowledge of properties held in antecedent epochs may be essential for understanding the properties held in the current epoch. For example, the differences in income and wealth of individuals and groups of individuals can be understood only by taking into account both the current background and the historical antecedents [B2000]. Ignoring these considerations may lead to various fallacies.

A change in an epoch does not change all properties of individuals. Important cultural symbols (such as "Brutus") that denote certain cultural traditions, certain realms of common memory, are usually stable. Although these symbols may change their meaning from one epoch to another (and still another), and even within the same epoch depending upon the context in which they are used, they penetrate through epochs. In other words, the same cultural symbol may acquire and lose types (including the type "being active in the culture of that epoch") in different epochs, but its "meaning invariant" remains the same [B1987].

Epochs are properties of individuals, in the same manner as are names, types, and templates. The individuals may include composites such as contracts, communities, and so on. More often than not, the individuals of interest are composites or communities; the composition invariant may require the epochs of all components of such a composite to be the same as the epoch of the composite. An example of three epochs in a specific banking community (in the U.S. environment) may be in order: before the Glass-Steagal Act, after it was passed by Congress and signed by the President in 1933 (the act separated banking from the securities industry and established deposit insurance), and after this separation was repealed (by the Gramm-Leach-Bliley Financial Modernization Act of 1999) when banks became free to provide almost all financial services. Of course, some components of banking communities might have been "ordinary" banks and therefore might not have changed during these epochs. Other components of banking communities might have substantially used the properties of, and thus changed during, all these epochs. Such banking communities dealt with the same kinds of properties of these three epochs, so we may recall the definition of a type as a predicate characterizing a collection of individuals and define three epoch types for banking communities as described above. This approach also leads us to the concept of *epoch composition*.

Epochs may be composed by means of ordered compositions. The change of an invariant that defines an epoch is not arbitrary: it is an action that preserves the invariant that defines a higher-level (composite) epoch. For example, a bank could have changed through the three epochs the types of which were described above, but during all these epochs it still would have to satisfy the invariant that defines that financial institution as a bank. For another example, when a company changes its type from a renter to a homeowner (and then perhaps again to a renter of 42 office spaces) these changes may be considered relevant to the modeling of that company, and they may be modeled as changes of epochs in the life of the company. At the same time, no matter what changes of this kind are made (for example, a company may become an owner of two homes) the context (i.e., the invariant of a higher level epoch) is preserved. This invariant states, for example, that the company is a taxpayer, i.e., that it has to pay taxes in each locality where it is a renter or a homeowner.

The concept of an epoch, perhaps under different names, is well known in the history of culture. For example [L1992], the (pre-historical) epoch of repeatable collective behavior of a society with a strictly organized (ritualized) structure having almost no distinctions between individual behaviors of the same type was replaced with the historical epoch when individual behaviors became, within some type-determined constraints, distinct and unpredictable (which made history possible). Within the historical epoch, the types of behaviors could also be changed, so the historical epoch, as well as its component epochs, could be appropriately decomposed, depending upon the abstraction levels and viewpoints (such as those that describe different coexisting subcultures). Of course, this epoch change itself can be also considered as an epoch that took quite a long time. At the same time, behavior within any epoch is governed by the appropriate invariants and is often repeatable, so we again encounter the *stability of the domain model* for that epoch.

How to Treat Environments

> "Well, in *our* country," said Alice, still panting a little, "you'd gener-
> ally get to somewhere else—if you ran very fast for a long time, as
> we've been doing."
>
> "A slow sort of country!" said the Queen. "Now, *here*, you see, it
> takes all the running *you* can do, to keep in the same place. If you
> want to get somewhere else, you must run at least twice as fast
> as that!"
>
> *Lewis Carroll, Through the Looking Glass [C1872]*

In the same manner that individuals (objects, actions, or relationships) do not exist in isolation, systems (business, IT, or other) are not isolated and exist in the context of their environments. Thus, we should discover and model not only the internal structure of a system (a non-empty collection of relationships between its components) but also its *external structure* [B1999]. The external structure of any system is specified using the concept of a *community* in which that system fulfills some role. Communities are established in order to meet objectives. Some objectives may be ongoing (such as the objectives of a financial firm or a married couple), while others are achieved once met (such as the objectives of a coalition in a war). The structure of a community is specified using the same approach as the structure of any system: by means of invariants to describe the relationships and, for example, by means of pre- and postconditions to describe the relevant actions. Clearly, an individual may participate in several communities at the same time and will have to satisfy all the corresponding invariants. As described elsewhere, this may lead to the need to formulate and solve the feature interaction problem because the invariants of communities in which the individual participates (i.e., fulfills roles) may be inconsistent. (For example, the same action of buying/selling a service using the Internet may be legal in the seller's community and subject to a legally enforceable contract, and illegal in the buyer's community and subject to a legal punishment.) More details about communities are provided later, in the discussion of the enterprise viewpoint of RM-ODP.

Thus, the external structure of a system is a non-empty collection of relationships between components of the system and components of its environment. The external structure of an *open system* is not fixed and possibly not completely available. Therefore, the outcome of an action in the context of an open system is always uncertain—an observation made by von Mises [M1949].

Various kinds of risk management strategies (and tactics) may be used to deal with such uncertainties.

Let's look, for example, at a strategy of a business firm. The output—products or services—of that firm must be adjusted to the (future and uncertain) most urgent needs of its customers. Anticipating this fragment of the future state of the market is difficult and much more important for the firm's well-being than the technological ability of the firm. Clearly, the firm itself contributes to the determination of the future state of the market by the collective effort of all participants of the market economy (all kinds of businesses, all kinds of customers, government bodies, and so on). Thus, the environment of a business firm—or of a business community, for that matter—is determined by the composition of relevant rules and regulations, market prices, contracts, and communications (such as news, opinions, proposals, and so on). Of course, a good strategist does not make serious errors in determining which components are, and which are not, relevant in the short run and in the long run.

The relationships of the internal structure and of the external structure themselves do not exist in isolation and should be considered in their contexts. In many modeling situations most of these contexts are abstracted out, in order to make our specifications understandable and manageable. But everything cannot be abstracted out. Some well-known examples of the need to consider certain external structures of systems in an explicit manner include computer viruses, legal issues of using MP3 file sharing, and globalization. (The concept of a context for human activities has been considered as an anthropological one [B2000b], and perhaps properly so.)

When we establish the environment of a system, we use abstraction in the same manner as when we discover the structure of the system itself. Depending upon the abstraction viewpoint and level, some parts of the environment may be relevant to the model and some may not be; the relevance is decided, collectively, by the stakeholders and the modelers. The properties or even the existence of some parts of the environment may not be known, and the relevance of some parts may not be determinable. Different viewpoints and levels may emphasize the relevance of different parts of the environment. In addition, the relevance of the specific parts of the environment may be dependent upon the epoch (determined by the system, by the environment, or collectively by the system and its environment): some parts of the environment may become, or cease to become, relevant in a new epoch. For example, from the viewpoint of a U.S. bank strategy, the environments in the epochs before and after the Gramm-

Leach-Bliley Financial Modernization Act of 1999 are different. For another example, some changes in a political environment may change the legal status of an existing business system. The relevant context of a specific environment is defined by its invariant.

Multiple and Dynamic Contexts

Context is a relative, not an absolute, concept. To quote Mario Bunge [B1999], a context is "any domain or universe of discourse in which a given item belongs, or in which it is embedded. ... Example: The context of turbulence is fluid dynamics, not politology (except metaphorically). More precisely, a context may be characterised by the ordered triple: <Statements, Predicates occurring in these statements, Domain of such predicates> ..." These predicates define the invariant of interest of their domain, and different domains are defined by different invariants.

An item (if we use Bunge's terminology), including a system, may clearly belong to more than one such domain (in terms of RM-ODP, to more than one community), and the properties of a domain may change with the passage of time. Therefore, an item can have many contexts, both in "space" and in time. This happens, for example, because that item is of more than one type (such as employees of a firm who are also owners of that firm). Properties, including names, of the item may be context-dependent.

The choice of a modeling context implies a corresponding choice of facts and structures significant for that context. In some modeling contexts, certain important classes of individuals may not be considered at all. For example, Yuri Lotman [L1990] and others observed that, in the cultural context of chronicles written in the Middle Ages in Scandinavia and Russia, only military conflicts were recorded as events; all other events were not deemed significant and were not recorded (they were abstracted out). We have encountered many examples of this kind in more modern specifications where various "default constructs" and events were considered obvious and not worthy of explicit articulation. These Middle Age chronicles were inadequate as models because they contained no texts—or contained only texts such as "everything was peaceful"—corresponding to the years without military conflicts. This absence of texts clearly affects our understanding of cultural history and cultures in general, in the same manner as any substantially incomplete model affects our understanding of (and actions related to) the modeled world.

In any domain that includes decision making, a context may be changed as the result of managing (creating, using, or changing) some important text in that, or another, possibly unforeseen, context. Such a text changes the relevant knowledge or perception[71] of the decision makers in the domain. For example, business decision makers may look at a precise and succinct model of their business (that is, at a new text); they may say, "Aha! Now we see ... we should change the following in our services. ...!", and they may act accordingly. This kind of change of the business context may also be known as a "business process change." For a more general example, business decision makers may look at a precise and succinct model of a fragment of some other business, recognize the similarities between that model (created in a different context!) and the context of their own business, and then make appropriate decisions, changing a context different from that in which the original text[72] of the model was created. And for a final example, marketing texts are created with the objective of changing the contexts of the potential buyers of the marketed product or service, as well as the context of the seller of that product or service. Therefore, good marketing texts are context-specific; each type of potential buyer characterizes the context that determines, together with the product or service itself, the properties of the marketing text. The determination of the relevant types of potential buyers may be of great importance for marketing success.

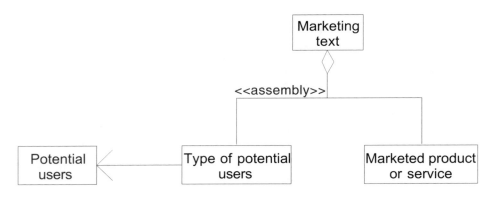

---

71.   The perception may be changed, for example, by attaching a specific kind of a name—a text—to an individual thing, action, relationship, community, and so on. Naming may change behaviors.

72.   As Umberto Eco noted, a text is a kind of tool requiring from both its maker and its user a combination of workmanship and creativity, skill and imagination [G2000a]. Therefore good business decision makers are good readers.

We often are interested in time-dependent contexts within which we consider an individual; the context represented by a large epoch differs from contexts represented by smaller epochs—components of that large epoch. For example, context-aware applications (used in mobile devices as well as in more traditional situations), in order to be successful, should consider several contexts: relatively static (such as roles, skills, and tasks), evolving (such as credit history, purchase history, or the calendar of a customer), and instantaneous (such as recent actions, time of day, location, and so on) [Z2001]. These contexts are, of course, combined in appropriate ways as components of a single context used by the application, as shown in the figure below. We also observe that evolving contexts are composed of instantaneous ones, but relatively static contexts are probably not composed of evolving ones; a relatively static context, or some important properties of that context, may be imposed by external considerations determined by some context (such as a specific employer, country, contract, and so on) very different from the one of the application. This external context, as well as the application itself, is not shown in the figure below.

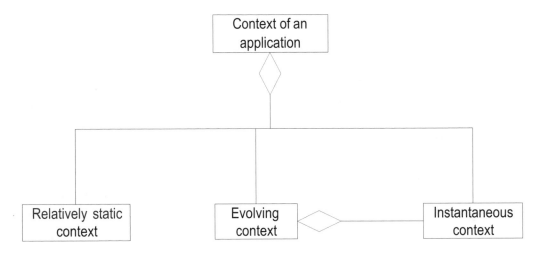

Contexts are essential for understanding and handling of names. For a simple example, using a person's first name to refer to that person is possible only in a context in which such usage will be unambiguous (and otherwise appropriate). For another example, when we decompose a contract as an action into its invariant, precondition, postcondition, and triggering condition, we use terms like "invariant" to specify the component names because the meaning of these abbreviated names was clear from the context that was explicitly determined, in this case, by the composition and by the composite name. And for another example, we often wish to specify that other components exist in a specific composition, or that other subtypes exist in a specific subtyping hierarchy, while the names and the nature of these "others" are temporarily of no interest. In this case, we may use "..." or "other" to denote a name that will be correctly understood only in the context of the corresponding relationship. Names are described in more detail below, in the section "How to Treat Names."

If a template (a business pattern) may be used in various contexts, and if these contexts are of importance for the instantiation of that template, then a context may be specified as a parameter of the template. For example, a real estate purchase-and-sale contract exists in the context of some government structure that must register the contract. This government structure may impose various conditions on such registration, and some of these conditions may not be explicitly specified. We may consider this government structure and the contract registration rules to be a context for the contract; this context will explicitly participate in contract negotiation in the (new!) registration step that is to be executed after the acceptance step.

Recognizing and modeling contexts is not trivial. Understanding a problem outside of a context may be very difficult. At the same time, the same situation may be reused in different contexts, and when we discover the common properties of such contexts, we significantly enhance our understanding and make modeling much easier. A simple example is provided by persistence—the property that a thing continues to exist across changes of contractual context, or of epoch [RM-ODP2]; note that properties of the thing may change. These persistent things include not only database records, but also contracts valid across very substantial social and political changes, programming and modeling concepts valid across changes in sets of fashionable buzzwords (and even across changes in information system properties such as pencil-and-paper or computer-based), and so on.

We often take into account "smaller" contexts, for example, those of a specific relationship—not considered important enough to be defined as a community—in which an individual (thing, action, or another relationship) participates. As an example, we may look at the collective, rather than separate, evolution of a book and a bookshelf described by Henry Petroski in [P1999]. Any composition is a context for the composite and the components. We often reason about properties of an individual relevant in the context of this individual being a component (or a composite) in a specific composition. The existence of such a context implies that the individual fulfills the role of a composite or of a specific component in that composition, and therefore acquires the properties of that role in accordance with the invariant of that composition. In other words, the individual acquires the type that characterizes that role in that composition. This type of an individual is determined not by the individual itself but rather by the relationship (such as composition) in which the individual participates.[73] As simple examples of a contractual composition, consider properties of a legal entity in general compared to the properties that the legal entity acquires as a party of a real estate lease contract, or properties of a person compared to the properties that the person acquires as a party of a marriage contract (or as a party of an employment contract). For a non-contractual composition example, we may look at a book instance sold as (that is, fulfilling the role of) a decoration in the context of an antique furniture store as opposed to the same book instance bought to be used as (that is, to fulfill the role of) a source of inspiration in the context of a private library.

Stamper [S2000] used the concept of ontological[74] dependency to describe an invariant formulated in terms of, and depending for its existence on, another invariant. These ontological dependency relationships are in fact compositions-subordinations: the more specific ontology is a component of the more general one, and it can be defined only in the context of that more general one. For example, the ontology of a society subject to the rules of a market economy provides a context for nation-specific ontologies, which, in turn, provide contexts for various ontologies of more specific contracts, and so on. At the same time, an ontology of financial products and services within the context of a society subject to the rules of a market economy in itself provides a context for various nation-specific ontologies of rules enforcing the handling of financial contracts.

We owe to Yuri Lotman the revealing metaphor of a *boundary* used to describe the collective structure of a text (such as a business model) and its context. The same metaphor can clearly be used, as a boundary between contexts,

---

73. These types also have been called "dynamic types" [KR1994]. Similar ideas were discussed in the context of agent systems, for example, in the very interesting paper [PO2001] and in the context of programming languages, for example, in [KLR2002].

74. Ontology studies "what is there" [V1990] in some domain. Similarly, Dines Bjørner describes ontology as "a study and the knowledge of what there exists!" [B2000c]. It is a formal, declarative semantic model that provides for shared understanding of the domain by people and thus for person-to-person communication. It can also be used for other purposes, e.g., in computer-based systems, by agents, etc. It is developed, collectively, by the SMEs and the modelers. For a modern example, successful enterprise content management requires the knowledge of "what is there," that if, of the corresponding ontology. For another modern example, ontology is essential for successful semantic search on the Web ("semantic Web").

to describe the collective structure of several contexts. Boundaries control, filter, and adapt the external into the internal. On the one hand, the context is external to its text; on the other hand, the text is external to its context! There may be a temporal boundary between contexts (a boundary between epochs), or a geographical, or a cultural boundary, and so on. In the example of marketing texts adapted to a specific type of potential buyers it may be useful explicitly to look at the penetration of the semantics of those marketing texts through the boundary between those texts and (cultural) contexts of those potential buyers.

Examples: Purposeful Behavior and Valuation

Handling invariants that define contexts becomes more complex, and perhaps more interesting, when we recognize that for open systems not all such invariants have been, or even can be, explicitly specified, and not all criteria used in formulating invariants are objective. Some of these criteria are established by subjective human judgment (possibly formulated as judgments of legal entities) and are unpredictable, i.e., they cannot be determined from the specification.[75] Subjective judgment is a specific type of human action, that is, a voluntary choice made by people or legal entities (modeled as parties) and directed toward some anticipated future state. (Lotman observed that semiotic behavior, in which "value is attached not to the acts themselves but to their symbolic meanings," is always the result of a choice.) Subjective judgment results in *purposeful behavior.*[76]

The anticipated future state is chosen from a set of possible future states as a postcondition of *valuation* by the parties (which itself is a subtype of purposeful behavior). This set of possible future states should include more than one element. Different objects fulfilling the same party roles, or the same objects fulfilling these roles in different epochs, may direct purposeful behavior toward different anticipated future states. The realization of purposeful behavior may lead to a postcondition different from that anticipated future state. Purposeful behavior is not predictable, i.e., it cannot be determined from the specification whether an action of purposeful behavior will or will not occur in a given state. The anticipated future state and the objective toward which purposeful behavior is directed may be left unspecified.

---

75. This does not preclude the determination of these criteria from some other specification which may or may not be easily available.

76. The description of purposeful behavior was formulated in the context of preparing the US contribution to the standardization of the enterprise viewpoint of RM-ODP and has been extensively discussed with William Frank and Joaquin Miller.

Most actions in which a party participates are purposeful because the set of possible future states in most cases includes more than one element (for example, due to possible violations of prescribed behavior). This contrasts with actions in which only non-parties participate. Therefore, the specifier, together with the owner of the specification, must decide which of these party actions are of interest to be included in the specification as elements of purposeful behavior.

An example of purposeful behavior of interest to the specifier includes the offer, counteroffer, and acceptance of an agreement that may be modeled as a contract. Another well-known example is shown in the subjective change by a person (for example, fulfilling the role of an underwriter) of the result of a presumably non-subjective valuation performed by a credit assessment algorithm (the process by which a person without a credit history may get credit). Still another example includes modeling of regulatory violations by financial institution employees; it is the specifier's (and specification owner's) choice which of these possible violations should be modeled in the specification.

When a person or legal entity delegates a purposeful behavior to an information system, that system will choose from a predetermined set of future states according to predetermined criteria. (When the information system is able to generate new behaviors or new choice criteria, the set of all those behaviors and choice criteria is predetermined in the specification of the system.)

Valuation is context-dependent due to human and voluntaristic character of value judgements. As von Mises stressed in *Human Action*, the value of a thing or a service exchanged on the market is not objective; rather, it is an expression of the eagerness of various people to acquire that thing or service. The disparity in the values attached to the things or services being exchanged results in their being exchanged [M1949]. Thus, valuation means expressing a preference.

For example, as observed by von Mises, an evaluation of all non-cash assets and liabilities of a business account has an uncertain and speculative character. In more modern times, the high valuation of "dot-com" stocks represents an example that many consider to be disadvantageous. For a more advantageous example in the same general context, a party (person or company) often finds an e-commerce exchange (that is, a trader described in more detail below) valuable in a situation with many buyers and sellers who differ in their valuation of products. Indeed, those who buy (or sell) antiquarian books find that the valuation (process and result) of those books changed rather substantially as the result of opportunities provided by the antiquarian book e-commerce exchanges. The user of such an exchange can even try to be an arbitrageur, although this may not be trivial because liquidity at the antiquarian book market does not always happen (when needed by a specific market participant). More generally, both buyers and sellers at an e-commerce antiquarian book exchange can often create and execute contracts that improve the future conditions of these buyers and sellers (according to von Mises) to a greater extent than in the absence of such an exchange. This happens because markets are more effective when there are more choices—various anticipated future states. Of course, this kind of observation is not new. A similar template was described by Adam Smith:

> As by means of water-carriage a more extensive market is opened to every sort of industry than what land-carriage alone can afford it, so it is upon the sea-coast, and along the banks of navigable rivers, that industry of every kind naturally begins to subdivide and improve itself, and it is frequently not till a long time after that those improvements extend themselves to the inland parts of the country. [S1776]

Contracts and Their Contexts

We have already described a contract as a composite in the composition of several parties, subject matter, and consideration, and we have used this description extensively. We also looked at some other viewpoints on a contract: for example, we considered the contract negotiation process and a contract as an action, with its invariant, pre- and postconditions, and triggering condition. There may be other viewpoints on a contract: for example, it may be important whether a contract is ongoing, that is, valid until explicitly destroyed by an action specified in the subject matter of that contract (such as a marriage contract, a partnership contract, or an employment contract), or a contract serves a particular purpose that is achieved once met (such as a purchase-and-sale contract). A contract can include quality of service requirements (in its subject matter or consideration), for example, temporal constraints such as deadlines, location constraints, failure probabilities, and so on.

Let's make some observations about these kinds of specifications. In all the viewpoints above, we described generic contracts rather than specific ones. Even when we considered more specialized contracts, such as a real estate purchase-and-sale contract, we still dealt with generic contracts. These specifications were contract templates that should be instantiated for a specific contract. As in any template, instantiation includes actualization of parameters, so that we need to provide for the following:

- specific people or organizations as actual parameters fulfilling the roles of contractual parties,

- specific subject matter (such as a checking account with interest as specified in the following reference: [XXX]) fulfilling the role of subject matter, and
- specific consideration (such as specific fees for handling the account and specific interest paid to the accountholder(s)) fulfilling the role of consideration.

Note that the specification of a contract—like any template—may include an invariant that places restrictions on the properties of the actual parameters that fulfill some of the roles; for example, in the U.S. only a person with a valid social security number may be the owner of an individual checking account.

RM-ODP defines a contractual context as "the knowledge that a particular contract is in place, and thus that a particular behaviour of a set of objects is required." This definition corresponds to the more general definition of a context discussed earlier. It describes (defines) the invariant of the contractual context that must be collectively satisfied by the objects of that set of objects. A contractual behavior changes some properties of the relevant set of objects, but does not change the contractual context. Of course, eventually the contract may terminate: "The [terminating] behaviour ... repudiates the corresponding contractual context and the corresponding contract." Thus, when we consider a contract as an action, the contract's invariant defined as the contractual context is the same as the action's invariant. Moreover, the same individual may be in several contractual contexts at the same time, and in this case we may compose these contexts into a composite single context. The invariants of the component contexts should be consistent, and if they are not, then we again deal with the feature interaction problem when a human decision becomes essential for resolution.

As an example, a specific person is not always a part of a specific contract (does not fulfill the role of a party of that contract). Becoming a part of such a contract by virtue of fulfilling the role of contractual party changes some properties of a person and may be specified as starting a new epoch for that person. (Some contracts are clearly more important than others in this respect; the value of "importance" is defined by the viewpoint.) The properties acquired by a person by virtue of becoming a party to the contract clearly influence other existing or potential properties of that person. For example, a bank or some other organization may consider marketing and selling certain products or services to a newly established owner of a checking account ("cross-selling"). This kind of marketing is usually not person-specific, but rather specific to the particular role of a particular template and, as such, may be described by another ("marketing") template. For another example, the person's behavior in the new epoch may change in some ways that are not immediately apparent from the contract template itself but follow from the composition of the newly acquired properties with the already existing properties of that person. Of course, such behavioral patterns that describe the possible new interests of a person in the context of the person's existing properties are of great interest in market research.

Trading

Contracts are not established in a vacuum. Parties look for each other in order to negotiate and establish a contract, and specifically they search for information about the types of products or services provided or sought by other parties. This kind of search may be non-trivial if the product or service is not a commodity. The information about such products or services may be recorded and provided by a "trader": for example, several Web sites collect and provide information about antiquarian book sellers.

A trader was specified as an international standard [T1996] within the family of RM-ODP standards. We only scratch the surface of some fragments of this specification here. It is written using the Five Basic Viewpoints (described in more detail below, see the corresponding section), and its fragments exhibit excellent approaches to specification writing. More specifically, the substance of the trader specification in its information viewpoint is written using the formal specification language Z (itself an international standard) and translated into structured English. Each fragment of the information viewpoint specification—an invariant or an action specification—is written in both languages, so that readers who do not want to read Z can skip the Z fragments,[77] while in cases of doubt or possible misunderstandings, of course, the Z fragments should be relied upon.

A trader can be viewed [T1996] as an object through which other objects can advertise their capabilities (that is, offer services claimed to meet some statement of requirements—i.e., offer a potential contract—or "export") and match their needs against advertised capabilities (that is, discover such services in order to allow the establishment of a contract, or "import"). To export, an object gives the trader a description of a service and the location of an interface at which that service is available. To import, an object asks the trader for a service having cer-

---

77.   In the same manner, a reader who does not want to look at pictures can skip the figures and read only the translation of the specifications from the pictorial representation into a structured English one. There are no pictures in the information viewpoint specification of the trading function.

tain characteristics, that is, a service of a certain type. The trader checks against the descriptions of services and responds to the importer with the location(s) of the selected services interface. Clearly, there may be more than one trader, and we can imagine a trader that, among other things, provides information about specific trading services.

In our antiquarian book example, the Web site *www.abebooks.com* points to a trader that collects information about specific antiquarian (and used) books from book dealers and publishes this information. In this manner, book dealers advertise the books they offer for sale. Customers ask the trader for antiquarian (or used) books having certain characteristics, and the trader responds with a list of books (if any) satisfying these characteristics and the location(s) of the book dealers offering these books. Further contractual negotiations may be accomplished between the book dealer and the customer. In addition, other traders provide the same kind of Internet services about antiquarian books, and certain traders provide information about such trading services.

The enterprise and information viewpoint specifications of the trader in [T1996] are probably the most interesting and important for us to understand the semantics of the trader.

The three-page enterprise viewpoint specification defines the purpose, scope, and policies of the trader, as well as the trading community in terms of its roles and policies. In particular, the trading community is defined in terms of the roles of a trader, an exporter, an importer, a trader administrator, a trader policy maker, and a service offer. Policies—sets of rules related to a particular purpose—are defined for export, import, arbitration, service offer acceptance, type management, offer placement, and search. The export policy, for example, may include an obligation for a service offer to be described in a specific way (as the antiquarian book vendors do when they describe the books they offer), a prohibition of specified service import activities from discovering the service offer, and a permission for the service export to be propagated to an interworking trading community. Further, the enterprise specification defines various structuring rules of the trading community, such as "a single trading community (at one level of abstraction) may be refined into a number of interworking trading communities at a second, more detailed level of abstraction."

The thirteen-page information viewpoint specification defines the things and relationships of the trading community, and then defines actions referring to these things and relationships. Actions are defined by means of pre- and post-conditions. In particular, a service description is composed of an interface signature type and a set of service properties, while a service offer is composed of a service description, an identifier of that offer, an identifier of an interface, and a set of service offer properties. Further, the search action uses three kinds of specific search criteria to determine the set of acceptable service offers: matching criteria—a set of service offers defining the essential properties that cannot be violated (in our antiquarian book example, it may be a specific edition of a specific book), preference criteria—a partial function from a set of service offers to an ordered sequence of acceptable service offers (for example, ordered by price), and scope criteria—a set of service offers that restrict the service offers to be compared with matching rules (for example, only members of antiquarian book dealer associations of their countries). In addition, the interface signature type and criteria types for all service offers that satisfy a search request must be subtypes of those specified in that search request. For example, the search request may specify first editions of any book by Lewis Carroll, and the service offers that satisfy the request will include offers by dealers proposing the first editions of the *Alice* books, *The Hunting of the Snark*, *The Game of Logic*, and so on. Applying matching and scope criteria means intersecting the corresponding sets of service offers while taking this subtyping into account.

Finally, the trader pattern can be used in situations when the number of buyers and sellers is large, as in antiquarian book exchanges, and in business-to-business exchanges when, for example, there are many sellers and only a few buyers (demand oligopsonies) [S2000a]. The contract negotiation mechanisms (such as bidding and reverse auctions) and possible cooperation between buyers and sellers in product specification and design becomes possible by using and expanding the trader pattern.

How to Treat Names

Names are arbitrary tags attached to things in order to refer to these things. RM-ODP defines a name as a *term* (linguistic construct) that, in a given naming context, refers to an entity. (Of course, we also use names to refer to actions, relationships, predicates, and so on, as well as to abbreviate concepts.) A context is essential for using names.[78] This context may be time-dependent: the term "services that may be provided by a bank" in the U.S. referred to different things in

---

78.   "Only in the context of a proposition has a name meaning" [W1933].

the epochs before and after the Gramm-Leach-Bliley Financial Modernization Act of 1999.

Usage of a particular name (even together with a context) by itself does not mean understanding of the semantics of an individual or individuals denoted by that name. William Kent presents an excellent discussion with numerous convincing examples in [K1979]. Different naming contexts may evoke different connotations for the same name by different readers (as in the UML-specific example of using the name "composition," see below; or in using the name "model"), and the name writer cannot control this [vG1990]. Substantially different connotations are relatively easy to determine. However, somewhat different connotations are notoriously different to discover, and such discoveries require clear and explicit specifications of contexts.

As an example from the financial domain, consider "trade confirmation." After a trade contract has been agreed upon between parties, that trade is considered to be "done," and all subsequent steps in trade processing should be based on this mutually agreed upon contract. However, misunderstandings happen (humans make mistakes), so the specification of the trade contract apparently agreed upon verbally should be confirmed in a more visible manner. To do that, the perceptions of the properties of the contract by the parties of that contract must be compared. When this was modeled in a large financial institution, the analyst and the SMEs had lengthy discussions about trade confirmation (eventually resulting in several non-trivial diagrams about that). And it was very instructive how the SMEs at the beginning said that confirmation was very simple ("everyone knows that"), and then, when the analyst started asking questions *based on the definitions of generic relationships*, these same SMEs realized that what they were telling was only a part, and possibly not the most important part, of the story. Different SMEs have different viewpoints on the structures of trade and trade confirmation, so different departments (in front and back office) of a financial institution may *implicitly* refer to subtly different things named "confirmation" or "confirmed trade." In order to discover these differences, it is necessary to specify, explicitly and precisely, the viewpoint-specific appropriate details of the trade contract and trade processing. Only after such specifications became explicit was it possible to look at the various viewpoint-specific contexts of "confirmation" explicitly, and as a result to consider the business processes of trade processing and to improve these processes, specifically their trade confirmation steps. This was extremely important for improving the business processes, and the SMEs, without the explicit model, could not even get a handle on that, although they wanted to do something for several years! There was a clear "Aha!" feeling among all participants in the modeling process.

A name need not refer to a unique entity: consider a name such as "customer service representative." In such a situation, we choose an element of a set in accordance with some choice criteria, and if more than one element satisfies these criteria (so that "the delivery of any object which answers to the generic description will satisfy the terms of the obligation" [A1832]), we do not care which specific element is chosen, but we often want to reason about that element and refer to it; so we use a name for this purpose. This non-determinism happens quite often in business.

Some names—*identifiers*—are unambiguous and do refer to a unique entity, but again, this happens only in a given context. The same name may refer to different entities in different contexts. For example, "this book" refers to a context-specific book. As noted earlier, a first name can be used to refer to a person only in a very restricted context. Also, identifiers of formal parameters in the specification of a procedure, or of a relationship (such as "parties" in the specification of a contract), refer to unique individuals only within the context of the specification of that procedure or that relationship.

Clearly, an entity may have several names (and several identifiers) even in the same context. Consider three identifiers of the book you are now reading in the context of an e-commerce book trader: *Business Modeling* by Haim Kilov, published by Prentice-Hall in 2002; ISBN 0-13-062135-8; the book by Haim Kilov published by Prentice-Hall in 2002. There may also be other identifiers. In the context of a tutorial based on this book, the name "the book" may well be an identifier. (These identifiers do not refer to a specific instance of the book, so the term "identifier" is also context-dependent!)

Can We Discover "The Only Correct Name"?

It is neither possible nor even desirable to determine that a specific name of an individual (or a property) is "correct" and all other names are not. A name is defined only in its context. Therefore, if a thing has different names in different contexts, then any determination of a name as being "correct" will make the owners and users of that context happy and will make the owners and users of other contexts less so. (Consider, for example, different linguistic contexts determined by different natural languages used in specific locations in space and time.) Moreover, declaring a specific name or a structure of names to be "correct" may seriously restrict possible behaviors because the action of naming may change existing or permitted behaviors.

If any name will be used only as a qualified name, i.e., only together with its context, then there will be no need to determine which of several names of an individual is correct. All names will be correct in their contexts. Of course, in some situations the default context may be specified only once (e.g., to oversimplify, "U.S. English," "French," or "risk management in a financial firm"), and after that an explicit qualification of names will be needed only when the context will change.

As an e-commerce example, we may consider the stock-keeping-unit (SKU) nightmare as described by John Jordan in his interview in *The Wall Street Journal* [T2001]. It includes different names for the same widget, different distributors' codes, and frequent changes of these codes. Textual names may not help either because, as Jordan notes, "it's often impossible to get current, accurate commercial information out of text-based search." The inadequacy of a keyword-based search has been well known for a long time. This is why, for example, good reference librarians who have excellent information models in their heads, and work with customers to formulate their questions in terms of these models, are so valuable. Human interventions solved most name-related problems before the emergence of business-to-business e-commerce, but for e-commerce to succeed, good *explicit* business information models of the named things and relationships between them are needed.

Different abstraction levels (or viewpoints) often provide contexts for using different names to denote the same thing. At a higher abstraction level, some specifics of a thing may be of no interest or importance, and this is often reflected in the choice of a name for that thing. At lower abstraction levels, it may be possible or necessary to distinguish between similar things by referring to these things using different names. For example, this book is being written using a thing named:

- a computer-based information system
- a Macintosh computer-based information system
- a word processor compatible with Quark Express on a Macintosh computer
- the Nisus word processor on a Macintosh computer
- the Nisus word processor version 5.1.3 on a Macintosh computer
- other possible names (note that most hardware specifics are of no importance in these contexts).

An Example of Contexts: "Each"

Reliance on "meaningful names" without considering the context of these names may lead to serious negative consequences. A news story in mid-November 1999 told about a food processing firm with two divisions—ordering and delivery. The IT system of one division was Y2K-compliant, but the IT system of the other division was not. The IT system that was not Y2K-compliant was successfully replaced with a compliant one. However, the firm had substantial problems: in one of these systems, "each" referred to a case of a product; in the other system, "each" referred to a single instance of that product. It was supposed that everyone knew what "each" meant; in reality, "each" meant different things for different people, and making these two IT systems work consistently together was going to take lots of effort, time, and money.

An explicit specification referring to the business domain of the firm as a whole would have easily prevented this waste.

Synonyms and Homonyms

> As to have wrought seven years under a master properly qualified was necessary in order to entitle any person to become a master, and to have himself apprenticed in a common trade; so to have studied seven years under a master properly qualified was necessary to entitle him to become a master, teacher, or doctor (words anciently synonymous) in the liberal arts, and to have scholars or apprentices (words likewise originally synonymous) to study under him.
>
> *Adam Smith, The Wealth of Nations [S1776]*

In general, we cannot rely on "meaningful names" in specifications and in reasoning. Extreme attempts to do that lead to extreme results. The constructs of Newspeak described by George Orwell are just one example that includes both (what we consider as) homonyms like "truth," "love," and "peace," and the absence of names to refer to undesirable constructs.

In modeling, we often encounter stakeholders who insist on using their favorite terminology as "the only correct one." As we have seen above, this is neither possible nor desirable. Therefore, modelers should explicitly handle synonyms and homonyms. In order to succeed in this activity, the structure of the business domain should be expressed in a clear, precise, and explicit manner. The appropriateness of a name at this stage is of secondary importance (remember, "structure over content"), and it may even happen that in order to discover the structure of a fragment of the domain, it becomes necessary to invent artificial "meaningless" names—such as "XYZ"—for temporary use in order to avoid deliberations about the "real meaning" of terms close to the hearts of the holders of a particular viewpoint. These artificial names are especially useful if some of the existing stakeholder's names are not well-defined or are homonyms (that is, are used to denote different things perhaps even in the same phrase) or if some stakeholders do not have a name for the element. In practice, the number of such artificial names is very small, usually not more than one or two per a sizable fragment of a model. Of course, if a name is used at all, then it should be used consistently throughout the model. When the structure of the model fragment becomes clear and agreed upon, it is possible to map the names favored by different stakeholders to the elements of that structure. In doing so, synonyms will be discovered and mapped to the same element, while homonyms will be discovered and mapped to different elements.

In some cases, stakeholders' names could not be reasonably and consistently mapped on any elements of a properly structured model. This may happen if such names do not denote single well-defined elements. Better definitions are then required for these names to be usable at all. As an example, it may be very useful to map the terminology of various buzzword-compliant approaches to a well-defined structure, such as the one for RM-ODP. As a result, stakeholders of some approaches have said that their approaches were "semi-precise."

The attachment of synonyms and homonyms to model elements may lead to an information overload. In order to avoid this, various context-dependent viewpoints may be used in which the same model structure is used with different viewpoint-dependent (or context-dependent) names. Such approach has been successfully used, for example, for contexts determined by different natural languages. The proliferation of synonyms may also be due to the kinds of abstraction used in the model; what is considered as a single concept with a single name at a high level becomes refined into several concepts at lower abstraction levels, as in the example described by Adam Smith above.

Identifiers

As noted earlier, a name need not refer to a single element (thing, action or relationship). For example, each of the names "a nice book," "a thought-provoking book," and "a nice thought-provoking book about programming" usually refers to more than one thing. At the same time, we need to be able to identify specific elements uniquely, so we use a special kind of name, that is, an identifier. Therefore, each element of interest should have at least one identifier. Observe that, at different times, the same element may have different identifiers: the same house may have different addresses at different times because street names, street numbers, and even town and country names (and natural languages) may change.

Some approaches to assigning identifiers are not workable. First, such an approach may be applicable only to a subset of the elements that need an identifier. For example, identifying hospital patients (or students) in the U.S. by their social security numbers does not take into account that some people who are legitimate hospital patients (or students) do not have social security numbers. For another example, a mailing address may not uniquely identify a house because in some villages houses on some streets do not have numbers. Second, an approach to assigning identifiers may not deal adequately with synonyms and homonyms. For example, codes assigned to two identical items may be different, while codes assigned to different items may be the same. Finally, the identifier of a thing may not correspond to the identifier of a computer-based representation of that thing because of various errors: for example, the record apparently representing a person in an information system, computer-based or not, may denote a different person, a non-existing person, or the same person with different properties.

There exists no simple recipe for dealing with these problems. In some cases, identification errors have important negative business consequences, and it may be necessary to apply human assessment in order to resolve various problems. For example, in a large hospital environment, it was necessary to determine whether a patient admitted to the hospital was already known. Patient numbers were used for identification, but many patients did not remember their numbers or did not have their patient IDs. Names and addresses were clearly insufficient for identification because people may change names, the names may be represented in somewhat different manner, people move, and so on. So the hospital SMEs and the modelers decided to consider the complete form filled in at admission as an identifier of the patient, and if this form could not serve as an identifier because it denoted more than one patient known to the hospital, then a hospital representative would ask the admitted patient questions based on the histories of homonym patients and would make appropriate decisions.

Names Used to Abbreviate Concepts

When we use a (perhaps arbitrary) term to name a concept, we abbreviate the definition of that concept by replacing the definition with the term. Thus, when we reuse that term later to denote the same concept, we may always replace the term with its definition. This approach goes back to Plato.

We have to be very careful in this reuse: we must replace—explicitly!—the term with its definition in the appropriate context rather than with a definition valid in some other context. As a simple example, the term "patient" in some hospital environments had about 60 different context-dependent meanings. In a certain context, a patient was defined as a person who pays for medical insurance. In a different context, statistical information had to be provided about patients, and the same definition was *implicitly* used (since "everyone knows what *patient* means"). As a result, the statistical information included such statements as "40% of male patients have at some time been pregnant."

As a modern-day and UML-specific (!) example, consider the usage of the terms "composition" and "aggregation" to denote the concept of a certain kind of relationship. RM-ODP defines composition (of objects) in a very precise manner as "a combination of two or more objects yielding a new object, at a different level of abstraction. The characteristics of the new object are determined by the objects being combined and by the way they are combined." Similar definitions are used in the General Relationship Model [GRM] and in philosophy. We have used this relationship throughout the book. The closest approximation[79] to this kind of relationship in UML is named "aggregation" (the term "composition" is reserved in UML for the hierarchical aggregation). Clearly, various discussions about the "real meaning" of composition (or of aggregation) have no merit: as long as a definition of a concept is provided, using this—or that—term to denote the concept often is a matter of context-dependent convenience. Temporary usage of artificial names to denote an element discussed in a modeling session, if there is no agreement on a name between stakeholders, is another example on concentrating on concepts rather than on word play.

Lewis Carroll demonstrated using names as abbreviations in his famous fragment from *Through the Looking Glass* [C1872]:

> "I don't know what you mean by 'glory,'" Alice said.
>
> Humpty Dumpty smiled contemptuously. "Of course you don't—till I tell you. I meant 'there's a nice knock-down argument for you!'"
>
> "But 'glory' doesn't mean 'a nice knock-down argument,'" Alice objected.

---

79. The definition of UML aggregation in UML 1.3 [UML 1.3] does not refer to any property determination. However, the UML profile for EDOC [EDOC2001] includes precise specifications of generic relationships in which the specification of UML aggregation explicitly includes the determination of properties of the "whole" in the manner prescribed by RM-ODP and GRM and described in this book. See also the eloquent paper [HSB1999].

> "When *I* use a word," Humpty Dumpty said, in rather a scornful tone, "it means just what I choose it to mean—neither more nor less."
>
> "The question is," said Alice, "whether you can make words mean so many different things."
>
> "The question is," said Humpty Dumpty, "which is to be master—that's all."

Thus, meaning is dissociated from "its" name, making it possible to rely only on characteristics explicitly specified and explicitly abbreviated in the model rather than on warm and fuzzy tacit assumptions.

How to Treat "Exceptional" Situations

Exceptions, and exceptions to exceptions, ought to be treated explicitly, i.e., as ordinary situations occurring when certain conditions are met (or not met). Otherwise, we may have the same kind of unmanaged complexity as in explaining planetary motions using "epicycles" (circles with centers that describe other circles), with the same (often doomed-to-failure) result. In either case, substantial simplification helps. This simplification is obtained by treating all situations in a uniform manner rather than considering some situations more equal than others. After all, what is considered to be an exception from one viewpoint may well be considered to be a normal situation from another viewpoint; the humans who deal with "exceptional" situations in insurance or other kinds of underwriting hardly consider their activities to be exceptional. Generally, exceptions are not exceptional at all: as David Parnas noted in his talk at ICSE 2001, undesired events may take up to 80 percent of a complete specification (and code).

In this context, we can stress again the need to be explicit and uniform in articulating all situations, including those that may be forgotten or that "should be ignored because they are not supposed to happen." Dines Bjørner provides many examples of such situations, such as when a seller, after receiving a buyer's order and confirming it, may, as an alternative to actually carrying out the order, realize that the promised merchandise is no longer available, or may forget to follow-up on the confirmation, or may go out of business, or may—at his own initiative and without any order—deliver goods to an unprepared customer [B2001a]. In a more detailed specification of this fragment, below, you will see that a seller's action is subtyped into a seller's follow-up (properties of which are determined by the properties of the buyer's confirmed order) and a delivery to an unprepared customer. The seller's follow-up is subtyped as requested by the

SME, so that carrying out the order is only one of several subtypes, while carrying out the order is subtyped further into carrying out as requested and carrying out incorrectly. As seen from the example, being explicit in such situations clearly suggests the use of subtyping, rather than "exceptions," resulting in clean and lucid specifications.

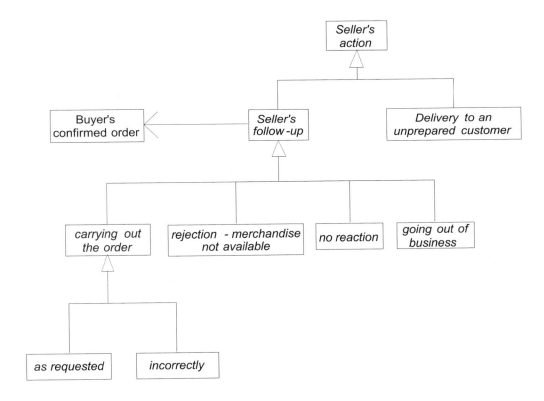

Similarly, in the specification of a trader, we should not forget that the information recorded in and handled by a trader may not be correct (for example, it may be outdated or just wrong for various reasons). Unfortunately, the trader standard [T1996] does not deal with these issues.

Document input may be used as another good example. In most cases, handling of "normal" situations represents only a small fraction of input processing. The essence of document input is in proper handling of "abnormal" (incomplete, incorrect, etc.) data input of various kinds from a screen or otherwise, e.g., from a different human or computer-based system. Clearly, error handling (including error message text handling) is a very important part of the job. This book does not deal with document input, instead referring the reader to the excellent book [GW1977] published a while ago.

Failures, Errors, and Faults

Systems may behave in a manner different from the one prescribed by a contract in which they participate. This kind of behavior leads to failures, that is, violations of a contract [RM-ODP2]. Failures may be observed when the postconditions of some actions are not satisfied or when the required actions do not happen. Failures may be perceived differently by different observers: in particular, some observers may not perceive a failure at all. For example, when an automated withdrawal from a customer's checking account is posted in such a manner that the telephone banking subsystem informs the customer about the withdrawal only a day or two after it happened, this is a failure from the customer's viewpoint, but may not be considered as a failure by the bank because the bank branch is able to provide timely information.

Failures may happen due to errors [RM-ODP2], that is, some undesirable characteristics of state. Some errors may be detected and corrected, and as a result some failures will not happen. This is why appropriate error messages delivered to and understandable by the parties who can correct the errors are essential for successful work. At the same time, some errors may disappear even before being detected (for example, as a result of detecting and correcting other errors). In addition, failures may be prevented by appropriate actions even if errors were not corrected. For example, when a customer's monthly statement has a typographical error in the street or town name but is nevertheless delivered correctly by the post office, the non-delivery failure does not happen. A compensating transaction requesting the customer to disregard an incorrect statement and replace it with the attached correct one, if delivered promptly, is another example of a failure-preventing action.

Errors, in turn, may be caused by faults [RM-ODP2]. A fault in some epoch may cause an error in a later epoch (RM-ODP uses an example of a design fault leading to an execution failure). Not all faults cause errors: active faults do, while dormant faults do not. An expected postcondition of an action may be violated, causing an error and possibly leading to a failure, due to some fault in the technological infrastructure (for example, an interrupted connection or an event represented as a "severe database error") used in that action. A software virus is an example of an intentional human-made external fault that may cause errors possibly leading to failures.

Various Viewpoints and the Five Basic Viewpoints

In order to understand a large or complex specification, we need to provide an explicit structure for that specification. The structuring mechanisms include viewpoints that focus on particular concerns within a specified system [RM-ODP2], as well as levels within a viewpoint.

Viewpoints are chosen by specifiers, specification stakeholders, and users. At the same time, certain important concerns within a system are common to many (if not all) systems, so the semantics of the corresponding viewpoints can be described once and reused. Notably, within the context of an information management project, we distinguish between the business viewpoint, the technological infrastructure viewpoint, and the IT system viewpoint. We may further say that the IT system viewpoint is a composite in a composition of the other two. In each of these three viewpoints, we concentrate only on viewpoint-specific concerns and suppress all others; thus, each of these viewpoints taken in isolation does not provide for a complete specification.[80] (The technological infrastructure and the IT system need not be computer-based; the technological infrastructure of the nineteenth century, for example, incorporated file cabinets and files, as well as actual ledgers, and was used quite successfully as a basis for the non-computerized IT systems.)

RM-ODP chose and defined five viewpoints—enterprise, information, computational, engineering, and technology—as the necessary and sufficient set of viewpoints "to meet the needs of ODP standards" [RM-ODP3]. In order to distinguish between these and other viewpoints, we will collectively name these five RM-ODP viewpoints the *Five Basic Viewpoints*. Some interesting aspects of these viewpoints are summarized below. The Five Basic Viewpoints can be applied to the specification of any system or its component, as well as to the specification of any viewpoint, if the specifiers or the specification users so desire based on the complexity of the specification and on concerns they want to deal with in the specification.

A viewpoint specification uses a set of concepts and constructs—a language—appropriate for that viewpoint. Some of these concepts and constructs may have been introduced as being of interest only within the corresponding viewpoint. Nevertheless, it may happen that certain concepts and constructs

---

80.   This is as it should be: some of us remember the excellent illustration by Grady Booch [B1991, p. 39] of two viewpoints on a cat—the owner's one and the veterinarian's one—which do not have a lot in common but which still are very useful in their respective contexts.

introduced only for a specific viewpoint are of wider interest and applicability and may be used in other viewpoint specifications as well. For example, the constructs of the engineering viewpoint specification are defined in [RM-ODP3] using, among others, concepts and constructs from the enterprise and information viewpoints.

Various viewpoint specifications of the same system should be consistent. This consistency should be demonstrable, so all viewpoint languages should have a common foundation, that is, should use *the same set of basic concepts and constructs*. The structure of this foundation is based on mathematics. Within the context of RM-ODP, this common foundation is presented in [RM-ODP2]. The most important of these common concepts and constructs are described in this book.

Viewpoints are needed for human understanding. As mentioned above, the Five Basic Viewpoints are not the only ones possible. Moreover, we often want to separate concerns within a particular viewpoint specification, so it is possible to provide for specifications of several or all of the Five Basic Viewpoints within one of them, for example, within an enterprise (or an engineering) viewpoint specification. For example, an enterprise viewpoint specification is centered around the specification of communities (those in which the ODP system fulfills a role, and possibly others)—configurations of enterprise objects that describe collections of entities formed to meet the objectives of those communities. The specification of communities and the relationships between them is best formulated using the information viewpoint concept of an invariant schema, while a specific observation about the state of a community is best formulated using the information viewpoint concept of a static schema. For another example, the specification of semantics of "operations"—that is, interrogations and announcements—defined in the computational viewpoint is best formulated using the information viewpoint concept of a dynamic schema.

We ought to remember that "people try too hard to ascribe deep meaning to the [Five Basic] viewpoints" [H1997]; I am not trying to do that in this book.

How to Choose Viewpoints

Viewpoint specifications of a system include those characteristics of the system that are of interest to the owners or users of that viewpoint. We use viewpoints in order to enhance the understandability of our specifications. Viewpoints permit us to concentrate only on the important (within some context) characteristics of a system and ignore all others.

Consider as a simple example three different viewpoints on a contract. First, a contract is a composite in a fixed composition-assembly of (several) parties, subject matter, and consideration. The composition is fixed because changes in components imply the need to create (negotiate) a new contract; the composition is an assembly because the components must exist for the contract to exist. Second, a contract may be considered as an action and as a composite in a composition-assembly of the action's invariant, precondition, postcondition, and triggering condition. And third, a contract expresses the objective of a community, i.e., of a configuration of objects formed to meet an objective, in accordance with the enterprise viewpoint of RM-ODP; the contract specifies how the objective can be met. Clearly, each viewpoint specification of a contract is focused on its viewpoint-specific characteristics and is chosen based on the relevance of these characteristics to the viewpoint users.

In the context of this example, consider IT development. The contractual model of each phase of IT development, from "requirements analysis" to "implementation," in accordance with which such a phase is regarded as a subject matter of a contract between two parties, the customer and the supplier, was proposed by B. Cohen in 1982 [C1982a, CHJ1986]. The postcondition of a successful completion of each contract is similar to the postcondition of a successful completion of any contract: the customer's acknowledgment that the deliverable of the contract satisfies the terms and conditions specified by the subject matter of that contract, and the supplier's acknowledgment that the consideration was appropriately handled.

All viewpoints are not equal. There may be inadequate viewpoints of a system that do not include any interesting semantic properties of that system. As an example, consider the viewpoint of a contract as an action that includes only the signature of that contract, i.e., that specifies only the contract name and the number, "meaningful names," and types of its arguments:

```
contract (house, first_party, second_party, money)
```

The semantics of a contract specified in this manner may be chosen quite arbitrarily: for instance, the first_party may buy (or rent) the house from the second_party (or *vice versa*), or the first_party may build the house for the second_party, or the first_party may babysit for the second_party (in all cases money—per year? per month?—is the consideration), and so on. Clearly, the specification of the signature does not tell us much about the semantics, although it may be supposed by some that "the developers" will be able to "figure out" what the semantics is. A more meaningful specification of a contract as an action—for example, if the contract is for buying a house—would, for example, include an invariant (a house has exactly one owner, the owner is a party,[81] and a house has monetary value), a precondition (the first_party owns the house, the second_party does not own the house, and the first_party has at least the "value of the house" money), a postcondition (the first_party does not own the house, the second_party owns the house, the first_party has "the value of the house" more money, and the second_party has "the value of the house" less money), and a triggering condition (the first_party and the second_party have agreed upon the buying/selling the house for the amount of money equal to "the value of the house"). Clearly, properties of the precondition, postcondition, and triggering condition are determined, in part, by properties of the invariant.

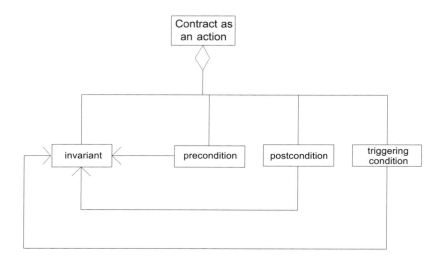

Observe that the specification above applies to any kind of a contract as an action and to any action in general. When we consider different (semantically important) viewpoints on a contract specification, we have to make sure that these viewpoints are consistent. It is useful to look at the contract negotiation described earlier and note that the acceptance leads to satisfaction of the triggering condition of the contract, while the invariant and pre- and postconditions are

---

81.   This is an oversimplification: in reality, it may be possible for a house to be owned by a composite in a composition of parties. In this case, the invariant, pre- and postconditions will be somewhat (but not a lot) more complex. Observe that reasoning in these terms would be hardly possible by considering only the (existing) signature.

implied by the subject matter of the contract with reference to the parties and the consideration.

Finally, it may be interesting and important to note that various viewpoints on the same specification often may be represented together as various decompositions of the same composite or various subtyping hierarchies of the same supertype. We have seen examples in the sections about multiple and dynamic subtyping, and multiple compositions.

The Five Basic Viewpoints

As noted elsewhere, the same specification artefacts (such as things and the relationships between them) may and often are described using more than one of the Five Basic RM-ODP Viewpoints. This is recommended for human understanding: the concerns of different viewpoints are separated in different viewpoint specifications. Different aspects of the same specification are better characterized using different viewpoint languages, but these aspects are not mutually independent. As an example from the RM-ODP standard itself, we may consider the usage of purpose and federation (enterprise viewpoint concepts) in the engineering viewpoint. And, we may consider using the information viewpoint invariant schemas to describe the properties of and the relationships between the "boxes" of an existing technological system in the technology viewpoint.

The Five Basic RM-ODP Viewpoints may be used to specify any system, be it a business one or an IT one. Some interesting examples are provided below.

The Enterprise and Information Viewpoints

These two RM-ODP viewpoints are the most important ones for any specification. They provide the framework within which other RM-ODP viewpoint specifications for a business may be created if need arises. Concepts specific to the computational, engineering, and technology viewpoints have been rather widely used in information technology, but are of limited significance in business specifications. Moreover, an IT specification with fragmentary or defective enterprise and information viewpoints often leads to failures and even disasters.

The business specifications in this book (and elsewhere) have been formulated in terms of the fundamental concepts and constructs of RM-ODP, together with a very small number of important concepts and constructs specific to the enterprise and information viewpoints. As noted elsewhere in this book, these concepts and constructs collectively determine the very small subset of an industry-available language (UML™) that can be used for business specifications, as well as the specifics of enhancing the fragments of this subset of the language characterized by "ambiguities, inconsistencies and lack of rigor" [SKB2001].

The enterprise specification of a system focuses on the scope and purpose of that system and the policies that apply to it in the context of its environment. The information specification defines the semantics of information and of information processing. Below I describe some viewpoint-specific concepts used in these viewpoints. You may observe that many of these concepts have been already used in specifications elsewhere in this book.

Let me reiterate that a viewpoint specification, including an enterprise or an information viewpoint specification, uses three kinds of concepts and constructs: the fundamental ones described earlier in this book (they are always used), the ones specific to that particular viewpoint, and those that are specific to other viewpoints but are convenient for the expression of the viewpoint specification at hand.

The Enterprise Viewpoint

The enterprise viewpoint [EV2001] is used to describe the behavior expected of a system by other individuals within its communities, that is, what the system is expected to be—and to do—in the context of those communities. It describes the behavior assumed by the users of a given system, the purpose, scope (the behavior that the system is expected to exhibit), and policies of the system, with an emphasis on contracts describing the objectives of the communities, various kinds of roles, relationships between roles and between communities, resources, owners, policies, etc.

A fundamental structuring concept for enterprise specifications is that of *community*—a configuration of enterprise objects that describes a collection of entities that is formed and continues to exist to meet some *purpose*. These entities are subject to a contract governing their collective behavior. The system that is specified fulfills one or more *roles* in one or several communities. These communities are the (possibly multiple and dynamic) contexts of the system. Each role stands as a placeholder for some enterprise object that exhibits the behavior identified by the role. For each role, there is an assignment rule that sets requirements for objects that may fulfill that role. Such an approach to roles corresponds to the one used elsewhere in this book.

A purpose (or "objective") of a system is its practical advantage or intended effect, expressed as preferences about future states.

It is reasonable to follow the proposal by Mario Bunge [B1990d] that a purpose can be ascribed only to humans ("highly evolved brains") or sets of humans. In this manner, we avoid anthropomorphism and strive for precision. Specifically, instead of reasoning about the purpose of a firm,[82] we reason about the purposes of various sets of people—stakeholders of the firm, such as its creators (entrepreneurs), investors, shareholders (including institutional investors and pension funds[83]), directors and managers, workers (both employees and consultants), especially knowledge workers (in von Mises' terms, "technicians"), customers, regulators, and so on. Most of these stakeholders were described by von Mises in [M1949] in a somewhat simpler context. Even within a specific set of stakeholders, the purposes of individuals of that set may be different, and different subsets of these sets may be precisely defined as classes of people satisfying certain types. As an example, consider employees who are customers, or consider customers interested only in a specific product or service of the firm. Consequently, for instance, the composite purpose of all knowledge workers of the firm may substantially differ from the purpose of an individual knowledge worker. As in any composition, this composite purpose emerges from the individual purposes and from the way these purposes are combined; this way may include lobbying, marketing, "becoming indispensable," influencing the formal or informal practices, and so on.

The top management of the firm and, ultimately, the owners of the firm will have to "balance" the conflicting demands of these stakeholders [D2001] and sets of stakeholders. This balancing is clearly a composition in which the composite purpose of all sets of the firm's stakeholders is determined in the same manner as the composite purpose of a specific set of stakeholders such as knowledge workers. The definitions of these sets of stakeholders and of their compositions help in understanding and formulating the properties of the (planned) future states of the firm and of the purposeful behaviors of stakeholders. In order to do that, we may consider only the common properties of the purposes of all stakeholders of the firm and may abbreviate the result as "the purpose of the firm." This kind of abstraction is probably overly simplistic and insufficient in our context because it suppresses details relevant for the determination of the result. A better approach would be to recognize the differences and to specify the purpose of the firm as a composite in the composition of the purposes of all stake-

---

82. The same considerations apply, to an even greater extent, to the personification of collectivities such as cities, states, and countries: decisions are taken by persons or groups of persons [B2000d].

83. Of course, "the purpose of an institutional investor" is similarly an abbreviation of the composition of purposes of its own stakeholders.

holders of that firm; in doing so, we explicitly will have to determine the (emergent) properties of the composite from the properties of its various components and the way these components are combined, in accordance with the definition of a composition.

Similarly, instead of reasoning about the purposes of an IT system, we reason about the purposes of its inventors, entrepreneurs, designers, developers, users, and so on. We compose these purposes (using criteria from the definition of the specific composition relationship) and may abbreviate the result as "the purpose of the IT system."

A purpose need not be something that, once achieved, is considered to be accomplished. As von Mises noted, a society is much more than a passing alliance concluded for a definite purpose and ceasing as soon as its purpose has been realized. Even on a much smaller scale, a firm usually has an ongoing purpose rather than one that can be considered as achieved after it is met (unless, for example, the purpose of a firm was to sell it to the highest bidder). And as to an IT system example, the purpose of the Internet is (most probably) ongoing.

The enterprise specification uses other important and interesting concepts. For example, consider the concept of a *resource*—an object essential to some behavior that requires allocation or may become unavailable. Allocation of a resource may restrict some other behavior. Also, consider the concept of a *process* (used elsewhere in this book)—a collection of steps taking place in a prescribed manner and leading to an objective. (Note that a step is an abstraction of an action that may leave unspecified the objects that participate in that action.) In addition, the enterprise specification uses the concepts of *policy* (a set of rules related to a particular purpose, where a rule can be expressed as an obligation, authorization, permission, or prohibition) and a set of accountability concepts such as party (again, used elsewhere in this book), commitment, declaration, delegation, evaluation, prescription, and so on. Usage of these concepts in an enterprise specification is subject to structuring rules described in detail in [EV2001]. I will not describe these concepts and structuring rules in detail.

As an example of a community, we may consider the financial community that includes financial products and services; participants who do or may enter contracts with these products or services as the subject matter; contracts; templates of these contracts or of these products and services; various processes in which these participate and templates of these processes; regulations that constrain the invariants and the process assertions; resources, both consumable and non-consumable (for example, templates are non-consumable resources); and various relationships between these. Note that a contract's consideration is also a subtype of a resource. The diagram below demonstrates a drastically simplified overview of the financial community (in which, for example, some important relationships are not shown).

This financial community specification is a context for any individual (such as person or organization, specific contract or template of a contract, specific product or template of a product, and so on) that fulfills one of the roles indicated in the specification.

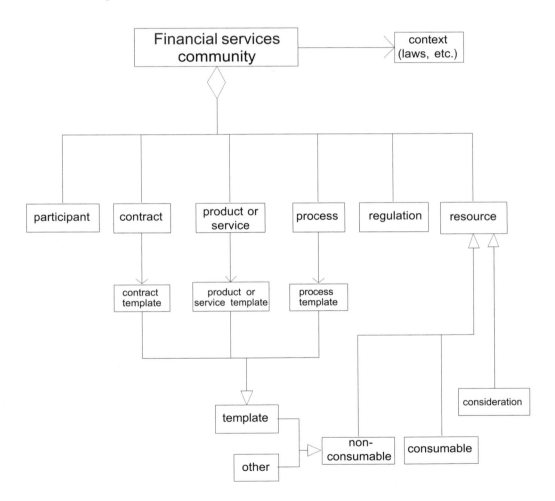

We distinguish here between the context within which the financial community exists (this context includes laws and informal customs "enforced" on the community from outside) and regulations internal to the financial community. In this manner, we observe that the financial community itself is, at a higher abstraction level, an object fulfilling a role in a higher-level community, such as in a society governed by some specific policies corresponding to market economy. Several such societies, such as political entities, may impose different and inconsistent policies on an object fulfilling roles in all these societies. Thus, we again encounter the familiar, but not easily resolvable, feature interaction issues.

The Information Viewpoint

The information viewpoint is used to describe the things, actions, and relationships between them, with an emphasis on *invariants* that define their stable properties. Practically, a substantial portion of the information viewpoint specification is done in terms of (combinations of) instantiated generic relationships. It includes the specification of the generic invariants and of such more specific fragments of the invariants as the actual rules for determining properties of composite and reference individuals, for distinguishing between subtypes of a particular supertype, and so on.

The information viewpoint specification [RM-ODP3] includes not only invariants, but also dynamic schemas, that is, specifications of allowable state changes of information objects, subject to the constraints specified as invariants. Because an allowable state change may happen only as an action, a dynamic schema specifies an *action*. This is usually accomplished by means of pre- and postconditions. (Of course, here we can recall that von Mises defined an action as the exchange of one state of affairs for another state of affairs.) At the same time, actions may be characterized by relationships between them. We have seen processes composed of steps, for example.

In addition, the information viewpoint includes static schemas, that is, specifications of the state of one or more objects at some point in time, again subject to the constraints specified as invariants. Static schemas specify single observations and are generally less interesting than invariants and dynamic schemas, although (as noted elsewhere) they are used in test specifications. At the same time, a static schema may be used to specify only some properties of an observation, for example, in terms of types (predicates).

The Computational, Engineering, and Technology Viewpoints

These viewpoints include a more substantial amount of concepts and constructs mostly of interest to information technologists. Therefore, I will not provide a lot of details here, but I will enumerate some of these concepts that may be of interest in business specifications.

The computational viewpoint [RM-ODP3] is used to describe behavior in terms of *operations*, that is, of interrogations or announcements. An operation is a subtype of an action. It is an interaction between two objects, a client (an object requesting that a function be performed by a server) and a server (an object performing a function on behalf of a client). An announcement is initiated by a client and results in the conveyance of information from that client to a server object, requesting a function to be performed by that server. An interrogation is an ordered composition of an announcement and its termination; the latter is initiated by the server and results in the conveyance of information from the server to the client in response to the announcement. Thus, operations correspond to the approach to behavior specification used in the legacy, message-oriented, object model. Actions in business specifications are not restricted to being operations: they may be collectively performed by several individuals, and there is no need to determine which specific participant of an action is the "owner" or the "initiator" of that action. In addition, the computational viewpoint includes other interesting constructs, such as *flow*—an abstraction of a sequence of interactions (including a continuous interaction) resulting in conveyance of information from a producer to a consumer (compare with a process as a composition of steps). The computational viewpoint is distribution-independent, although it makes distribution possible.

The engineering viewpoint is used to describe various detailed aspects of system distribution configuration, emphasizing the specifics of the infrastructure required to support functional distribution of an ODP system, checkpointing, cloning, recovery, etc. This does not necessarily require IT-related automation because, for example, distributed banks with branches existed in the nineteenth century. For another example, the concept of a checkpoint (defined as an object template derived from the state and structure of an engineering object that can be used to instantiate another engineering object, consistent with the state of the original object at the time of checkpointing[84]) has been used for a very long time and is not specific to computer-based IT systems.

The technology viewpoint deals with implementation defined in RM-ODP as "a process of instantiation whose validity can be subject to test." It identifies spec-

---

84. Checkpoints can only be created when the engineering object involved satisfies a precondition stated in a checkpointing policy [RM-ODP 3]. Clearly, the specifics of that policy belong to the enterprise viewpoint, while the specifics of the precondition belong to the information viewpoint.

ifications for technology relevant to the construction of systems and describes relationships between them, as well as specifies the information required from implementors to support testing. Technology is not the same as computer-based information technology: in particular, implementation may be accomplished by humans using pencil-and-paper. Thus, the "how" of implementation is hidden as it should be: for example, a specification of an accounting process may, and at least at the top level should, be written in such a manner that it does not matter, it is not visible from outside, and it cannot be tested, whether that specification is implemented by accountants, by an IT system, or by an IT system with some accountant intervention. At the same time, a technology specification realizing a specification written in other viewpoint languages must (for testing purposes, as well as for *traceability* purposes) interpret the atomic terms of those other viewpoint specifications [RM-ODP3]. (We recall that the fundamental concepts and constructs used in all viewpoint specifications are the same.)

In certain situations, we may wish to describe technology in substantially greater detail. In order to do that and to separate various concerns in the technology specification, we may use viewpoints, including the Five Basic RM-ODP Viewpoints. We may do that, for example, when we need to describe an existing technological system that we want to—or have to!—assess and use in our work. Such a precise and explicit specification of an existing technological system (which may be realized by humans or may be computer-based) may not be readily available. In this case, discovering and formulating it may be difficult, especially when the owners or authors of an existing technological system are unwilling or unable to act as SMEs in providing the essential information.[85] This is where "the system does what it does" must be replaced with a much more usable specification, that is, a specification explicitly demonstrating that "the system does what it should."

Synergy between Business and IT Specifications

As I have noted many times, the basic concepts and constructs used in any kind of specifications are the same. Moreover, we may well consider not only the traditional businesses, but also the business of a virtual machine, such as a relational database management system, or the business of an information

---

85.   In a trade, rather than in a profession, the apprentice had to spend "seven meagre years" (E.W. Dijkstra) to observe and absorb by osmosis the (technological) magic done by the Master.

technology project. Thus, the names "business specification" and "system specification"—as, of course, any other names—are context-dependent. In many situations, the context is clear, and when we use the names "business specification" or "business model," we often (but not always!) imply traditional businesses.

The specifics of a "business" may differ, but the general approach to specifying all businesses and the structure of all such specifications remains the same. In particular, a specification may be of an existing business, a newly created business, or a business some properties of which will be changed. Most (but not all) traditional business specifications are of the first or third kind, while many (but not all) traditional IT specifications are of the second kind.

Because all kinds of specifications use the same approach, it becomes possible and natural to handle these specifications in a similar manner. Specifically, we may reason about traceability from a traditional business specification to a traditional IT specification realizing a fragment of that business on a virtual machine defined by a traditional technology infrastructure specification. We may also reason about traceability "back" where for each fragment of interest of a traditional IT specification, we determine "why it is there," that is, what specifically it supports. These ideas are not new and, explicitly or not, are based on mathematics, specifically on category theory.

The Business of the Business, the Business of the IT System, and the Business of the Technology Infrastructure

The specification of any business, traditional or not, may be structured using the RM-ODP Five Basic Viewpoints. In doing so, some viewpoint specifications may be more important than others, depending upon the specifics of that business. It may even happen that some viewpoint specifications will not be important at all.

Let's consider how the Five Basic Viewpoints may be used in a specification of a banking clearing house in the nineteenth century, as described by Charles F. Dunbar in one of the best books on banking [D1901] and specified on the basis of this description in [K1999]. The enterprise viewpoint will specify the purpose of a clearing house (such as simplification of inter-bank settlements and stability of the banking system), the communities (such as the banking system including banks, clearing houses, assets, liabilities, rights to demand money, transfer of rights, etc.), the policies (such as the obligation "banks must meet checks drawn upon themselves"), etc. The information viewpoint will specify the things (such as banks, checks, liabilities, etc.), the relationships between them (such as "a change in liability for a single bank is a composite in a composition-assembly of checks against this bank and checks against other banks"), and the actions (such as, for a settlement, the action invariant "the total liability of all banks before and after the settlement is the same"). The computational viewpoint will specify the operations (interrogations and announcements, such as the delivery of checks by a bank to its clearing house) using pre- and postconditions, etc. The engineering viewpoint will specify the distribution characteristics (including checkpointing) of the banks and clearing houses. And the technology viewpoint will specify the implementation of various invariants, actions, and so on (whether manual or using the technology of the nineteenth century eloquently described by Dunbar). As we have seen, there was no computer-based information technology here.

Similarly, let's consider how the Five Basic Viewpoints may be used in a specification of a relational database management system (DBMS)—an important component of a technological infrastructure, that is, of a virtual machine on top of which various IT systems are being built. The enterprise viewpoint will specify the purpose of a relational DBMS (such as structuring data in a representation- and access-independent manner), the communities (such as the schema describing tables (with rows having keys and columns) and domains,[86] as well as val-

---

86.   The concept of a domain was described by E.F. Codd in his famous paper [C1970]. Several attributes (possibly of different objects, or of different columns of relational tables) may be defined on the same domain (an "application-specific type of an attribute"). Domains are more semantically rich than just "base types" in a computer system [K1989]. They define, for example, valid names of US states, valid colors, valid publishers, valid sizes, and so on. They need not be elementary; an address may be an example of a non-elementary domain. In many cases, these sets of valid values are not fixed. Synonyms of these values also belong to their corresponding domains. All this can be defined precisely, and a fragment of this definition will look like:

  A domain can exist independently of anything, but in order for an attribute to exist, the domain of that attribute has to exist (hierarchical subordination), and an object for which that attribute would be an attribute of that object has to exist (a composition-subordination).

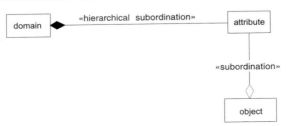

ues), the policies (such as the obligation "a foreign key should refer to an existing primary key"), etc. The information viewpoint will specify the things (such as values, domains, tables, keys, etc.), the relationships between them (such as "a table is a composite in a composition-subordination of rows"), and the actions (such as, for deletion of a row from a table, the precondition "there should be no foreign key in any row of any table referring to the primary key of the row to be deleted") including ways of constructing complex actions on the base of simpler ones (such as the ones described by SQL). The computational viewpoint will specify the operations (such as interrogations about foreign keys referring to a specific primary key), etc. The engineering viewpoint will specify the distribution characteristics including checkpointing. And the technology viewpoint will specify the implementation of the database schema and data (whether using hardware or software or a combination of the two).

Similarly, let's consider how the Five Basic Viewpoints may be used in a specification of an IT system. Instead of repeating how the same approach could be reused, we observe that the most important properties of an IT system specification will be demonstrated in its enterprise and information viewpoints. An IT system specification does not exist in isolation; it exists in the contexts of the business specification and the technological infrastructure specification. Thus, an IT system specification is a composite in a composition of the relevant fragments of the business specification and the relevant fragments of the chosen technological infrastructure specification[87] [C1997, K1999]. It follows from the definition of the composition relationship that properties of the IT system specification are determined not only by its business specification but also by the chosen technological infrastructure specification. In fact, modern technological infrastructures, such as those providing opportunities for instantaneous information exchange, often help to solve (using IT systems) business problems that could not be solved earlier.

Several observations are in order in this context:

We are (becoming) used to good business specifications of traditional businesses. At the same time, specifications of technological infrastructures and their fragments (a.k.a. components) are frequently missing, incomplete, or inadequately structured, leading to substantial economical losses. This problem is

---

87.   The same considerations, in a somewhat different manner, were presented in the excellent textbook by Bauer and Wössner: "Program development ... is open-ended, its methods should be flexible enough to adapt to different, technology-dependent machine styles." [BW1982].

often referred to as the problem of technological complexity. Clearly, existing systems such as the ones sold by middleware (or other) vendors may and should be specified in the same manner as businesses. Such specifications should be understandable by their users; understandability will make it possible for users to make informed decisions based on explicit assessment of and comparison between systems provided by competing vendors.

We must distinguish between specifications of generic components of technological infrastructure (such as a generic relational DBMS defined, together with the relational data model, in [C1970]) and their specific realizations (such as specific relational DBMSs sold by various vendors). A specific realization of a generic component often refines or expands some properties of that generic component. At the same time, a crisp specification of a generic component is a good foundation for comparison between its various (existing and planned) vendor-based realizations. (Note, however, that in many cases the descriptions of existing component interfaces including interfaces of so called COTS (commercial off-the-shelf) systems—are informal, ambiguous, incomplete, and at wrong abstraction levels.)

The same approaches to component specifications have been successfully used in traditional engineering.

Traceability

Let's look at an overview of an information management project. This specification is adapted from [KA1998], with earlier ideas also borrowed from [KS1996a] and [KS1997].[88] It is an abstraction in which, for example, we pay only limited attention to the fact that a business specification is realized by a composition of automated (IT) systems and systems realized by humans.

This is where we show how to get from here (a business specification) to there (an implemented system). The deliverables of a successful information management project are among the means by which an organization improves business process efficiency or effectiveness through achieving specific business objectives. (More often than not, effectiveness is of greater importance.) Usually, this results in a new computer-based IT system, because technology is a powerful way to improve efficiency and effectiveness. At the same time, even a "low-

---

88.   Many thanks go to Ian Simmonds and Allan Ash for a lot of discussions.

tech" or "no-tech" solution to a problem can be a cost-effective, and sometimes preferable, way to deliver these improvements.

An information management project is a complex effort with a specific set of objectives. For our purposes here, it is composed of the processes (and deliverables) of *business specification, business design, systems specification,* and *systems implementation,* as shown in the diagram below. We use the same name for the process and its deliverable.

We say that these processes (and deliverables) are components of an ordered composition-assembly because we need to move through these processes generally in the order they are listed above and because the information management project is not complete until the processes have all been done.

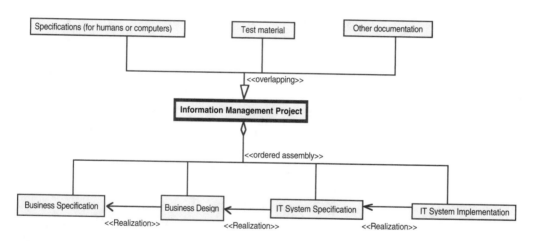

Business specifications are the subject matter of this book.

The business design—showing "who does what when"—is a *realization* of its business specification. It refines existing business rules and may add new ones. It specifies which fragments of the business specification are supposed to be realized by humans, which by automated IT systems (current or future), and which by a combined effort of humans and IT systems. (Proper enforcement of business invariants is of special interest and importance in this context. Checking the correctness of these invariants is an essential and often the most important component of system testing.) It also specifies which fragments of the business specification will be realized internally in the firm and which will be outsourced. And it determines which fragments of the business specification will be of interest from the viewpoint of the future (IT or manual) system specification within the framework of the information management project under consideration. A business design is still at the business, and not technological, frame of reference. It firmly relies on the business domain specification and on those most important action specifications that were included in the business specification. Realization is a special kind of reference relationship. It relates a "source" to its "target" (see below), where the source is made more concrete, or "more real," and results in the target. We show realization as a single relationship and abstract out its specifics in order to reuse it later when we similarly realize, for example, the business design (as the source) by a systems specification (the target).

The IT system specification is the result of taking those business things, relationships, and processes that the business design decided to support by an automated IT system, and transforming them into the IT system things, relationships, and processes that will realize them in the context of the technological infrastructure—the virtual machine on top of which the IT solution is built. The frame of reference here is technological, so the IT system things, relationships, and processes may be substantially different from the business things, relationships, and processes. (The business processes deal with "business things and relationships" and the IT system processes deal with "IT system things and relationships.") The transformation is "many-to-many," and it preserves the overall structure of the specification. This is where IT system specifiers make decisions like transforming several subtyping hierarchies of the same supertype into (for example) a single database record with appropriate attributes. The IT system things may be computers, DBMSs, Web Servers, objects, files, communications protocols, and the relationship patterns that we use to tie these things together. Alternatively, and similarly, the system specification may be for a manual implementation (pencil and paper), in which case, the implementation will be a collection of manual procedures and interrelated things needed for these procedures.

The system implementation produces the computer programs and operating procedures necessary to realize the IT system specification. Alternatively, the "objects" that implement a manual (or "no-tech") system might include ledgers with red and black pencils.

To conclude this small specification, we notice that some types of material are developed and delivered in each phase of an information management project. They include specifications (for humans or computers), test material, and other documentation. This is shown using an overlapping subtyping relationship because sometimes the material may satisfy more than one type; for example, a test driver program is both test material ("data") and code, that is, a specification for the computer. Specifications for humans or computers are the deliverables that, within their viewpoints and project stages, lead directly from a discussion of the business needs of the business area to an automated IT (or manual) system that implements them. Test materials are test specifications and test data that allow for validating the deliverable, as well as experimentally verifying that the next process has realized it properly. Note that test materials are composed of validation and verification materials; at the early stages of the project, validation will prevail (and will be the only kind of testing for the business specification). Other documentation refers to project plans, reviews, contracts, budgets, and all other materials that frame the project. Different kinds of documentation are provided to different users.

Thus, convincing structures for traceability between the stages of an *intellectually manageable* information management project provide an excellent heuristic guidance [D1972] for correct realization of these stages and for being able to convince ourselves and the stakeholders that these realizations are correct. Testing, described below, is a complementary process to increase the level of confidence.

Let's now look at the specification of the *realization* relationship.

As noted above, realization is a subtype of reference relationship (between the source and the target), so it satisfies the invariant of the reference relationship. Specifically, properties of the target are determined by properties of its source. Additional details about realization are shown in the specification at the top of page 150.

The source and target (in fact, collections of source and target elements) are shown as components of realization. (This composition is an assembly because both source and target are needed in order for the realization to be completed.) Realization is a human activity in which a few different approaches—realization variants—are evaluated, and the "best" one (for the benefit of the project) wins. A target is not uniquely determined by its source (for example, there is usually more than one business design realizing the same business specification). Rather, each realization variant takes into account elements of the source, along with some environmental and strategy considerations, to generate its own particular target material (such as specifications and other documents). The overall structure of the source is preserved in the target, but the transformation from the source elements to the target elements is "many-to-many." The target material of the best realization variant becomes the resulting target of the realization relationship.

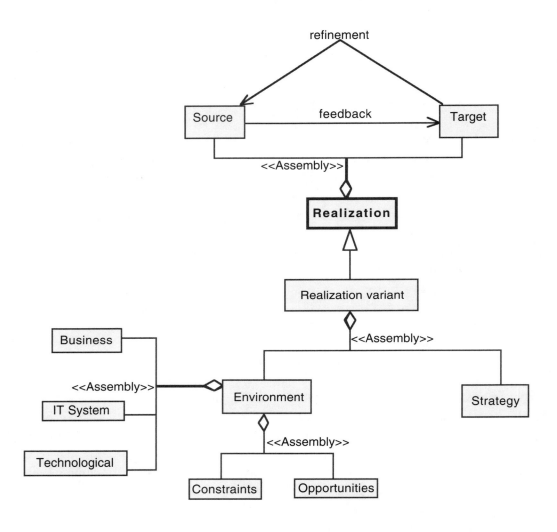

The realization (and therefore each of its subtypes, realization variants) is composed (in a composition-assembly) of an environment and a strategy, so that the emergent properties of the realization (and its variant) are collectively determined by the properties of the (variant-specific) environment and of the (variant-specific) strategy. These properties include not only the properties of the target (because the source is generally fixed), but also, for example, the decision about which properties of the source will be realized by the target. Given the various strategies and environmental constraints that apply in any particular project, however, only one variant will be perceived as the best fit. The environment is in a similar manner composed of the business, IT system, and technological environments[89] because these kinds of environments participate, collectively, in determining the overall properties of the environment. Further, the environment is composed of constraints and opportunities: for example, certain properties of the technological architecture may be considered as (business!) opportunities for realization, leading to substantial competitive advantages for the business. Clearly, all components of the environment should be explicitly taken into account during realization.

In addition, the source and target are related by means of the *refinement* and *feedback* reference relationships. The refinement reference demonstrates that the source is refined into the target, with appropriate property determination of the target. The feedback relationship shows that, in some cases, changes to the *source* may be needed as a result of creating the target. During business design, for example, a deliberate and explicit decision may be made to solve a business problem somewhat different from the one described in the original business specification (for example, due to various constraints or opportunities resulting from the choice of a technological architecture).

We observe, among other things, that by abstracting the realization specification, we determine that the IT system specification is a composite in a composition of its business specification and the chosen technological infrastructure (that is, the virtual machine) specification.

Finally, the reference relationships between the source and target describe the traceability path of an information management project. For each identifiable part of the solution (target), it should be possible to determine why it is there: it should participate in satisfaction either of one or more particular collections of requirements from the previous project phase or of an environmental requirement of the current phase. Although many collections of requirements will have identifiable target solutions, it is also possible that a particular collection of requirements will not be worth solving at this time and will lead to a null solution.

Source or target collections should be chosen so that it is easily understood which set of requirements is realized by which solution set. Each individual

---

89. The characterization of a particular component as "business," "system," or "technological" is context-dependent, so that, for example, a component considered "technological" in a business context (of the realization from a business specification to a business design) may be considered "business" in a technological context (of the business of realization from a system specification to a system implementation).

requirement should be traceable to the set of elements that implement it, and each element of design, or each implemented program should be traceable to the set of requirements from the immediately preceding project step that it realizes.

How to Test Systems

What be th' observations of this neadle, by whiche you affirme that it doth not exactlye poynte Northe and Southe?
W. Cuningham, 1559

To be correct, a program must be just a subset of the observations permitted by the specification.
C.A.R. Hoare [HJ1998]

Any proposition true in a specification must be true in its implementation [RM-ODP2]. Testing determines whether the statements in the implementation are true, that is, whether they satisfy their counterparts in the specification. There is absolutely no need to wait for a system (computer-based or not) to be implemented before writing test specifications for that system. As early as 1967, the (U.S.) Air Force Management Concepts assured that test specifications were written concurrently with the system definitions (Jules I. Schwartz, [SE1970]).

When we have a specification and an observation (including a measurement or an experiment) referring to the implementation of that specification, we must be able to put them together (including using the same concepts as well as determining the referents for which the observer will be looking) in order to find out whether the observation, that is, the very specific statement about the implementation, satisfies the specification. Thus, in order to create a test specification, it is necessary to map from terms of the original specification to observable aspects of the system implementation. This is, of course, what traceability must provide.

From the business viewpoint, it is essential to test with respect to the business specification rather than with respect to the IT system specification, so the mapping of interest must be from concepts and terms of the business specification (business invariants together with pre- and postconditions of business actions constitute the most important generic business concepts) to observable aspects of the system implementation. This mapping is often not trivial, especially if the business specification is written at a sufficiently high abstraction level. It requires transformation of the more abstract propositions of the business specification into more specific propositions about the implementation.[90] Of course, such transformation is not unique, and it is not just a refinement because, as noted earlier, it is determined not only by the business specification but also by the technological architecture chosen for the IT system specification and its implementation. This kind of transformation is described in more detail above, in the section about traceability. Because a business specification is often realized by a composition of IT systems and human systems, we may say that testing with respect to the business specification is an abstraction of testing with respect to the IT system specifications and of testing with respect to specifications of systems realized by humans. (As noted earlier, human decisions are unpredictable, so specifications of systems realized by humans may prescribe only some properties of human decisions rather than the specifics of these decisions.)

Testing a system implementation is accomplished only at the systems predetermined reference points. The system under test is observed (as a black box) at these points, and the observation involves collective behavior between that system and the observer (a human or another system). This behavior may be originated by the system under test ("in nature") or by the observer (in an experiment). In many cases, the observer records a collection of statements about the state of the system in terms of the observable aspects of system implementation that must be compared with the expected collection of observations (static schemas), that is, specifications of these states, in terms of the business specification. Clearly, there may be too many observations in testing, and in order to avoid semiotic pollution we must make (and justify) choices about "what to test." Satisfaction of the appropriate business invariants and of pre- and postconditions of the appropriate business actions should influence these choices in a substantial and demonstrable manner. At the same time, the behavior of a computer-based system is described by discrete, rather than continuous, mathematics, so for such a system, it is generally *incorrect* that a small change in

---

90.   The very useful concept of linking invariant introduced by C.A.R. Hoare comes to mind: "The general technique for crossing a level of abstraction is to define the way in which an observation at one level of abstraction corresponds to one or more observations at the other level. This relationship can itself be described by a predicate (often called a linking invariant) $L(c,a)$.
which relates an abstract observation a (in the alphabet of the specification) to a more concrete observation c (in the alphabet of the implementation)." In the context of legacy object-oriented development, it has been "tough to verify invariants of any real importance"—this certainly includes business invariants—because they "reach beyond a single method or even a single class" [I2002]. Approaches like aspect- and subject-oriented programming [HKOS1996, I2002] appear to help: they acknowledge the need to not only understand but code a system in more natural terms than those of legacy OO approaches and provide constructs that support non-isolated objects.

inputs will lead to a small change in outputs. Thus, testing for a discrete computer-based system *cannot* be accomplished in the same manner as for an analog system governed by the rules of traditional engineering mathematics.

In accordance with E.W. Dijkstra's observation that testing can only demonstrate the presence of errors in a program but not their absence [SE1970], the role of a good tester is to *think of cases that will likely fail.* Therefore, a good tester is an experimenter rather than a passive observer. This approach is in very good agreement with the general principle of falsifiability of scientific theories and the impossibility of their verifiability (Karl Popper, about 1935). The objective of testing is to find errors, that is, cases in which observations of the implemented system do not conform to the business specification. The test specification should include experimental actions in which the tester attempts to "break" the system under test, for example, by attempting to introduce faults as a result of which the system under test may be expected to fail. A stable system under test will not fail in these circumstances, that is, it will satisfy the specification "garbage in—error messages out," as opposed to an unstable system that will satisfy the specification "garbage in—garbage out."

The conformance community includes the specifier, the implementor, the tester, and the business stakeholders (including the owner) who establish constraints on the use of the specification. Observe that in creating test specifications—and even in experimenting with the system under test—it may be possible to establish that some situations were not dealt with at all, or were not dealt with properly, in the business specification.

Testing can fail for the following reasons [RM-ODP2]: the business specification is inconsistent or incomplete in a manner that makes testing impossible; the observations made by the tester cannot be related to or interpreted in terms of the business specification; or these observations yield propositions that are not true in the business specification. In the first situation, the business specification should be corrected; in the second situation, the traceability mappings should be created or corrected; and in the last situation, the implementation (or some earlier stage in the information management project composition) should be corrected. Testing can never provide absolute confidence; the level of confidence in a tested system, as in a scientific theory, is determined by the criticality and repeatability of experiments (tests).

Finally, when we specify and create information systems, we should reuse the approach of traditional engineering. To quote David Parnas, "[m]uch of engineering education is devoted to learning how to perform both mathematical analysis and carefully planned testing of their products" [P2001]. In other words, testing is not an alternative, but *complementary* to the usage of relevant mathematics in order to write valid specifications (and correct programs) and know it.

Chapter 3

Putting It All Together

A business is any serious activity in which humans are interested. When we understand, analyze,[91] and model a business, we become familiar with its various fragments and distill its *essential* characteristics. In order to be effective, we do not start from a blank sheet of paper: we recognize and reuse business patterns—precisely defined structuring concepts and constructs—in the context of the specific business. We do this by asking questions in terms of the appropriate business patterns and getting definite ("yes," "no," "not applicable") answers from the business SMEs (subject matter experts). The result of understanding and modeling a business is a business specification. It must be convincing for the stakeholders of the business, that is, it must be a demonstrably correct and complete description of the relevant characteristics of the business. Convincing the stakeholders is accomplished by validation: the stakeholders read the specification and agree (or disagree) with it, that is, with its structural and behavioral predicates.

For any business domain, we can reuse fundamental and generic (common) business patterns, such as "invariant" or "composition." For some domains, such as financial, we also have accumulated and reused business-specific patterns such as "contract," "Internet sales contract," "option trade," and so on. These and other business patterns have been precisely defined, and some of these definitions are provided and used in this book. At the same time, domains perceived

---

91. "Analysis: breaking down a whole into its components and their mutual relations" [B1999].

as technology-oriented often have not been specified in such a manner, leading to a symptom often formulated as "the system does what it does." It is possible to solve this problem by modeling all kinds of domains as businesses, starting with the basics of the business domain and reusing the same generic and then business-specific (if they exist) business patterns.

The *invariant* is probably the most important, most foundational business pattern. As noted in [B2000b], the process of cognition fixes "the permanent flux of the continuum that surrounds us by placing invariants." Using invariants clearly solves the problem of requirements that "always change" because invariants determine a stable foundation for all requirements. By using business patterns based on invariants, we may be able to "trap the real world into a system of differentiating symbols" [B2000b], that is, into a business specification. Discovering invariants is not difficult when we start with the basic structures of the business domain of interest; these structures are defined by means of invariants.

The following section provides an overview of business patterns used in modeling. You have seen them in specifications throughout this book. These patterns are based on the foundations presented in the previous chapter.

Business Patterns: From Basic to Specific

The need to discover, distill, formulate, and reuse concepts and constructs has been around for a long time, both in business and in IT. Such concepts as market, division of labor, price, contract, tax, money, and so on have been recognized and reused in quite different contexts. In some situations, it has been necessary to generalize the existing concepts and subsequently provide for appropriate context-specific parameters to instantiate these concepts. The discoveries of more general and more abstract concepts and constructs have led to much better understanding of various systems.

In information management, the usage of procedures has been around since the very first activities of programming: for example, Turing distilled the idea of subroutines. The need to introduce and reuse appropriate abstract constructs together with operations on them was made explicit in the late 1960s: "...introduction of suitable abstract data structures ... is greatly analogous to the way in which we can understand an ALGOL program operating on integers without having to bother about the number representation of the implementation used. The only difference is that now the programmer must invent his own concepts (analogous to the 'ready-made' integer) and his own operations upon them (analogous to the 'ready-made' arithmetic operations)" (E.W. Dijkstra, *Structured Programming*, in [SE1970]). And in order to reuse such a construct (a concept with operations), also known as a pattern, from a library of constructs, we do pattern matching, i.e., we recognize situations in contexts.

The same approach applies to all kinds of specifications and to (business) patterns used and reused in specifications. This book demonstrates and widely uses some basic "ready-made" business patterns, as well as certain more specific ones. These basic patterns (such as composition or invariant) are perceived as less well known than integers, but are used in a variety of situations, as are integers. And in the same manner as integers, the basic (business) patterns are used in information management and in many other areas of human endeavor. Specific business patterns are built on top of more basic ones by means of structuring operations. The most important of these structuring operations—composition and generalization[92]—have been well known for a long time both in business and in information management and have been described in detail in this book.

Basic business patterns are "small" and often can be explained on the back of the proverbial envelope. More specific business patterns are complex and may require more (or much more) effort for their explanation and representation. For example, a reasonably complete high-level specification of exotic option trades, their context, and their processing—composed of (partial) instantiations of a few business-specific patterns such as a trade, an option, a tradeable, a confirmation, and so on—took more than fifty pages of terse text and diagrams. This specification [G2001a] has been successfully used by the business SMEs and decision makers in the environment of a large financial institution for various purposes, only some of which were IT-related.

Note that the library of constructs (such as business patterns), as any other library, should be well structured in an explicit manner; otherwise, only a very highly qualified librarian will be able to find a library construct needed in a specific context. In other words, an explicit model of that library must be provided. Inadequately structured libraries of constructs often lead to low (or accidental) reuse.

Finally, specific business patterns should be represented in substantially the same manner as more basic business patterns of the same kind. For example, a specific relationship—such as *realization*—should, in a convenient representa-

---

92. The classical paper by Smith and Smith on database abstraction [SS1977] can also be mentioned here.

tion, not look very different from a much more basic relationship—such as *composition*. This happens because specific relationships are created using subtypes of generic ones.

The Very Basic Concepts and Constructs

> The body is a system or constitution: so is a tree: so is every machine.
>
> *Joseph Butler, 1729*

> But to explain these proposals, and to gain a full understanding of many arguments that have been used, we must look more in detail at the component parts of Lombard street, and at the curious set of causes which have made it assume its present singular structure.
>
> *Walter Bagehot, Lombard Street [B1873]*

As noted earlier, the basic underlying concepts and constructs used in all specifications, and in all businesses, are the same. These concepts have come from mathematics in general, rather than from any specific branch of mathematics. And in the same manner that we can speak about the unity of mathematics as "the dominant feature of current mathematics" [D1998], we can speak about the unity of all kinds of specifications.

The common concepts of mathematics have been discovered mostly by abstraction—which helps to form intuition—and by transfer of intuition and ideas from one branch of mathematics to another and still another. In doing so, we often want to make precise our intuitively useful but somewhat vague ideas. In most cases, the structure of the concepts remains the same, while the nature of elements of that structure is very different. The same approach to discovery and reuse of concepts is perfectly applicable to business and other kinds of specifications. Basic business patterns (such as *system, structure, invariant*, and so on) were discovered and transferred from one business area to another a long time ago. We can see, for example, how the pattern "invariant" has been used in mathematics, traditional architecture (Christopher Alexander), computing, business, philosophy, and so on. Also, we can see how the pattern "structure" has been used in all kinds of human endeavor, and how, specifically, the invariant that defines a particular kind of structure (such as the structure of a particular kind of relationship) is independent of the nature of elements of that structure.

Relationships

A useful model of any domain must capture the structure of that domain, i.e., the set of all relations among the individuals of that domain, as well as among these individuals and environmental items [B2001b]. This applies to both basic relationships (such as subtyping) and more specific ones (such as contracts). The relationships usually are expressed at the abstraction level of common properties of collections of individuals (such as all real estate purchase-and-sale contracts in a particular locality) rather than at the level of properties of specific collections of individuals (such as the specific contract of transferring the title of a house at 123 Maple Street in Anytown from XXXXX Construction Company to Ms. YYYYY on 29 February 2001[93] for the consideration of $234,999.43).

Relationships are perfect candidates for business patterns. Indeed, it would be extremely unreasonable to try to reinvent the properties of a contract, or (more specifically) of a real estate purchase-and-sale contract, in the context of specifying such a contract. It would be even more unreasonable to try to reinvent the concept and the properties of composition and its various subtypes. Instead of reinventing, we discover and reuse the existing relationship patterns in their contexts.

When specifying and reusing relationships, we note that their structure is much more important than their specific content: for example, the same real estate purchase-and-sale contract template[94] (a complex relationship based on a few simpler relationship templates) can be used for various kinds of parties, various kinds of real estate, various kinds of consideration, and in various contexts. If some repeatable specifics (valid at some locality, for example) are of interest, then we may create a more detailed template (for example, to satisfy the regulations of that locality). At the same time, if the same (specific) constructs with some changes could be used in different situations, then we may generalize our original template and reuse it; for example, a U.S. real estate purchase-and-sale contract may be generalized and this generalization reused for parties residing in other countries, or for parties buying/selling something else.

A relationship is defined by its invariant. The General Relationship Model [GRM]—an international standard—defines this invariant as "[a] logical predicate that must remain true during ... the lifetime of a ... relationship." In other words, violation of the relationship's invariant means that the relationship no longer

---

93.   Something may be wrong here with the instantiation of one of the "date" parameters.
94.   As noted earlier, the terms "business pattern" and "template" are used interchangeably.

exists (and is possibly replaced with some other relationship(s)). For example, the relationship s invariant becomes violated as a postcondition of the successful termination action applied to the participants of that relationship.

In the same manner that things and actions are characterized by their types and templates, so are relationships. For example, the real estate purchase-and-sale relationship described in the example above (with the consideration of $234,999.43) can be instantiated from the following templates: composition; composition-assembly; contract; real estate purchase-and-sale contract; contract for transferring a property title in Anytown; and many others. Some of these instantiations are quite simple "fill-in-the-blank" ones, while in some others, the action of filling in the blanks is not so trivial because the specifics to be filled in may refer to various context-dependent laws, regulations, customs, and so on.

Most interesting relationship invariants describe various ways of property determination based on characteristics of the relationship structure.

Generic Relationships

Some relationships—namely, composition, subtyping, and reference—are encountered everywhere, are called "generic relationships," and serve as building blocks for other, more complex relationships. These complex relationships are either partially instantiated generic relationships or obtained by applying generic relationships to other complex relationships. For a simple example, a contract is a composition in which the number of components is made specific (three) and components (several parties, subject matter, and consideration) are partially specified, that is, some of the types of these components are established; a complete specification of the components will result in a very specific contract instance. For another example, reporting about a transaction in a financial institution is (partially) specified using three subtyping relationships: it is subtyped into real-time reporting and reporting on demand; independently, into providing feeds to computer-based systems and providing reports for human use; independently, into reporting formulated using the party's viewpoint and reporting formulated using the counterparty's viewpoint. In this manner, semantically the same report uses terminology appropriate for the party reading and handling the report.

When we try to discover the properties of a relationship, we ask questions about the relationship in terms of various relationship templates. When we succeed in discovering a business pattern of a complex relationship, we obtain the properties of that relationship "for free": actualization of parameters is the only remaining step. However, even when we cannot find a template of a complex relationship that corresponds to the fragment in our model, we still can always use the more simple generic relationship templates. Because the semantics of generic relationships is far from trivial, when we discover how a fragment in a model can be described by means of some appropriately parameterized generic relationship, we contribute much to the semantics of our specification.

Generic relationships have been used for a long time and have been described in various texts, including mathematical and philosophical ones. The semantics of generic relationships (and of their important subtypes) is described in detail in Appendix B.

CRUD Operations

As we have seen, the properties of a relationship are defined by its invariant. These properties include the specifications of the generic Create-Read-Update-Delete (CRUD) operations[95] applied to the participants of that relationship. Specifically, such operations include creating or deleting a participant of a relationship, as well as changing the properties of a participant of that relationship. The generic CRUD operations for various generic relationships are specified in substantial detail in [KR1994].

Each operation applied to the participants of a relationship must preserve the invariant of that relationship (unless, of course, the operation terminates the relationship). This consideration shows how we created the specifications of the generic CRUD operations. But what happens if we want to consider changes of the relationship, i.e., CRUD operations applied to the relationship specification itself rather than to the relationship participants in the context of the existing relationship invariant? After all, we know that invariants may change when the business so requires.

The approach we take here is determined by the abstraction level, i.e., by what is considered "atomic." If at some abstraction level the changes of the relationship invariant are not visible, then these changes are treated as CRUD operations applied to the participants of that relationship. If, however, the changes of the relationship invariant are visible at some abstraction level, then the old relationship invariant becomes invalid, that is, the old relationship is terminated, and

---

95.   These are actions as defined in RM-ODP rather than interrogations and announcements as defined in the computational viewpoint of RM-ODP. We retained the name "operation" in the context of CRUD because this usage has been traditional.

a new relationship template (with its new invariant) must be instantiated. This new relationship invariant implies new specifications of CRUD operations to be applied to the participants of that relationship. Moreover, the participants of the old relationship (which satisfied the old relationship invariant) may or may not (collectively or individually) satisfy the new relationship invariant, so the instantiation of the new relationship template may require some changes of the (collective or individual) properties of these participants.

As an example, consider again a contract defined as a composite in a composition of several parties, subject matter, and consideration. In this context, consider the business need to add an arbitrator to the set of existing parties[96] together with appropriate operations in which an arbitrator should participate. How can we deal with this need? The preferable approach here would probably be to consider the "parties" component of the contract as being decomposed into the original party ("us"), the counterparty ("them"), and a set of other parties ("third parties") of which the arbitrator will become an element. Therefore, adding an element to the set of other parties (or deleting such an element) at this abstraction level will not change the invariant of the contract relationship. Of course, another approach is possible in which the invariant of the contract relationship is considered to be changed as the result of the addition of the arbitrator as a "third party" to the contract. The choice of the approach here is determined by the level of *relevance* of such changes to the business (keeping in mind that abstraction means suppression of irrelevant detail); therefore, such a decision is usually made by the business stakeholders.

The Uniform Commercial Code

Several important business patterns are precisely described in the (U.S.) Uniform Commercial Code (UCC) [CS1990]. We have seen and reused the business pattern of a contract, both as a composition of several parties, subject matter, and consideration and as a result of negotiations—an offer, possible counteroffer(s), and acceptance. Of course, we used only the top-level templates of these constructs; we may be interested in refinements as well. These refinements may include delegation of performance, warranties, delivery, "sale on approval," handling of various risks, consideration installments, and so on.

We can also use other patterns described in the UCC, such as commercial paper (drafts of which checks are a subtype, certificates of deposit, and notes)

---

96.   This example was initiated by Joaquin Miller.

and its handling including transfer and negotiation, as well as bank deposits and collections. This includes a substantial amount of precisely defined constraints governing the actions in a clearing house environment. The Uniform Commercial Code also includes various specific patterns about secured transactions, such as a collateralized loan the existence of which is usually a precondition for a success-ful execution of a real estate purchase-and-sale contract.

More Specific Patterns

There is no need to repeat the descriptions of various specific patterns some examples of which were presented in the section about templates and elsewhere in the book. At the same time, it is important to reiterate that libraries of specific business patterns save lots of intellectual effort, time, and money. For example, when we need to model exotic foreign exchange options, it is clearly easier to reuse the business pattern of an option than the business pattern of a general financial contract. At the same time, if a specific business pattern does not exist (or could not be discovered!), then it is always possible to reuse a more general one. Even in a totally new business area, it is always possible to reuse generic relationships and probably other business patterns such as "contract."

Business-specific business patterns are composed of business-generic (such as "contract") and other business-specific ones, and these compositions use fun-damental (such as "invariant") and generic (such as "composition") business pat-terns. For example, "composition" itself is a generic business pattern defined using the fundamental business pattern of "invariant."

Business patterns do not appear magically. More abstract ones, such as "invariant" or "composition," are difficult to discover but can be applied every-where. More specific ones, such as "foreign exchange option" or "life insurance annuity," are easier to discover and formulate, although they are usually applica-ble only in their specific context. If a precise and explicit specification of an important business construct (that we want to use and possibly reuse) is not available, then we probably will want to create such a specification and general-ize it as a business pattern for future reuse. This is why the business pattern of a contract was distilled and formulated in the Uniform Commercial Code.

Reuse: Pattern Matching in Context

The "instinctive skill at pattern matching" [H1989] noted by C.A.R. Hoare in the context of category theory makes modeling so effective. As noted by Dusko Pav-lovic, categories dam the flood of structure in software engineering. This is extremely important because it lets a software engineer get rid of "too much stuff" and tame complexity. I agree with Dines Bjørner who considers business modeling and, specifically, domain modeling as an essential part of software engineering.

In a manner *somewhat* similar to category theory (although not as abstract!), this skill of pattern matching can be acquired and developed. And it appears to be conceptually simple: non-experts in analysis including business SMEs such as traders, back office specialists of financial firms, and insurance underwriters have appreciated and successfully practiced matching not only business-specific patterns, but also general patterns described in this book—such as "composition" or "subtyping"—in the contexts of their specific businesses.

As in [H1989], in modeling, the emphasis is on the concepts underlying the patterns and on the similarities of their usage rather than on the technicalities. We have observed, for example, how the same composition pattern has been used in very different areas of human endeavor, or how substantially more specific patterns—such as "contract" or "contract negotiation"—have been used and often have been a foundation of models of apparently quite different business fragments. But there is nothing unusual here: the conceptual unity of different areas of activity in which humans are interested (i.e., of different business areas) was observed centuries ago, for example, by Francis Hutcheson (contracts) and Adam Smith (the "invisible hand" that defines the emergent properties of a market economy, and many others), and what we see now is just a more detailed refinement of these general constructs defined and recognized as patterns.

Pattern Structuring and Instantiation

Like a good reference librarian, a good business modeler is aware not only of various business patterns available for reuse, but also—more importantly—of the internal and external structure of the system of patterns, that is, of relationships between them and of various contexts in which they can be instantiated and used, individually or collectively. We can even use the term, "a business model of business patterns." In this manner, it is possible and desirable to create and maintain an ontology ("what is there") of business patterns. This (extensible) ontology helps us to determine what things and relationships to model and how to model them.

As we have seen, business patterns can be classified into:

- fundamental (such as "invariant"),
- generic (such as "composition" or "subtyping"),

- business-generic (such as "name in context" or "contract"),
- business-specific (such as "financial contract," "derivative," or "option" in finance).

Business-specific business patterns are constructed from business-generic and other business-specific ones using composition, subtyping, and other fundamental and generic business patterns. Observe that generic business patterns such as "composition" and "subtyping" are themselves defined using fundamental business patterns such as "invariant."

As a relatively simple example of using the business model of business patterns, we can look at the business pattern of a financial contract. A financial contract is a subtype of a general (business-generic) contract in which the subject matter is a financial product or service. Further, this financial product or service—a component of the financial contract business pattern—is itself a business pattern. A financial product can be subtyped into fungible (i.e., not unique[97] and therefore, in this context, readily tradeable in the marketplace) and not fungible (and therefore not so readily tradeable). Further, and independently, a financial product can be subtyped into primary (such as common stock, i.e., issued in accordance with the issuer's structuring rules) and secondary (such as options, i.e., based on some underlying—a primary (fungible or not) or secondary product[98]—and issued in accordance with structuring rules determined by the financial industry). The essence of this financial product pattern is shown in the diagram at the top of page 166.

Clearly, a more detailed refinement of these business patterns is possible and useful for modeling in any financial area.

For a more specialized example, we can look at exception requests arising when a customer having a good relationship history with a financial institution requests an extension in the amount or conditions of payment to that institution (for example, in some margin calls or in repaying a mortgage loan). The extension, if granted, is a contract, and granting an extension is an instantiation of the contract negotiation pattern composed of an offer (an extension request by the customer due to temporary extenuating or unusual circumstances), possible counteroffer(s), and acceptance. The financial institution may agree to such a

---

97. "Grain and coin are fungibles, because one guinea, or one bushel or boll of sufficient merchantable wheat, precisely supplies the place of another" (Erskine, 1765).
98. For example, an underlying for an option may be another option.

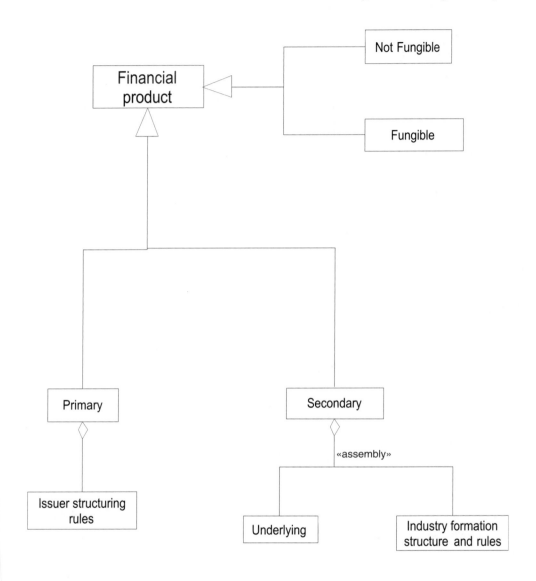

contract because it wants to retain a customer with a good history; retaining is the consideration from the financial institution's viewpoint.

Any business pattern reveals the common properties of its instantiations. For example, realtors take the business pattern of a real estate purchase-and-sale contract (*represented* as a document with some slots to be filled in) "off the shelf" and instantiate it for their customers, so that the specifics of the parties (buyer and seller), the actual property, and the consideration (and possibly some others) are filled in for each particular instantiation of that pattern. This is a rather straightforward activity. A real estate builder who is also a seller will probably use a much more specific pattern of a real estate purchase-and-sale contract with an even more straightforward instantiation. At the same time, more generic business patterns—such as the one of a general-purpose contract—are simpler but require more substantial work in their instantiation because the specifics to be filled into their slots are much more complex.

There are usually many ways to structure and instantiate patterns to reach the same result. The total amount of detail in the result is the same, no matter how the structuring and instantiation are accomplished. More abstract patterns can be used in many contexts, but they require more intellectual effort during instantiation. More detailed patterns can be used in more limited contexts, and they require less intellectual effort during instantiation.

Metaphors and Notations

A notation, like a metaphor, is a tool for thought. Joseph Goguen observed that "[a]nalogy, metaphor, representation and user interface have much in common: each involves signs, meaning, one or more people, and some context, including culture; moreover each can be looked at dually from either a design or a use perspective. [...] Metaphors can be seen as semiotic morphisms from one system of concepts to another. [...] The purpose of semiotic morphisms is to provide a way to describe the movement (mapping, translation, interpretation, representation) of signs in one system to signs in another system." [G1999]. A good metaphor preserves as much of the essential source structure as possible.

Metaphors may be very beneficial[99] but should be used with caution. On the one hand, "[i]t is no exaggeration to say that metaphors are the most significant tool we use for understanding and communicating in many key areas of life" [G2001]. (The term *metaphor* was coined by Aristotle.) Most essential aspects of

---

99. For example, consider E.W. Dijkstra's metaphor: "if I have to describe the influence PL/I can have on its users, the closest metaphor that comes to my mind is that of a drug. [...] within a one-hour lecture in praise of PL/I, [its devoted user] managed to ask for the addition of about 50 new "features," little supposing that the main source of his problems could very well be that it contained already far too many "features." The speaker displayed all the depressing symptoms of addiction, reduced as he was to the state of mental stagnation in which he could only ask for more, more, more ..." [D1972]. This metaphor can be reused for various more modern specific languages.

user interface with modern computer-based systems are explained using meta-phors. Metaphors often are an excellent source of inspiration. For example, they may be very helpful in discovering the commonalities between apparently differ-ent situations and therefore for the process and the result of abstraction. On the other hand, metaphors may be misleading when they are based on incomplete, unclear, wrong, or non-essential analogies, and in these situations, to avoid con-fusion, they should be replaced with better metaphors or with literal expressions. E.W. Dijkstra observed that metaphors do not and cannot apply at all in drasti-cally novel situations, such as the pill, nuclear weapons, and computer-based information systems. More generally, literal expressions are propositions the cor-rectness of which can be asserted or denied, while metaphors are not.

Similarly, choosing an inadequate notational tool, or a tool inappropriate for an audience, leads to serious problems in communicating about the semantics—either in general or with that audience. A notation can transform thinking: "users of markedly different grammars are pointed by their grammars toward different types of observations—and hence are not equivalent as observers, but must arrive at somewhat different views of the world" [W1956]. Some of these nota-tional problems may be perceived as serious but can be solved very easily, while some others may not be immediately apparent but, in fact, may be much more serious.

As an example of the former problems, we may consider the need to repre-sent business specifications in a notation like UML perceived by some to be inap-propriate for (having the reputation of "not understandable by") business SMEs. All too often, specifications are presented to business SMEs and decision makers using stories, slides[100] with box-and-line diagrams, and handwaving, although such presentations are properly considered to be not sufficiently precise for IT developers. This approach is counterproductive and condescending because good business SMEs perfectly understand the importance of precision and make precise decisions in their everyday work. In making these precise decisions, business SMEs refer to the essentials of the business in the appropriate contexts rather than to various accidentals.

Arguments in favor of specific decisions are used in order to influence some fragments of the business model of the decision makers, and so they must refer to

---

100. "Was the dot-com bust engendered by people who had suddenly realized that they had invested a fortune based on a few beautiful graphics that were laughably called a business plan?" [L2001].

this business model. If the model is not made precise and explicit, then any argumentation becomes fuzzy and may result in "talking at cross purposes." The discussion participants, in order to succeed in decision making, should always refer to the same business model presented in such a manner that they understand it. Therefore, our specifications should demonstrate the essentials in which the specification users are interested, no more and no less. This includes the essentials of the notation itself, so that the unnecessary complexities of the required notation should be abstracted away.[101] In order to do that, we can choose a very small but powerful subset of the required notation and consistently use only this subset (an improved variant syntax) for presentation. When we choose such a subset, we often must provide precisely defined clarifications or extensions of some existing notational elements or relationships between them, as demonstrated in Appendix A for our tiny subset of UML for business modeling.

As an example of the latter, much more serious problems, we may look at the misunderstandings that happen when business specifications are represented using metaphors and notations based on message-oriented object models. Metaphorically, such representations require handling the structure of a "rich soup" (Joseph Goguen) of objects and messages—a very demanding adventure. Usage of these representations implies making premature and irrelevant decisions about the "owners" of invariants or actions. In some cases, such decisions cannot be made at all because some invariants or actions are inherently joint. Even the concept of a participant of an action (as opposed to sender and recipient) was considered less obvious in the context of such inadequate notations; this often leads to anthropomorphic expressions such as "a transaction sends a message to an account" (or "wants to send a message ...") that alienate business SMEs.

Experience

> If the final form appears ugly, and if reason does not bring appreciation of beauty therein, we may be certain there is something illogical in the design, and it is this instinctive feeling that something is wrong ... that often will suggest a better solution for the problem.
> *H. Kempton-Dyson, Design, in [S1904]*

---

101. Semiotic considerations may be successfully used for this purpose, as demonstrated, for example, in [GF1999] and in the discussion about notation and usage of names in [vG1990].

A "typical"—but detailed enough—top-level business specification may comprise ten to forty diagrams of the kind shown in this book (or in [K1999] and many other sources). Some of these diagrams may be more complex than shown here; the permitted (or tolerated) complexity is determined, among other things, by the convenience of the business customers of the specification. Clearly, a narrative that explicates the diagram in a carefully phrased stylized natural language is required for each of the diagrams because some people don't like diagrams, and also—more importantly—because some things cannot be conveniently represented in a diagram.

Some fragments of a top-level business specification may be refined into more detailed business specifications. This is determined by the customers. In particular, those fragments that describe parts of the business requiring support by an IT system (determined during business design) need to be specified in sufficient detail so that the IT system specification could be created with explicit traceability to that business specification, as well as to the corresponding technological infrastructure specification.

Clarity and explicitness in writing such specifications are absolutely essential. Examples may and often should be added as illustrations, especially elegant ones because they encourage understanding, but no specification should be based on examples.

A business specification is the base document used by all stakeholders in discussing and making decisions about the business. It is used at least for the following purposes:

- to make strategic, tactical, and operational business decisions that demonstrably support the objectives of the firm,
- to demonstrate the competitive advantage and core competencies of the firm,
- to increase adaptability due to changes in the firm's regulatory environment and market conditions,
- to ensure proper handling of existing and future business processes, including business process change and business process automation,
- to serve as a guide to procedures and manuals for training employees,
- to serve as a source for all business information needed to create or change IT systems essential for automation of some business processes.

Walkthroughs and Reuse

> At the same time, though one Player is enough, a good deal more amusement may be got by two working at it together, and correcting each other's mistakes.
>
> *Lewis Carroll, The Game of Logic [C1887]*

Working in small groups—such as groups of two people—and reviewing each other's work, both in creating specifications and in realizing them, is a "highly effective way of organizing the software work" (Peter Naur, [SE1969]). The same approach was independently invented and successfully used by Ber Levi in Latvia in the mid-1960s and thereafter; this author was fortunate to be a student and later a member of Ber Levi's programming team.

When we try to discover the semantics of a business—be it a traditional business or a business of technological infrastructure—analysts and SMEs need to work together to understand and precisely specify the semantics of that business. In doing so, analysts carefully listen to business people; ask questions about the business in terms of various business patterns that they think are appropriate; and, together with business SMEs, abstract out the essential characteristics of the business. We need immediately to record the common understanding (because people tend to forget very quickly), so a scribe is essential. At the same time, the scribe can participate in the discovery process only in a limited way, so it is desirable to use some technological means to improve the quality of recording. Fortunately, this is possible: our experience suggests that using an ordinary whiteboard and a digital camera solves the problem of recording. This requires writing "everything" (as much as is reasonable) on the whiteboard in such a manner that the walkthrough participants would be able to agree on the contents of the fragments of the whiteboard. As soon as such an agreement has been reached, the fragments are recorded using a digital camera. Of course, some or all participants may later disagree with the recorded fragments, but this is only natural, especially in the context of "precision over correctness." It is desirable to be able to print and distribute the recording to the participants immediately after it is made. All recordings made during a walkthrough (or modeling) session will collectively represent the minutes of that session.

The agreed upon results of the session are represented in the chosen tool (pencil and paper or something else). There is no need for all participants to work on that. These representations are then quickly distributed to the participants for their review and feedback.

The results of walkthroughs may be abstracted out (as business patterns) and reused. Such abstraction may not be easy; however, reuse pays off rather quickly (possibly in other engagements, but often in the same engagement as well). Abstraction leads to the discovery of important commonalities between apparently different things or situations. Of course, reuse is possible only if the reusable material is clearly specified and is, to an even greater extent than a "more ordinary" specification, a *small deliverable with large information content*. Most specifications in this book, including all generic business pattern specifications, are the result of such abstraction.

Existing Material

In quite a few situations, various documents about the business already exist. These documents may include (a large amount of) prose descriptions as well as "data models" and other kinds of specifications. Lots of useful information may be included, but it often happens that this information is semiotically polluted: not well-structured, incomplete, or unclear. The concerns of the business and the IT implementation of some of its fragments (including user interface) may not be properly separated. More often than not, the semantics of "relationships" shown in the existing materials is not clear because these (binary) "relationships" are specified using links with, at best, "meaningful names." The term "relationship" in the previous sentence was used in quotes because the semantics of a relationship is determined by its invariant, and when the invariant is absent, the semantics is unclear and the construct may or may not be a relationship. In many cases, the construct is a fragment of a non-binary relationship.

To understand the semiotically polluted existing material, we observe that—in accordance with the general approach of modern semiotics—the semantics of existing texts should be discovered by taking into account the encoding mechanisms that generated these texts. In the semiotics of history, this is called discovering facts from a story. Therefore, in order to create well-structured, precise, and explicit specifications based in part on this existing material, it is advisable to use the services of a guide—a subject matter expert in this material—who will provide a roadmap (based on these encoding mechanisms) and who will answer questions formulated in terms of various business patterns. In this manner, it will be possible to clean up and restructure the relevant fragments of the existing material and to discover the semantics that was not included in these fragments or that remained unclear.

Discovering the relationships is usually the most important aspect of clarifying the structure of the business domain. In many cases, it is possible to reuse various business-specific patterns to do just that. If business-specific patterns appear to be unavailable, it is still always possible to reuse generic relationships within the context of the existing models, even if all "relationships" shown in the models are in fact just (named or unnamed) binary links. Because relationship semantics usually describes property determination, it often will be necessary to discover and demonstrate which binary links collectively constitute the structure of a newly discovered composition or a subtyping. In doing so, based on the explicitly specified semantics of the relationship, it will be possible to determine missing links (to components or subtypes). It will also be possible to determine and resolve, together with the SMEs, various defects of the existing models, such as incomplete, unclear, or inconsistent semantics. At the same time, sometimes creating fragments of a new business model from scratch may be cheaper than salvaging fragments of an existing polluted model that has been stored on paper, "out there in these two boxes."

As an example, a huge existing model within a large pharmaceutical company environment contained lots of binary "relationships" such as an "experiment" related to a certain biological entity by a "relationship" called "tests." In order to resolve the semantic defects of this model, it was noted that specific relationships were (partial) instantiations of generic ones. Therefore, the invariant that precisely defines the semantics of a specific relationship is a (partial) instantiation of the invariant that defines the semantics of the appropriate generic relationship. Thus, it was proposed to reconsider the binary "relationships" in the model, look at which of them were fragments of single non-binary relationships, and in doing so think in terms of generic relationships. For example, the "tests" relationship above probably indicated a composition that would probably need to include the following components: "what is to be tested" (such as the biological entity), the properties being tested, the testing (success) criteria, the testing methodology or something like that (all or some of these may be components of "experiment"), many other things that any good SME can tell, and so on. Because the structure of a relationship is more important than its content, all testing relationships would be alike (this is in part what the regulatory bodies want); if important differences exist, then these would determine interesting subtypes of testing.

Much can be reused from existing materials, even if these materials are of less than stellar quality. However, some information and approaches are best avoided.

What to Avoid

Some experiences—technological and other—are best avoided, in particular, because they lead to semiotic pollution. To quote Dijkstra, "it is well known that we don't gain automatically from every experience, on the contrary, that the wrong experience may easily corrupt the soundness of our judgement" [D1969].

The best way to avoid the wrong technological experiences that often stand in the way of understanding the business—unless the business we consider is precisely the business of technology—is to ignore technological details altogether. And the best way to do that is to start with a real or hypothetical pencil-and-paper-based business domain and its processes, such as described in the best books about economics, banking, and finance published centuries ago. The basic structure of businesses mostly remained the same since then; and for those, mostly local, fragments that changed, these changes can be specified in a clear and crisp manner suggested by a good technology-neutral specification of these basics.

Some additional advice about avoidance follows. It is mostly based on the need to create and use abstract and precise specifications understandable by humans.

- Avoid excessive detail even in describing traditional businesses, especially in business process descriptions. This specifically applies to avoiding the operational approach to modeling when the modeler and the business SMEs collectively drown in a sea of avoidable and inadequately structured details.
- Avoid complex notations. If these notations are required for some reason, then choose a very small and well-defined subset.
- Postpone unnecessary decisions. The same approach is used by good traditional engineers and business decision makers. A precise specification does not need to be detailed. Even in specifying a solution of a problem, postpone the temptation to bind any particular technology into the solution, much as Dijkstra would warn against solving a programming problem in terms of a particular programming language.
- Do not strive for complete specifications at the early stages of modeling: simplicity and precision are more important than completeness and even correctness.
- Never rely on meaningful names even if the customers like them and appear to recognize them. Different customers may and often do use the same name to denote (substantially or somewhat) different things.
- Avoid requirements (of all kinds) in terms of solutions.
- Avoid hacking—the urge to deliver something, anything. Hacking is possible not only in programming but also in analysis. The programming prov-

erb "Think first, program later" is clearly applicable in analysis. There may be no visible progress in analysis deliverables for some time, but better understanding takes time to be distilled and formulated.

The examples presented in this book (and in actual engagements referred to throughout the book) applied this avoidance discipline.

An Example: *Human Action* and the "New Economy"

Let's start with some essential functions of a living and acting person as described by von Mises in *Human Action* [M1949]. Any person fulfills many roles in life, and from the viewpoint of economics, the ones of substantial interest are the roles of a consumer and a money earner. We show them as components of the functions of a person. Further, there are several mutually overlapping ways to earn money, and von Mises enumerates the most important ones as entrepreneur, landowner, capitalist, and worker. We will discuss some of these roles in more detail. The subtyping of a money earner into these four roles is overlapping because the same person can at the same time fulfill more than one of them, and by virtue of doing so can acquire the properties of the corresponding types. For example, in a start-up company, the same person may be a promoter of a new profit-generating idea (and thus be an entrepreneur), provide some amount of money to invest for the new company (and thus be a capitalist), lease some facilities such as an office for the new company (and thus be a landowner), and finally do some technical, managerial, or bureaucratic work for hire to benefit the new company (and thus be a worker). Of course, these money earner roles fulfilled by a particular person need not be within the same company!

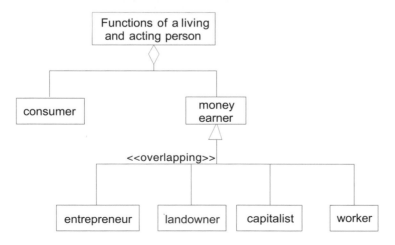

Let's continue with considering a single enterprise. It includes participants of various kinds, and so we will look at various types of such an enterprise participant. In accordance with von Mises, these types are of a promoter, capitalist, manager, technician, and bureaucrat. (Landowners may be included here together with capitalists.) Because any human action is directed toward influencing the future state of affairs, the outcome of an action is always uncertain, and therefore "all are entrepreneurs" in a functional distribution, that is, all fulfill, to a certain extent, the role of entrepreneur. (Entrepreneurs and all other types here "describe not men but a definite function" [M1949, p. 253]. Specifically, an entrepreneur is "an acting man in regard to the changes occurring in the data of the market," while a capitalist and landowner act in regard "to the changes in value and price... brought about by the mere passing of time as a consequence of the different valuation of... goods," and a worker acts in regard "to the employment of the factor of production human labor.") Promoters ("those who are especially eager to profit from adjusting production to the expected changes in conditions... who have more initiative... and a quicker eye than the crowd... the pushing and promoting pioneers of economic improvement") are considered by von Mises as a subclass of entrepreneurs. As noted above, these subtypes of an enterprise community participant are overlapping because the same person can acquire properties of several or all of them. We do not include here other stakeholders of the enterprise, most importantly, customers who ultimately determine the outcome of the activities of that enterprise, as well as regulators, competitors, suppliers, and others.

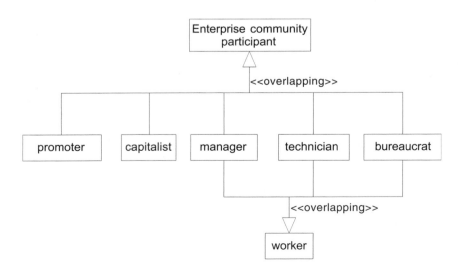

In an enterprise, von Mises specifically looks at three—overlapping—sub-types of a worker, that is, a manager, a technician, and a bureaucrat. All workers are hired by a promoter. A manager is hired to assist the promoter in the subordinate economic aspects of the promoter's general plan of adjusting production (and the discretion of a manager is restricted only by considerations of profit and loss), while a technician is hired to provide for the technological aspects of that plan. A bureaucrat, unlike a manager, does not consider any profit motive, and the methods of economic calculation are not applicable to the work of a bureaucrat. "No accountant can establish whether or not a police department ... has succeeded." Thus, the discretion of a bureaucrat is restricted by lots of specific rules and regulations, and bureaucratic methods are indispensable where economic calculation is unfeasible.

Let's find out whether this approach works in the "modern economy." More specifically, let's look at how *The Wall Street Journal* describes those in e-commerce enterprises who make e-commerce tick [W2001], and in doing so let's use the business patterns introduced by von Mises and described above. We notice that *The Wall Street Journal* describes representative examples of people fulfilling specific roles in e-commerce enterprises, that these roles usually differ from the more traditional specific roles in the "old economy," and that these new roles perfectly fit into a refinement of the business pattern of an enterprise community participant. We also notice some interesting and instructive peculiarities. First, many workers, such as a turnaround expert, are not hired to work full time by a single promoter but have contractual (often temporary) relationships with several enterprises. Thus, these contractual workers are their own promoters. (This might have been the default of an ordinary enterprise, although von Mises did not emphasize such arrangements as the only possible or even as preferable.) Second, there are no bureaucrats whatsoever. Third, the subtyping of important specific roles (such as a privacy officer) into a manager and a technician is clearly overlapping.

The figure at the top of page 178 demonstrates these new roles in e-commerce. Of course, *The Wall Street Journal* in its e-commerce report did not enumerate all roles but described only the most interesting ones. We show other roles of promoters, managers, and technicians by means of boxes labeled with ellipses.

In essence, from the viewpoint of economics, of "the business of the business," we see that an enterprise of the "new economy," as described in *The Wall Street Journal* in 2001, is driven by the same general kinds of participants as an

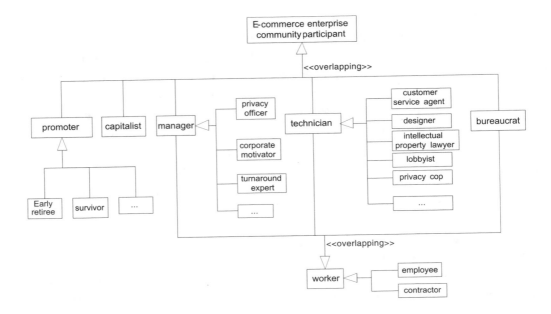

enterprise of the "old economy." This is as it should be: the business rules of a market economy (as described, for example, by Adam Smith and Ludwig von Mises) are valid independently of the technological peculiarities, although the specifics of these rules may differ.

Another Example: "Old" and "New" Business Enterprises

The previous example was mostly about commonalities. Now look at some important differences between enterprises of the "old" and the "new" economies. We will follow the approach of *Metacapitalism* by Means and Schneider presented in [MS2000] and the approach of Peter Drucker from [D2001].

On the one hand, a traditional enterprise has been based on its physical capital because existing companies have had a large base of physical capital. Further, the physical capital has determined various components of the company's working capital which, in turn, determined the human capital and, finally, the brand capital. Thus, the means of production have determined "everything." Such a company has tended to have as much as possible of its supply chain under its control. Efficiency of such companies often increased, but this was not always applicable to their effectiveness.

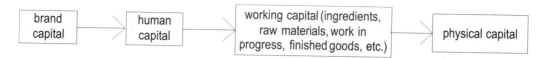

These companies, ultimately, were good at selling the customer "what the company made," that is, at "sales push."

In other words, the saleable units (products or services) of such companies—which were parts of their brand capital—determined the customer wishes. As an example, here is a quote from E.W. Dijkstra: "In June [1984], during my last preparatory visit to the USA, I tried to order a telephone to be installed upon my arrival in September. The lady reacted as if I had made her an indecent proposal: didn't I know that after 30 days I 'would be dropped out of the computer'? This was not incidental, this was characteristic; just think how often the bank has denied you a reasonable service on the ground that 'the computer won't let them do it'" [D1984]. These arrangements were not always convenient for customers, and in some situations the need for new or improved saleable units was determined by the need to keep up with competitors. Creating substantially new saleable units was not easy because too much had to be changed in the chain from physical capital to brand capital, that is, to the saleable unit.

On the other hand, from the customer's perspective, there is a better way in which customer requirements determine the saleable units:

To succeed here, it is necessary to reverse the direction of reference relationships in the model of a traditional enterprise. The new enterprise model will look like:

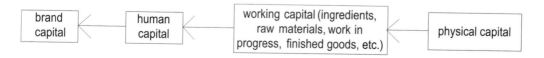

Clearly, in the new enterprise, the physical capital does not determine much, nor does working capital. Moreover, human capital (and creativity) here is of substantially greater importance, and the supply chain is no longer under the control of the enterprise. Means and Schneider call this kind of business model a *decapitalized* one. Such an enterprise does not need to manufacture or assemble any physical products; it invents and designs those that provide a clearly demonstrable competitive advantage (outsourcing all manufacture and assembly), and thus provides for industry leadership. We know examples of such excellent enterprises and are happy to use their saleable units. The same approach applies when the saleable unit is a service rather than a product. The creation of these saleable units is composed of human capital as well as working capital and physical capital, and the value added by the enterprise, as well as its competitive advantage, is often *in the composition*, that is, in the choice of components (often provided by someone else) and in the way these components are combined.

Ultimately, as noted elsewhere in this book, a knowledge worker with no physical capital can become an entrepreneur because this worker owns the means of production (and can easily create brand capital) necessary for success in the marketplace. Everything else can be outsourced to (bought in a competitive manner from) those enterprises that specialize in specific kinds of working capital and physical capital. The importance of the market is substantially increased (as it should be for a successful economy). This approach makes it much easier to prepare and realize strategic decisions based on knowledge about a company's business environment and its competitive position in the marketplace. As noted by Paul Strassman, 65 percent of the profit performance of corporations can be attributed to such knowledge.

From the modeling viewpoint, the difference between a traditional and a modern enterprise is similar to the difference between a hierarchical and a non-hierarchical composition. This also follows from the observations made by Peter Drucker in [D2001]: a traditional enterprise (or industry) is composed of enterprise-specific or industry-specific components, and this composition is *hierarchical* because the components pertain only to "their" specific enterprise or industry, while a modern enterprise (or industry) is composed of both generic and specific components, and this composition is *non-hierarchical* because many components are not specific to that enterprise or industry and are reused by various enterprises or industries.

To be somewhat more detailed, the composition corresponding to a traditional enterprise is a (hierarchical) *assembly*: the composite (the brand capital) can exist only if its components (specifically, physical and working capitals) already exist. These components cannot be used anywhere else. Contrariwise, the composition corresponding to a modern enterprise is a *subordination*: the components are bound into that composition only when the composite (the brand capital) already exists. These components can be used in composing other enterprises. In other words, the different kinds of composition describing a traditional and a modern enterprise determine "what comes first"—the components (as in a more rigid, traditional enterprise), or the composite (as in much more flexible, modern enterprise).

Conclusion: Debuzzwordification

He was thoughtful and grave—but the orders he gave
   Were enough to bewilder a crew.
When he cried "Steer to starboard, but keep her head larboard!"
   What on earth was the helmsman to do?
         Lewis Carroll, The Hunting of the Snark [C1876]

As early as 1968, R.W. Hamming observed in his Turing Award Lecture: "perhaps the central problem we face in all of computer science is how we are to get to the situation where we build on top of the work of others rather than redoing so much of it *in a trivially different way*." These trivially different ways often are differentiated by means of way-specific buzzwords. New technological buzzwords appear all the time, and, unfortunately, Hamming's observation is still valid today.

Technology by itself does not solve business problems: "the entrepreneur's technological ability does not affect the specific entrepreneurial profit or loss ... the specific entrepreneurial profits and losses are not produced by the quantity of physical output. They depend on the adjustment of output to the most urgent wants of the consumers. What produces them is the extent to which the entrepreneur has succeeded or failed in anticipating the future—necessary uncertain—state of the market" [M1949]. Of course, some technological artefacts, when appropriately used, make new business opportunities possible. A business specification of these artefacts in the context of the business domain under consideration demonstrates their business relevance.

When we specify or reason about business or technological artefacts (including apparent breakthroughs), we need to clearly understand what we are talking about and be able to express this understanding. Buzzwords may provide a warm and fuzzy feeling to some, especially to those who "got it" [W2000], but they are counterproductive and may lead to ("dot-com"-like or other) disasters. Some of these disasters became front page news. Lots of large, or smaller-scale, disasters happen due to attempts to replace a problem statement or a reasonable discussion about the problem with statements about an apparently new and all-encompassing fashionable technology, method, or tool. This leads to semiotic pollution and widens the proverbial gap between business and IT. Debuzzwordification gets rid of semiotic pollution and is essential for not becoming obsolete in 12 (or is it 18?) months when a new set of buzzwords will become fashionable.

With the development of new technological opportunities, new concepts and constructs (as opposed to new names of existing ones) may appear, but this happens quite seldom. Therefore, it makes perfect sense to consider the basic concepts and constructs first and instantiate them within the context of the current technology or business needs. Their usage leads to stable business models that stay relevant even with the appearance of new fashions. These concepts have become instantiable templates, and we have seen many examples of their usage in this book and elsewhere. The division of labor on which modern civilization is based [H1945], together with Adam Smith's "invisible hand," can be easily explained using the concepts of composition and of emergent properties of the composite [KRS1999]. No buzzwords were used or required in these specifications.

By debuzzwordification, we make the rules of the game precise and explicit and *bring them to the public domain*. They can and should be learned explicitly. This is the main distinction between a profession and a craft learned only implicitly, by observing a master (or a magician).

On Thinking

This book is about thinking. E.W. Dijkstra observed that the teaching of programming is the teaching of thinking; and of course, the same applies to the teaching of modeling. In both cases, the goal of thinking is to be able to tame complexity intrinsic in programming or modeling, that is, to reduce formalizable reasoning to a doable amount. In order to do that, it is essential to be able to understand (that is, properly structure) large amounts of information. This (abstraction) activity cannot be formalized.

When we teach or learn modeling, we should take into account that "building a software system is similar to developing a mathematical theory. Mathematics, as software construction, can be taught, including the general principles that help talented students produce brilliant results; but no teaching can guarantee success. As soon as you open up the problem domain, no simplistic approach will work; the designer must exert his best powers of invention." (Bertrand Meyer).

And another quote may be used to demonstrate whether the book's objective has been achieved: "It is nice when a reader finishes a book with an unerring feeling that now he does not know more than he did not know earlier" [G2000]. I hope that this book provides such a feeling.

Appendix A[102]

The UML Subset Used for Representation

This Appendix describes the UML subset used to represent specifications in the book.

Both the UML representation and (earlier!) the generic relationships have been widely used by the author and many others in multiple engagements in financial, insurance, telecommunications, document management, military, and other domains, as well as in the domains of information management project development and information system specification and design.

On Tools and Specifications

Specifiers use tools: we like, or are required to, use them. At the same time, tools are often a part of our problem set; a specifier who must understand and demonstrate the semantics of a complex subject matter does not need to struggle with the additional complexity of the technological infrastructure used to reason about the specification—a methodology, a set of buzzwords, or a tool.

When the tool is a programming language, its "powerful features," in E.W. Dijkstra's words [D1976a], often belong "more to the problem set than to the solution set," and as a result the programmer may become "an expert coder of trivial [usually given] algorithms." Thus, "the really tough problems are way

---

102. This appendix is an abridged incremental modification of [K2000b].

beyond his mental horizon." The same considerations clearly apply to all kinds of specifications. The tough problems, both in programming and in business specifications, are about understanding and proper structuring of large amounts of information. Clear thinking is essential to formulate and solve such problems. Tools should help, and to do that, a tool should be as simple as possible.

There exist many ways to represent a business specification. Choosing an appropriate representation mechanism and a tool is not trivial, especially taking into account that the readers and validators of a business specification—the business subject matter experts (SMEs)—appreciate precision but do not appreciate excessive representational complexity or technological terms.

At the same time, too often we must use a prescribed tool for various reasons, including non-technical ones. When the choice of a tool has been made for us, all is not lost: if the tool is powerful but overly complex, then only a relatively small essential subset of the tool can be used. This subset should be sufficient to represent the concepts and constructs used in business specifications. If certain concepts cannot be represented in the chosen subset of the tool, then it must be appropriately extended. In other words, there should be no methodology- or tool-imposed restrictions for representing a business specification.

This Appendix describes how UML has been successfully used to represent business specifications in real projects in insurance, financial, business process change, and other areas. A small subset of UML was chosen for this purpose, and it was possible to use UML stereotypes in order to represent generic relationships. The customers, including business SMEs, were willing and able to read and validate the business specifications represented in this manner.

What to Include in UML Diagrams?

Clarity and understandability are essential for a business specification to be accepted, i.e., read, validated, reasoned about, and used to verify its realization(s). Thus, all semantic concepts and constructs used in a business specification should have a clear and explicit representation, so that the semantics of the specification could be easily inferred by the readers of its representation without spending too much time to figure out the meaning of representation mechanisms.

Because a business specification includes business things, actions, and the relationships between them, our UML representation includes class diagrams and a similar representation of relationships between actions. We introduce only those bare essentials of notation that are needed to understand and reason about the specification's conceptual space. In doing so, we strive for simplicity and uniformity: similar but different semantic concepts should have similar but distinguishable representations.

Because a business specification must be explicit and complete (so that it is usable without the business SME around), its graphical representation (using UML or otherwise) should never be a "box-and-line" diagram. In a UML class diagram, all relationships should be precisely defined. Thus, for each relationship of a UML class diagram, we use an abbreviation, such as a UML stereotype, that denotes a (generic) relationship defined by its invariant. By doing so, we explicitly refer to the relationship semantics. Contrariwise, a named line does not define relationship semantics because a "meaningful" name possibly provides a warm and fuzzy feeling, but may mean (very) different things to different people, and also because most relationships are not binary.

This approach helps significantly: a precise UML specification in which all relationships have clear semantics helps to avoid handwaving and semantic-free warm and fuzzy feelings. Such a specification is in fact a question, "Is this a correct representation of your business; and if not what needs to be changed?," that the business SMEs must answer when they validate the specification. In other words, we prefer precision over correctness.

In the same manner as things do not exist in isolation, neither do actions (sometimes called "use cases"). Therefore, we need to discover and represent relationships between actions. We do this in precisely the same manner as relationships between things, using the same UML stereotypes for generic relationships with precisely defined semantics. Here again, the approach is based on utmost simplicity with the bare minimum of concepts. The invariants that define the structure of relationships are independent of the specifics of the relationship participants.

Each action (use case) itself is represented textually, using pre- and post-conditions, triggering conditions, and specific invariants that refer only to the context of interest. The same approach has been successfully used in [K1999], in the ISO General Relationship Model [GRM], and elsewhere.

Simplification

The rules defining a relationship type are often independent of the identity and nature of the related participants. (For generic relationships, this is always true.) These rules include the invariant that defines the relationship and also pre- and postconditions that define elementary (Create-Read-Update-Delete) operations applicable to the relationship and its related participants. The same kind of relationships (such as *composition* or *contract*) when instantiated using different parameters describes the similar properties of similarly related collections of quite different participants. (This is the approach used for template definition and instantiation in RM-ODP [RM-ODP2] and elsewhere.) In our experience, business SMEs appreciate this concept of "structure over content" and successfully use it; they recognize and appreciate familiar business patterns in various contexts.

UML has several different ways to represent relationship semantics. For example, it uses the "hierarchical" tagged value to represent hierarchy, the "ordering" attribute of the appropriate Association Ends to represent order, the triangle vs. diamond adornments to distinguish between subtyping and composition, and so on. These substantially different ways to represent the distinctions between similar, but different, relationship subtypes, may be tolerated by technologists who have been conditioned to learn what a tool requires, but they are intolerable for business people. Therefore, we use three adornments (triangles for subtypes, diamonds for compositions, and arrows for references) together with UML stereotypes to represent each relationship type. Relationships without adornments are prohibited.

Furthermore, a stereotype is an abbreviation of an invariant, and it is very desirable to use similar abbreviations for similar invariants—such as various kinds of subtyping—and different abbreviations for different invariants—such as for subtyping vs. composition. Here we have used abbreviations that slightly differ from the terminology used in UML. In particular, instead of using both "aggregation" and "composition," we use only one of these terms with a qualifier (e.g., "assembly") that denotes its subtype. We base these concepts on the clear and crisp definition of a composition from the ISO Reference Model of Open Distributed Processing [RM-ODP2], as well as on definitions used in philosophy such as [B1999].

In other words, only three UML constructs are used in graphical representations of business specifications: "things" (named boxes[103]), the relationships between them (with semantics always explicitly denoted by adornments and stereotypes), and notes. The details about thing and relationship semantics are provided by domain- or application-specific invariants represented either as notes or (more often) as separate text. OCL is not appropriate for business specifications; for more information, see the eloquent paper [VJ2000].

---

103.   These boxes are also used to represent actions, see below.

Separation of concerns is also essential for a specification to be understandable. Specifically, we describe both the structure of a specification and its content in terms familiar to business SMEs rather than in technological terms. In particular, we have not used message-oriented OO concepts (like "message" or "method") and often have not used the term "object." Contrariwise, concepts like "invariants" and "pre- and postconditions" were easily explained (e.g., using the context of legal contracts) and explicitly used.

A Simple Example (a Contract) and Lessons Learned

The UML specification of a contract reproduced below from the subsection "How Not to Get Lost: Abstraction Viewpoints and Levels" corresponds to the description of a contract provided in the Uniform Commercial Code. The three components of a contract are required for its existence, but may themselves exist without the need for the contract to exist. It is also essential to observe that some properties of a contract are determined by the properties of its components. Therefore, our relationship is a composition-assembly.

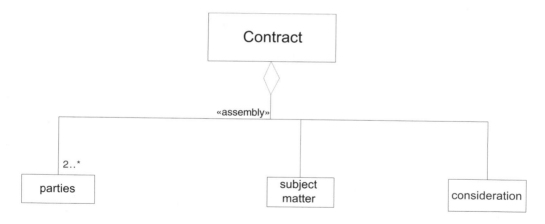

This example is typical for a (fragment of a) business specification. We make the following observations:

- The relationship is non-binary. We know that properties of the composite are determined by the properties of all components, not just some of them. (In our case, some details of property determination are provided in the Uniform

Commercial Code.) Moreover, there may be several composition relationships—as shown in the next subsection—for the same composite, with quite different rules for property determination, and we certainly want to demonstrate in our representation that these relationships are different.

In a business specification, properties of a relationship generally cannot be reduced to properties of its (UML) roles; and properties of a non-binary relationship generally cannot be reduced to properties of its binary fragments. The invariant that defines a relationship refers to all of its participants, rather than to just two of them.

- We usually do not need to include multiplicities. In this case, the multiplicities for subject matter and consideration are the default ones—those that follow from the invariant of our generic relationship (composition-assembly). We will need to include explicit multiplicities only when they differ from the default ones for the corresponding relationship stereotype: in our case, there should be at least two parties of a contract.
- We did not include attributes or operations in the boxes that denote things. In a business specification this is not needed. The decision as to whether a particular construct is a property (or attribute) or a thing usually need not be made in a business specification. (For example, in a large Human Resource project, the full UML was considered to be both too complex and too restrictive and forced the modelers to make decisions irrelevant to the overall goals of the project, such as classifying professional HR employees' knowledge between classes and attributes.) We describe important properties as explicit components in appropriate compositions. An action in a business specification is not owned by a specific thing: it is collectively owned by all its participants.
- In actual specifications, we use specific contracts such as insurance policy contracts, trade contracts, option contracts, etc. To do that, we instantiate this contract specification by replacing the formal parameters (such as "consideration") with the specific actual parameters (such as a composition of "Promised Consideration" and "Actual Consideration"). We see that the actual parameters are often not elementary. Thus, the specification of a general contract provides a solid foundation for asking questions about and thus discovering and formulating the relevant properties of contracts in various business-specific and application-specific factual domains.

Relationship Invariants Are About Property Determination

As we have seen in the example above, a relationship is interesting and its specification is important for the business (or system) because properties of some participants of the relationship are determined by some properties of other participants of that relationship.

More specifically (see also Appendix B), in the subtyping relationship, an instance of a subtype has all properties of its supertype and also subtype-specific properties. In a reference relationship (such as between a *person* and *a person's record in a database*), the properties of a reference entity (e.g., *person*) determine some properties of its maintained entity (e.g., *person's record in a database*). In a composition relationship, some properties of a composite are determined by the properties of its components and by the way in which they are combined. As an example, consider a drastically simplified specification of a document represented, on the one hand, as a composition of its content-based components, and on the other hand, as a composition of its logical layout-based components.

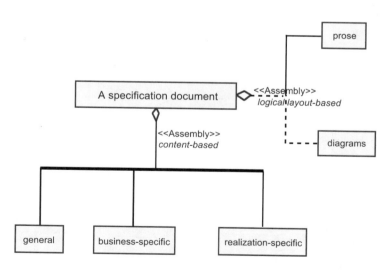

Here, each composition is named (the name is in italics). In the logical layout-based composition, the properties of components (and possibly their subcomponents) determine, for example, the table of contents of the document. In the content-based composition, the properties of components determine, for example, the abstract of the document. The former property determination may be calculated automatically, while the latter cannot.

We also observe that we made the representation of a business specification in a "received" notation (UML) isomorphic to its representation in a simple notation created on semiotic principles [K1999, Chapter 5].

The same considerations hold when we consider multiple mutually orthogonal subtypings of the same supertype. Numerous examples have been provided in this book.

These concepts are much more important for relationship semantics than multiplicities, and they have been easily understood by the business users.

Relationships Between Actions

The structure of relationships between actions (or operations, sometimes called use cases), for example, when modeling steps of a process, is specified in exactly the same manner as the structure of relationships between "things." There is no need to invent new concepts (and representations) if the existing ones can be successfully reused. A typical relationship between operations is an ordered composition, as shown in the simple example of a contract negotiation reproduced below.

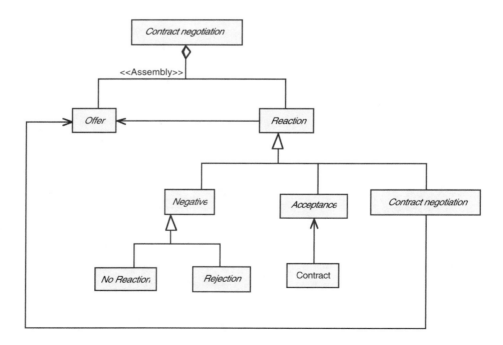

Here, we see two components of contract negotiation. Ordering is shown, by convention, from left to right; of course it is possible and sometimes—as above—desirable to show ordering using appropriate reference relationships between the components, especially when the ordering is partial. We also see that a reaction is exhaustively subtyped into negative, acceptance, and contract negotiation reactions. Further, we observe that action names are in *italics*, to distinguish actions from things.

Reading and Writing Large(r) Business Specifications

We clearly differentiate between being able to write and being able to read a business specification. The business SMEs do not have to write business specifications but should be able to read them, perhaps with some small help from the business specifiers at the beginning. To make this possible, we need to explain the semantics of the notation used, and also provide a clear written overview of the notation. The generic relationships and their abbreviated invariants can be presented in one page of English text and in one UML diagram that shows different generic relationship subtypes. This terse representation is consistent with the terse representation of the business domain and operation specifications.

The semantics of the required UML constructs has been easily introduced to the business users "on the back of an envelope" as and when needed, so, in E.W. Dijkstra's words, the specifiers and the users were able to spend their valuable time dealing with the business problem rather than spending "five days" to learn a (or "the") funny way to represent known or trivial problems.

Everything cannot (and should not) be shown in a diagram. More specifically, some actual parameters of invariants for generic relationships—such as those related to property determination for composites or specific distinction between subtypes—usually are presented in textual form. It is possible to create and then reuse appropriate stereotypes as abbreviations for commonly encountered relationships, of course. Various new stereotypes may be used as long as their semantics (invariants) is precisely and explicitly defined.

An English (narrative) description is provided for each domain specification UML diagram; our experience suggests that it takes approximately one page per rather "busy" diagram. In this manner, it is possible to represent a specification in a form appropriate for those readers who hate pictures and also to represent the semantics (such as the details of invariants) that could not be naturally shown in a diagram, but rather should be shown textually, in a table, or otherwise. The English used in the narratives is clearly not a "natural" language; rather, it is structured and highly stylized as in [RM-ODP2], or as in a legal document.

Separation of Concerns: Problem vs. Solution

Both in writing and in reading a business specification, we need to clearly separate the specification (problem) concerns from the realization (solution) concerns. No requirements should ever be provided in terms of solutions. No IT terminology and concerns should be present in a business specification.

In creating UML diagrams for business specifications, no IT constructs—and no artificial restrictions—should be used in the diagrams and class specifications. For example, no distinction between "public," "protected," or "private" should be referred to; no "friendship" should be mentioned. No UML "roles" should be used because they are realizations of relationship invariants for binary relationships. No navigability considerations belong here either. These IT-related fragments of a UML diagram (and related artefacts) are simply ignored in a business specification.

The business specification UML diagram is usually not the same as the realization UML diagram. There is no code generation accomplished using a business specification diagram, and most probably there will be a many-to-many mapping between business specification artefacts and the corresponding realization artefacts. For example, mutually orthogonal subtyping hierarchies may be realized as various attribute values of the supertype attribute(s), together with roles considered as separate objects appropriately contributing to the semantics of the realization. The emphasis of a business specification is on human understanding, while the emphasis of the realization is on the best (according to some criteria) way to compose the given business specification with the given (or chosen) technological architecture. Clearly, this technological architecture should be precisely and explicitly specified in the same manner (e.g., as described here) as any relevant business fragment.

Additional Practical Hints

The following guidelines may be useful in creating understandable and usable business specification diagrams in UML:

- A single specification diagram should never be larger than 8.5 x 11 inches. Do not include too much stuff, even into such a specification. Complex specifications should be split into fragments.

- Important properties of things are to be represented as components of these things. Realization of these properties is not in the scope of a business specification (and may in fact use attributes).
- Only compositions of horizontal and vertical lines are used for relationship links; other lines may be used for note connections and possibly for reference relationships. Rare exceptions are possible for better presentation. There should be no crossed lines: if this is impossible then, most probably, the specification is too complex and should be decomposed.
- Relationships may be visibly named if the analyst or the customer thinks names will make the specification more understandable. Relationships should be visibly named if there is more than one relationship of the same kind referring to the same supertype or composite.
- If some subtypes or components exist but are not known (or are not deemed to be important), then it is possible to denote them by "OtherXXX" where "XXX" is the name of the corresponding supertype or composite.
- In order to be explicit, it is preferable to use exhaustive ("complete" in UML) subtyping rather than incomplete subtyping.

Where Do These Ideas Come From?

Most of these ideas come from international standards—such as RM-ODP and GRM—together with practice and experience in telecommunications, document management, financial, insurance, and other areas. These ideas are simple and elegant and are based on the need to provide understandable specifications that are methodology-, technology-, and tool-neutral.

Representation mechanisms, such as UML, are technological artefacts, and we compose a representation of a specification from the semantics of concepts and constructs of the conceptual space(s), on the one hand, and the semantics of the technological architecture, on the other hand, where composition is an intellectual act [C1997]. In our composition described here, we have chosen a very small number of appropriate fragments of this technological architecture (that is, UML) and extended (including providing precise semantics for) some of the existing artefacts of this architecture. The objective was to preserve in the (understandable!) representation as much from the semantics of the conceptual space(s) as possible. Clearly, some important ideas from semiotics (such as described in [G1999] and elsewhere in this book) were also used in the same manner as earlier in [KR1994, K1999].

Among the foundational concepts, we consistently use the RM-ODP definition of a *type* (a predicate characterizing a collection of <X>s) and of a *class* (a collection of <X>s satisfying a type). These definitions are used for "things," for actions, for relationships, and for other constructs (such as contracts). Other RM-ODP definitions such as *composition*—of various kinds of components—are also consistently used (see above). And we use the RM-ODP definition of a template and instantiation, which usually requires actualization of parameters. This always happens when we instantiate a template of a particular generic relationship such as a composition-assembly; in these situations, the parameters—often non-elementary—will characterize property determination.

Appendix B[104]

Generic Relationships

A Generic Relationship: Generic Properties

This Appendix considers properties common to all generic relationships.

The few relationship types are encountered in, and reused by, all applications. Invariants that define a particular generic relationship type are provided in the section on taxonomy. Contracts for Create-Read-Update-Delete (CRUD) operations applied to (the elements of) these generic relationship types follow from these invariants. Some of these contracts are presented in [KR1994 and K1999].

The invariant of a generic relationship (e.g., a composition corresponding to an application-specific composition between a document and a set of its chapters) describes the stable properties of the "collective state" of the participants of the relationship. The same individual may participate in several (application-specific instantiations of) generic relationships. For example, the same person may fulfill the role of a component in several composition relationships such as *simple financial contracts* (a *checking account* and a *mortgage loan*), an *employment contract*, and so on. Such an individual becomes a participant in an application-specific relationship, the invariant of which is generally a conjunction of the invariants of its participating generic relationships. Contracts for operations in which such an individual participates will also follow from this (more complicated) invariant.

---

104. This appendix is an abridged incremental modification of Chapters 4 and 5 and Appendix D of [KR1994].

In order to define properties common to all generic relationships, we will use the concept of an elementary relationship. It is a supertype of which all generic relationships are subtypes. Therefore, each generic relationship satisfies the properties—the invariant—of the elementary relationship. We are describing these properties only once, below.

The Invariant

An elementary relationship is a binary (asymmetric) relation. A relationship type—a relation type—relates a source type to a target type [PST1990]. Any of these types may be (from the "generic" viewpoint) nonelementary: an instance of such a type may be a set, a set of sets, etc. If a nonelementary type is a set, then its corresponding elementary type will be an element of this set. An instance of a relation generally exists if and only if there exists an instance of its source type and an appropriate instance of its target type (for the only exception, see below).

Let's apply these features to the important generic relationship types:

- A **reference** relationship may be represented as a relation between the source type (maintained) and the target type (reference). An instance of the reference relationship exists if and only if corresponding instances of the maintained and reference types exist. In other words, the existence of an instance of the reference relationship is equivalent to the existence of corresponding instances of the maintained and reference types.
- A **composition** relationship may be represented as a relation between the source type (composite) and the target type (non-empty set of component types). In this case, the source type is elementary, and the target type is not. An instance of the composite type corresponds to a set of sets of instances for each of its component types. The cardinality of each set of instances of a particular component type may be arbitrary. Consider a *document* composed of *texts*, *pictures*, and *tables*. An instance of the document corresponds to a set consisting of three elements. Each element, in turn, is a set of instances of pieces of text, pictures, and tables, correspondingly. Each of these sets may be empty.
- A **subtyping** relationship may be represented as a relation between the source type (supertype) and the target type (non-empty set of subtypes). Again, the source type is elementary, and the target type is not. However, for any given subtyping relationship instance, the sets of instances of its source and elementary target types will have a nonempty intersection. This does not hold for any other generic relationship. More specifically, the set

of instances of an elementary target type will be a subset of the set of instances of the source type. Consider a supertype *employee* and subtypes *technical employee* and *managerial employee*. An instance of an *employee* may be an instance of either a *technical employee* or a *managerial employee*. The set of all instances of *technical employees* and *managerial employees* will be a subset of the set of instances of *employee*. If the subtyping is exhaustive, then the union of these sets of subtype instances will be equal to the set of supertype instances.

The following invariant is valid for all generic relationships, **except composition-package**:

The existence of a generic relationship instance is equivalent to the existence of corresponding instances of its source type and its elementary target type.

For a composition-package—and only for a composition-package—instances of the source and target types may exist independently, without the existence of a corresponding instance of the composition relationship. Thus, for a composition-package, the equivalence in the invariant above does not hold and is replaced by an implication: the existence of a composition-package instance implies the existence of an instance of the composite type and a corresponding instance of its component type.

The invariant above implies that a separate operation for the creation or deletion of a relationship instance is not needed and not available, except for a composition-package, in which instances of participating composite and component types may exist in isolation, so that separate operations are needed and available to create or delete a relationship between these entity instances.

This is not the complete invariant for an elementary relationship: we know more than that!

As stated above, for any given subtyping relationship instance, the sets of instances of its source and elementary target types will have a nonempty intersection, but this is an exception. The rule is quite different.

For all generic relationships, **except subtyping**, the following invariant holds:

For any generic relationship instance (and its transitive closure), the sets of instances of its source and elementary target types have an empty intersection.

Indeed, in an instance of composition, a composite instance cannot have itself as one of the components; and so on. Moreover, a composite instance cannot be, directly or indirectly, its own component.

More formally, the relation between a source type and its elementary target type is irreflexive. The same is true for the transitive closure of this relation.

Finally, let's provide an invariant satisfied by all generic relationships (no exceptions this time). Let's consider the sets of types of an instance of a source type and of an instance of an elementary target type (recall that an instance can satisfy several types). These sets should be different, although they may have a nonempty intersection. For example, in a composition between *widgets*, both a composite instance and a component instance will satisfy the *widget* type, but the composite instance will also satisfy the *assembly* type.

Therefore, for all generic relationships, the following invariant holds:

For any generic relationship instance, the set of types of an instance of its source type is not equal to the set of types of a corresponding instance of its elementary target type.

The conjunction of all these boldfaced invariants constitutes the invariant for any generic relationship. In the description of particular generic relationships, this discussion (and this invariant) will generally not be repeated. They have just been abstracted out.

How an Operation Changes the Sets of Associated Instances

Consider adding a new component to a composition.[105] It leads to a change in the set of composites associated with this component and also to a change in the set of components associated with this composite. In both cases, the elements of the new set include all elements of the old set and one new element. This postcondition of the create operation may be generalized for all generic relationships. Moreover, a symmetric postcondition exists for the delete operation. This section will formulate appropriate generalizations, and we will not repeat them later.

An instance of the source type may be associated with several instances of the target type (don't forget that these types need not be elementary). By the same token, an instance of a target type may be associated with several instances of the source type.[106]

---

105.   The ISO General Relationship Model [GRM] uses the term *bind* for this purpose
106.   In either case, we may deal with more than one relationship instance.

What happens after an instance of a relationship between an instance of the source type and an instance of the target type is created? Naturally, the new set of instances of the target type corresponding to this instance of the source type will consist of the old set of instances[107] of the target type and this new instance of the target type. By the same token, the new set of instances of the source type corresponding to this instance of the target type will consist of the old set of instances of the source type and this new instance of the source type. If the source or target types are not elementary, then this also applies to each element of the set of instances of these types.

Symmetry considerations suggest that analogous rules are applicable for deletion. For example, after an instance of the relationship between an instance of the source type and an instance of the target type is deleted, the new set of instances of the target type corresponding to the instance of the source type will consist of the old set of instances of the target type minus this instance of the target type. As a result, this new set of instances of the target type may become empty.

Consider our *document* example again (a document composed of *texts*, *pictures*, and *tables*). If a *table* is added to a particular *document*, then two predicates are true:

- The set of *documents* of which this *table* is a component will include the old set of such *documents* and this particular *document*.
- The set of *tables* for this *document* will include the old set of its *tables* and this particular *table*. (A *table* may be a component of several *documents*, and a *document* may include several *tables*.)

In the description of particular generic relationships, this discussion will not be repeated. It has just been abstracted out.

Mandatory/Optional Participation; Cardinalities

Let's refine the invariant of an elementary relationship presented in the preceding section. To do that, we will precisely define the traditional concepts of mandatory and optional participation.

The participation of an individual in a relationship may be mandatory or optional.

On the one hand, an individual has **mandatory** participation in a relationship if *the existence of an instance of the individual implies the existence of a cor-*

---

107. Evidently, the old set may be empty, consist of one element, and so on.

responding instance of the relationship. In other words, the relationship for this individual has mandatory existence. The *italicized* predicate conjoined with the invariant of an elementary relationship defines the invariant for mandatory participation of an individual in a relationship.

On the other hand, the participation of an individual in a relationship may be **optional**. In this case, the *existence of an instance of the individual does not imply the existence of a corresponding instance of the relationship.*

If the invariant of the relationship implies optional participation of an individual in the relationship, then this relationship may be subtyped. For some application-specific individuals in an application-specific instantiation of this relationship, their participation may be mandatory: the relationship invariant will be (satisfied and) strengthened. This stronger invariant describes a subtype of such a relationship—a relationship with mandatory participation of an individual.

This subtyping can be performed for any relationship with optional participation of an individual in the relationship. It implies—thanks to its invariant—corresponding sets of permissible operations applicable to the participants of the relationship. It leads, in particular, to the need to distinguish between the create operations for the first and non-first instances of this individual participating in the relationship, and the need to distinguish between the delete operations for the last and non-last instances of this individual participating in the relationship. Again, thanks to the invariant, contracts for these operations will have substantially different specifications. These specifications follow from the invariants in a straightforward manner.

When an Isolated Instance Can and Cannot Be Operated Upon

The invariant for an individual with mandatory participation in a relationship implies that both the individual instance and the first corresponding relationship instance must be created in the same action.[108] As shown earlier, the existence of a relationship instance is equivalent to the existence of the instances of related individuals of its source type and of its target type. Therefore, to create the first relationship instance, it will be necessary to create, in the same action, corresponding first instance(s) of the individuals with mandatory participation in this relationship. Similarly, the only instances of the related individuals with manda-

---

108. This is an indivisible unit of work consisting of possibly several elementary CRUD actions. An action at a particular abstraction level preserves the invariants of the appropriate relationships at that level.

tory participation in this relationship should be deleted in the same action.[109] Violation of these rules leads to violating the invariant of the relationship (i.e., the semantic integrity rules of the relationship) and is therefore inadmissible.

Recall that the only exception to the relationship-instance-related invariant for the elementary relationship is provided by the composition-package. This generic relationship subtype always has optional existence, and therefore the reasoning of the previous paragraph is not applicable to it.

The invariants for mandatory/optional participation of an individual in a relationship naturally imply corresponding preconditions for create and delete operations. Therefore, only certain creates and deletes are permitted:

- Optional participation of an individual in a relationship implies the possibility of creating (or deleting) an instance of this individual separately (in a separate action) from an instance of its associated individual in this relationship.
- Mandatory participation of both the source and the target in a relationship implies the requirement for creating the first associated instances (or deleting the last associated instances) of these individuals in the same action. It also implies the possibility of creating the not-first (i.e., not-only) associated instances, as well as deleting the not-last (i.e., not-only) associated instances of one of these entities separately.

These generic CRUD rules will be reused for all generic relationships.

Business rules for a particular application may require simultaneous creation (or deletion) of associated individual instances of both the source type and the target type, independent of whether these individuals have mandatory or optional existence in this relationship. In this case, the creation (or deletion) of the instances of the source type and the target type will happen in the same action (for deletion, the traditional name of the operation is delete cascade). In other words, this action will have to appear as an indivisible one at the chosen level of abstraction. Moreover, for deletion, some of the individuals to be deleted may not be explicitly mentioned in the action's signature, but will be explicitly mentioned in the action's assertions (i.e., in the definition of its semantics)!

---

109. Both the creation of the non-first instance and the deletion of the non-only ("non-last") instance by itself do not violate the mandatory participation invariant. Therefore, in these cases there is no need to create/delete instances of both related individuals in the same action.

Providing More Detail When Needed: Cardinalities

In most cases, specifying mandatory/optional participation of an individual in a relationship is sufficient for further analyzing a relationship of a particular generic type. As we have seen, this specification refines the invariant of the relationship (and may define the relationship subtype).

To be even more specific—if the need arises—the concept of cardinality may be used.[110] The cardinality of an individual in a relationship refers to the minimum and maximum number of instances of this individual that may participate in the corresponding relationship instance. The minimum cardinality for an individual with mandatory participation in a relationship is greater than zero, whereas the minimum cardinality for an individual with optional participation is zero. If the minimum and maximum cardinalities are equal, we just use the term "cardinality." Naturally, this specification belongs to the invariant of a relationship.

Default cardinalities may be defined for each generic relationship: they are implied by the corresponding invariants. Therefore, these cardinalities need not be respecified for application-specific instantiations of these generic relationships. We will omit default cardinalities from actual diagrams in order to prevent overloading them with clutter. However, in some cases, additional non-default "numeric" information may be needed. Here, an explicit specification of cardinalities must be introduced.

Let's consider a composition example: a document consists of texts, pictures, and tables. This is an example of a composition-package: each component may exist independently of whether the composite (that is, a document) exists and vice versa. Moreover, each component may be associated with any number of composites and vice versa (e.g., the same text may be used by several documents). Therefore, the cardinalities for each of the individuals will be "any number," that is, "0..*"—the default ones (more precisely, minimum cardinality of zero, and maximum cardinality of an unknown positive integer):

---

110. Cardinalities are defined in somewhat different ways by different sources. Our definition is close to the ones traditionally used in ER modeling.

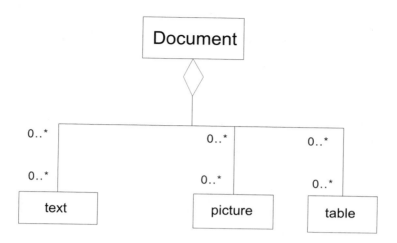

This picture is seriously cluttered: it contains too much (default) information. Because the default cardinalities are usually not shown, *no cardinalities should be explicitly shown here*.

Let's consider a small change: imagine that the SME wants to discourage documents with too many pictures and prohibits documents with more than five pictures (a somewhat arbitrary constraint). In this case, the appropriate cardinality "0..5" states that there may be at most five pictures in a document and must be explicitly shown in the invariant.

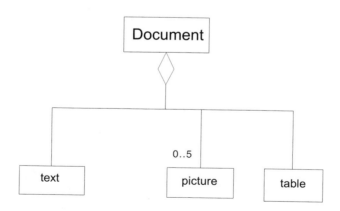

The (sub)type of the generic relationship (in our case, composition-package) does not change when any of the maximum cardinalities change. However, the mandatory/optional participation of an individual in a relationship may change the subtype of the generic relationship: the invariants of different subtypes of the same generic relationship may have different predicates referring to mandatory/optional participation. As mentioned above, these invariants determine which CRUD business rules (i.e., which generic contracts) are applicable to the relationship and its elements.

Generic Relationships: The Taxonomy

This section defines the generic relationships used in all applications. All these relationships are subtypes of the elementary relationship type described above. Therefore, they satisfy the properties—the invariant—of that elementary relationship. These properties may be referred to here, but will not be described in detail again: they will be reused.

Each generic relationship is defined by its invariant. The operations applicable to the relationship and its elements should preserve this invariant, so their definitions follow from this invariant. Most generic relationships can be subtyped (e.g., a composition may be hierarchical or non-hierarchical), and the description of the relationship includes the definition of its generic subtypes. The contracts for CRUD operations follow from the invariant of the (subtype of the) generic relationship.

The set of generic relationships described here is not intended to be complete; it can be extended if it will appear that different applications have certain other (reasonably fundamental) constructs in common. These constructs will have to be understood, specified, and then reused—in the same manner as the constructs already described in the specification of this generic relationship library.

Reference Relationship

A **reference** relationship associates a reference individual with a maintained individual. A reference individual in this relationship represents read-only instances used to determine properties of instances of other, maintained, individuals.[111] A reference individual participates in its own actions (not just read-only) within other relationships, possibly outside of the particular application area. In

---

111. The particular rules for using the reference individual instances to determine properties of corresponding instances of maintained individuals are application-specific. However, these rules have some important properties in common, and these properties are encountered often enough to warrant their abstract formulation and reuse.

other words, a particular individual is a reference individual only within the context of a particular reference relationship.

Actions applied to an instance of a maintained individual in a reference relationship should leave instances of its reference individual unchanged. More than one instance of a maintained individual may refer to the same instance of a reference individual. Moreover, an instance of a maintained individual may refer to several instances of a reference individual.

Reference individual instances may be used both to validate the preconditions for, and as information sources[112] for, creating/updating/deleting instances of its maintained individual. Values of some properties of an instance of the maintained individual should agree with (in the simplest case—but not always!—be equal to) values of some properties of an appropriate instance of its reference individual. The particular appropriate instance need not be prespecified in the operation.

When an instance of a reference individual is changed, all corresponding instances of its maintained individual must be examined (triggering condition) and, if necessary, changed. This should ideally take place in the same action, to satisfy the invariant of the reference relationship (see below). However, in practice there may be a delay, in which case you may want to keep more than one version of the reference and maintained individuals (and update the values of maintained individual instances later—"lazy update"). If more than one (e.g., both the "old" and the "new") versions of reference individual instances will simultaneously be of interest to the application, then an immediate massive update of maintained entity individuals may not be needed. In this case, a "lazy update" may happen when an instance of a maintained individual is updated only after it is referred to by any action. As a result, the "mass update" of a large number of maintained individual instances is diluted in time, and the delays become acceptable; instead of one long delay, the application will suffer many very short delays that its users will not even notice.

Two subtypes of the reference relationship exist. The ordinary reference relationship is supported during the lifetime of its associated individuals. Therefore, a change of properties of a reference individual instance will immediately or eventually lead to corresponding changes of properties of associated maintained individual instances.[113] Another subtype of the reference relationship, the refer-

---

112. By providing parameters and possibly an algorithm (postcondition).
113. The concept of versions may be used to delay these changes.

ence for create, is supported only during the create operation for an instance of a maintained individual. This instance may be created when the criteria described by the properties of the corresponding reference individual instance are satisfied (this is often accomplished using an instance of another reference individual, as in notification [KR1994]). After the maintained individual instance is created, any change in the property values of the corresponding reference individual instance does not affect this instance of the maintained individual. In other words, the invariant for the reference for create relationship applies only to the version of the reference individual that existed when the maintained individual was created. A "lazy update" of such a maintained individual instance never happens.

For an ordinary reference, the creation of an instance of the maintained individual is user-initiated. For a reference for create, this creation may be either user-initiated, or the condition for creation may be a triggering condition, in which case the creation is "system" -initiated.

If the participation of a maintained individual in a reference relationship is optional, then some maintained individual instances do not require a corresponding reference individual instance. However, after creation of a maintained individual instance, the reference-maintained instance property correspondence may subsequently be established.

The property updating of maintained individual instances initiated by a change of the corresponding reference individual instance is accomplished as follows: The validation of each maintained individual instance is an application operation. If this validation operation indicates property correspondence between a reference and maintained instances (i.e., the invariant for the reference relationship is satisfied), nothing happens (i.e., properties remain unchanged). If there is no correspondence, then the reference relationship invariant is not satisfied and must be restored: the maintained instance is updated or deleted, or a new version is created for it.

Invariant. *A maintained type corresponds to one reference type. The existence of a maintained instance implies the following:*

If a corresponding instance of the reference type exists, then the property values of the instance of the maintained type correspond[114] to the property values of an appropriate version of the corresponding instance(s) of the reference type. The appropriate version of the reference type should be its current version, or, in the

---

114. The result of an appropriate Boolean function with properties of the reference and maintained individuals as parameters should be TRUE.

case of a lazy update, a prior version, or, in the case of reference for create, the version that has been used for creating an instance of the maintained type.

As follows from the invariant for the elementary relationship, the existence of an instance of the reference relationship is equivalent to the existence of instances of both the corresponding reference and maintained individuals.

A graphical representation.

The arrow points to the reference, that is, to the information source.

First note: It is possible for an individual to be clearly outside of the scope of the current application area, that is, in its context, but to have (reference) relationships to individuals in this area. A reference individual may, but need not, be out of the scope of its application area.

Second note: Several (two or more) reference relationships in which the same maintained individual participates ("more than one incoming reference") are often better specified as a composition; this maintained individual becomes a composite, and each of the reference individuals in these reference relationships become components. This approach takes care of the collective participation of the components in the determination of the emergent properties of the composite.

Composition

A composite individual "consists of" (or, is an "aggregate of") component individuals. A component instance may or may not exist independent of its composite(s). A composite instance may or may not exist without its components. Structural properties of a composite are not inherited by components. Some operations applied to a composite individual propagate to its components. For instance, if a document consists of chunks of text and pictures, then operations such as "read," "copy," "move,"[115] and so on propagate to all components of the document. There exists at least one property of the composite individual the value of which is determined, collectively, by some properties of its component individuals. In our document example, these may be number of pages, abstract,

---

115. Considered as "updates," as certain property values will be changed.

and table of contents. There exists also at least one property of a composite independent of components' properties. The property of a composite's identity is always there; for many kinds of documents, the set of authors is also a good example.

A composite type corresponds to one or more component types, and a composite instance corresponds to zero or more instances of each component type. The sets of application-specific types for the composite and its components should not be equal (irreflexivity).[116] In other words, there should exist at least one type of the composite such that it is not, at the same time, a type of its components. Creating, updating, or deleting a component does not change the identity of the composite. In our example of a composition relationship between a document and its components, changing a chunk of text in a document, adding a new picture, or even adding a new type of component (e.g., table) does not change the identity of the document.

A component instance may relate to zero or more composite instances (e.g., the same picture may be a component of zero, one, or more than one document). A component type may relate to more than one type of composite; for example, a picture may belong to a document or a viewgraph.

A **composition** relationship may be subtyped by means of several mutually orthogonal hierarchies. The most important of them are presented below.

Serializability

- *Nonordered* components (default).
- *Ordered* components (i.e., it is possible to determine, at least for some components,[117] whether a certain component is before another component). The components may be ordered (i.e., the predicate *before* is defined) either only within a component type or across component types of the same composition.

Due to the possibility of using *before* in the pre- and postconditions of actions for ordered components, it is possible to define actions such as: *get next component after a given component, insert a component before a given compo-*

---

116. This follows from the invariant for the elementary relationship and should also be true for the transitive closure of the composition relationship.
117. The order may be partial, so that the determination is possible for some component pairs; or complete, so that the determination is possible for all component pairs.

nent, and so on. The definitions of these actions are straightforward and will not be provided here. For nonordered components, these actions are not permitted.

Changeability

- *Static* components—After a composition has been established, no dynamic entry/departure[118] of components into/from the composition is possible.
- *Variable* components—Dynamic entry/departure of components is possible (default).

Changeability refers to whether the collection of component instances may become established ("frozen"). For static components, there exists an action *freeze* that prohibits any further creations/deletions of components. The specification of *freeze* is straightforward and will not be discussed here. For variable components, an operation *freeze* is not permitted.

Hierarchy

- *Hierarchical*—A component instance may be associated with not more than one composite instance of the corresponding composition relationship.
- *Non-hierarchical*—The composition relationship is a network, that is, a component instance may be associated with more than one composite instance (in different instances of the same composition relationship) (default).

"The composition is hierarchical" is equivalent to "for every component instance, there may exist at most one corresponding composite instance."

Linkage

- *Assembly*—Composition is associated with the composite.
- *Subordination*—Composition is associated with the component.
- *Package*—Composition is not associated with either the composite or the component (default).
- *List*—Composition is associated with both the composite and the component.

---

118. To use ISO General Relationship Model terminology, binding/unbinding.

The existence of a composite instance for the *assembly* implies the existence of at least one corresponding component instance. The existence of a component instance for the *subordination* implies the existence of at least one corresponding composite instance. There are no additional rules for the *package*. The package is the only subtype of composition for which the operation "create a composition relationship" for existing composite and component instances is defined. Moreover, the package is the only generic relationship for which such an operation is defined. In other words, the package is the only generic relationship for which the existence of an instance of the relationship is not equivalent to the existence of the participating individual instances. Finally, for the *list*, the existence of a component instance implies the existence of at least one corresponding composite instance, and the existence of a composite instance implies the existence of at least one corresponding component instance.

The four subtyping hierarchies of composition presented above are mutually orthogonal. Therefore, they may be combined by explicitly picking one of the (non-default!) possibilities from several of these hierarchies. We may define, for instance, a hierarchy of variable ordered packaged components. Some of these combinations are more likely than others and may therefore deserve to have a specific name; for instance, a *containment* is a hierarchical subordination (with the other two subtypes being default, i.e., nonordered and variable). A particular composition relationship satisfies the invariants of the appropriate subtypes from each of its participating subtyping hierarchies. In this example, a containment satisfies the invariants of both subordination and hierarchy.

It may happen that component individuals associated with the same composite individual in the same composition have different properties (e.g., instances of one component type can be associated only with this particular composite, and instances of another with any composite), and therefore belong to different subtypes of composition. This situation becomes not worthy of classification because of the extraordinary complexity of the case analysis. Naturally, in every particular application-specific case, it is straightforward to combine (conjoin) the existing composition subtypes described in this section. Although every such case is straightforward, the enumeration and analysis of all of them are almost beyond human understanding.

Invariant (generic). *A composite type corresponds to one or more component types, and a composite instance corresponds to zero or more instances of each component type. There exists at least one property of a composite instance determined collectively by the properties of its component instances. There exists* *also at least one property of a composite instance independent of the properties of its component instances. The sets of application-specific types for the composite and its components should not be equal.*

The identity of a composite is independent of the properties of its component instances, so creating, updating, or deleting a component instance does not change the identity of the composite instance.

As follows from the invariant for the elementary relationship, the existence of an instance of the composition relationship—for all subtypes of composition except package—is equivalent to the existence of an instance of the composite and a set of corresponding instances of its component.

The invariants for subtypes of the generic composition follow. (Naturally, the generic invariant for composition is satisfied by each of its subtypes.)

Invariant for ordered components (serializability): *For a pair[119] of component instances in a composition relationship instance, it is possible to define whether one is before the other.*

Invariant for static components (changeability): *After a composition relationship instance has been established, the preconditions for creating or deleting a component are FALSE.*

Invariant for hierarchical composition: *For every component instance, there exists at most one corresponding composite instance in a given composition relationship.*

Invariants for linkage subtypes: *For an assembly, the existence of a composite instance implies the existence of at least one corresponding component instance. For a subordination, the existence of a component instance implies the existence of at least one corresponding composite instance. For a list, the existence of a composite instance implies the existence of at least one corresponding component instance, and the existence of a component instance implies the existence of at least one corresponding composite instance.*

A graphical representation.

---

119. "For every pair" in the case of a complete order, and "for some pairs" in the case of a partial order.

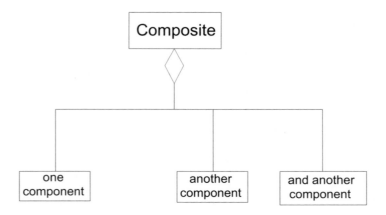

The non-default subtype of a composition, if necessary, is shown as a UML stereotype, within guillemets—quotation marks used in French writing. For example, a composition-assembly is shown as:

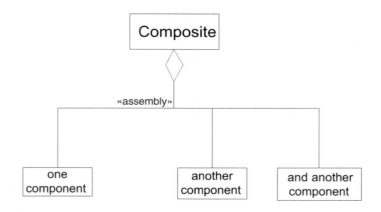

Subtyping

Instances can be grouped in collections using the notion of types. All instances of a type possess the same properties, and a type is a predicate that characterizes these common properties [RM-ODP2]. In other words, these instances satisfy the type. Common properties of different types may be abstracted out into a "super-type," and the types themselves are called "subtypes." Subtypes may also be obtained by adding (conjoining) interesting properties to the properties of a supertype. An instance of a (sub)type satisfies the (sub)type's predicate. An instance of a subtype has properties that distinguish it from an instance of another subtype. In other words, an instance of a subtype satisfies the invariant of (i.e., the predicate that defines) this subtype, in addition to the invariant of its supertype. Such an invariant may be application-specific. The predicate of a type may or may not be formulated by means of other explicitly specified properties. In the latter case, the predicate (of the type) must be explicitly specified, for each instance, by the user during "create" (i.e., by extensional inclusion).

A **subtyping** relationship need not be static. A new type (a supertype) may be dynamically attached to an instance of another type (a subtype). Of course, this dynamic supertype may also be detached from such an instance. The identity of an instance does not change when a new supertype is attached or detached (a person can become a homeowner and so acquire properties of a homeowner, but the identity of this person will remain the same). Specifically, a supertype is attached to an instance when that instance starts to fulfill a role in a relationship (such as a specific component role in a composition relationship). A type can participate in several different static or dynamic subtyping hierarchies (see below). The default subtyping is static.

For static subtyping, the set of instances of a subtype is a subset of the set of instances of its supertype. In other words, an instance of a subtype is an instance of its static supertype(s). The invariant of a (static or dynamic) supertype is satisfied by its subtypes. (Specifically, this includes the property of being an element of a (generic) relationship: if a supertype is a component entity in a particular composition, then all its subtypes will also be component entities in the same composition). Therefore, a subtype's properties are a superset of its supertype properties. For dynamic subtyping, this is true only for those instances of a subtype that are also instances of its dynamic supertype.

A subtype may have different supertypes within different subtyping relationships. In this case, the conjunction of all predicates defining all of the supertypes should not be false. More than one classification hierarchy for the same supertype may exist (e.g., an employee may be subtyped by gender or job classification).

The relationships between a supertype and its subtypes give rise to two mutually orthogonal constraints: the "exclusiveness" of the subtypes and the "exhaustiveness" of the subtypes.

The exclusiveness refers to whether a given supertype instance can be of (i.e., satisfy the properties of) more than one subtype. If it can, we say the subtypes are **overlapping**; if not, the subtypes are **disjoint** (the supertype *employee* may have overlapping subtypes *in-house lecturer* and *in-house student*). For disjoint subtyping, an instance of a supertype may have properties of, at most, one of its subtypes. *The default subtyping is disjoint.*

The exhaustiveness refers to the participation of all supertype instances in the subtyping hierarchy. If every instance of a supertype is of (i.e., satisfies the properties of) at least one subtype, we say the hierarchy is **exhaustive**; if not, the hierarchy is **nonexhaustive**. The latter is probably an incomplete specification. *The default subtyping is exhaustive.*

As mentioned earlier, subtyping may also be static or dynamic. For **dynamic** subtyping, if an instance of a subtype has the properties of its dynamic supertype, then—as for any subtyping relationship—the invariant of a supertype is satisfied by instances of its subtype (i.e., a subtype instance will acquire new properties—the properties of its new dynamically attached supertype). As an example, consider furniture, computers, cables, software, and so on in a company. These types are very different and modeled differently. However, instances of each of these types become inventoried items when they are assigned to some employee. This happens dynamically so that the properties of an inventoried item are dynamically attached to an instance of furniture, computers, or others. Of course, properties of an inventoried item can be dynamically "detached" from such an instance (when the employee leaves the company or does not need the instance anymore). If, however, the company decides to attach the properties of an inventoried item to only one type (e.g., computers), then it would be reasonable to model an inventoried item as either a dynamic supertype, or a nonexhaustive static subtype of a computer. Certainly, repetition of the exact same nonexhaustive static subtyping for several different types is not advisable; dynamic subtyping should be used instead.

For multiple static subtyping hierarchies, one action usually will have to handle all these hierarchies. For example, in creating an instance, it will be necessary to determine its subtypes in all exhaustive subtyping hierarchies, and it will be possible to determine subtypes in the non-exhaustive subtyping hierarchies.

When an instance is created, it has the properties of some static types (i.e., it satisfies the predicates of these types). When another (super)type is attached to this instance, the existing predicate is conjoined with the new one—with the predicate that defines the dynamically attached (super)type. Clearly, the conjunction of these predicates should not be false.

Dynamic subtyping cannot be exhaustive because it does not satisfy the invariant for exhaustive subtyping.

Invariant. *A supertype may participate in several subtyping relationships; a subtype may participate in several subtyping relationships. A supertype in a subtyping relationship corresponds to one or more subtypes. The set of instances of a subtype is a subset of the set of instances of its static supertype. If an instance of a subtype is also of its supertype, then the properties of a subtype constitute a superset of the properties of its supertype.* (This is always true for a static supertype. If subtyping is dynamic, then it is true only for those instances of a subtype that also are of its dynamic supertype.)

As follows from the invariant for the elementary relationship, the existence of an instance of the subtyping relationship is equivalent to the existence of an instance of a supertype having the properties of one of its subtypes.

Invariant for exhaustive. *The union of sets of instances of all subtypes is equal to the set of supertype instances.*

Invariant for overlapping. *There exist two different subtypes such that the intersection of the sets of instances of these subtypes may be not empty.*[120]

These invariants imply that it is possible to attach a subtype to, or detach a subtype from, an instance of a supertype if and only if the subtyping is overlapping or nonexhaustive. It is possible to attach a supertype to, or detach a supertype from, an instance of a subtype if and only if the subtyping is dynamic. And it is possible to change the subtype of an instance of a supertype, provided, of course, that the subtyping hierarchy has more than one subtype.

A graphical representation.

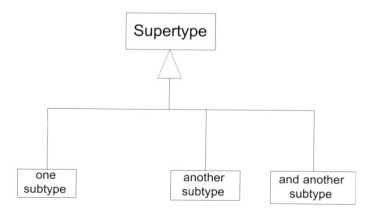

---

120. The careful reader will have noticed that these expressions are translated from a formal specification (e.g., written in Z) into English.

The non-default subtype of a subtyping (such as «overlapping»), if necessary, is shown within guillemets—quotation marks used in French writing.

References

[A1832] John Austin. *The Province of Jurisprudence Determined*. John Murray, London, 1832.

[A1979] Christopher Alexander. *The Timeless Way of Building*. Oxford University Press, 1979.

[AZ2001] Martin Aigner, Günter M. Ziegler. *Proofs from THE BOOK*. Second Edition. Springer Verlag, 2001.

[B1790] Edmund Burke. *Reflections on the Revolution in France, and on the Proceedings in Certain Societies in London relative to that event in a Letter intended to have been sent to a Gentleman in Paris*. Printed for J. Dodsley, London, 1790.

[B1873] Walter Bagehot. *Lombard Street: A Description of the Money Market*. New York: Scribner, Armstrong & Co., 1873.

[B1987] S.G. Barsukov, M.F. Grishakova, Ye.G. Grigor'eva, L.O. Zayonts, Yu.M. Lotman, G.M. Ponomareva, V.Yu. Mitroshkin. The problem "emblem - symbol - myth" in the 18th century culture: preliminary observations. *Sign Systems Studies (Σημειοττκη)*, Vol. 20, Tartu, Estonia, 1987, pp. 85-94.

[B1990a] Mario Bunge. Reply to *Wand and Weber on Information Systems*. In *Studies on Mario Bunge's **Treatise***. (Eds. Paul Weingartner and Georg J.W. Dorn). Rodopi, Amsterdam-Atlanta, 1990, pp. 593-595.

[B1990b] Mario Bunge. Reply to *Bartels on Sense and Reference, Models and Realism*. In *Studies on Mario Bunge's **Treatise***. (Eds. Paul Weingartner and Georg J.W. Dorn). Rodopi, Amsterdam-Atlanta, 1990, pp. 572-576.

[B1990c] Mario Bunge. Reply to *Kanitscheider on the Tense Relations between Science and Philosophy*. In *Studies on Mario Bunge's **Treatise***. (Eds. Paul Weingartner and Georg J.W. Dorn). Rodopi, Amsterdam-Atlanta, 1990, pp. 630-632.

[B1990d] Mario Bunge. Reply to *Mattessich on the Foundations of the Management and Information Sciences*. In *Studies on Mario Bunge's **Treatise***. (Eds. Paul Weingartner and Georg J.W. Dorn). Rodopi, Amsterdam-Atlanta, 1990, pp. 641-642.

[B1991] Grady Booch. *Object-oriented design with applications*. The Benjamin/Cummings Publishing Company, 1991.

[B1999] Mario Bunge. *A dictionary of philosophy*. Prometheus Books, 1999.

[B2000] Peter Bauer. Disregard of reality. In *From subsistence to exchange*. Princeton University Press, 2000, pp. 15-27.

[B2000a] Dines Bjørner. *"What is a Method?" An Essay on Some Aspects of Software Engineering*. Technical University of Denmark, DK-2800 Lyngby, Denmark. August 28, 2000.

[B2000b] Sabine Brauckmann. Steps towards an ecology of cognition: A holistic essay. *Sign Systems Studies (Σημειοττκη)*, Vol. 28. Tartu University Press, Tartu, Estonia, 2000, pp. 397-419.

[B2000c] Dines Bjørner. *Domain Engineering. Elements of a Software Engineering Methodology—Towards Principles, Techniques and Tools—A Study in Methodology*. Technical University of Denmark, DK-2800 Lyngby, Denmark. August 8, 2000.

[B2000d] Peter Bauer. Egalitarianism: A delicate dilemma. In *From subsistence to exchange*. Princeton University Press, 2000, pp. 139-148.

[B2000e] Peter Bauer. From subsistence to exchange. In *From subsistence to exchange*. Princeton University Press, 2000, pp. 3-14.

[B2001] Mark Bruno. Nothing's easy. *U.S. Banker*, Vol. 111, No. 7 (July 2001), p. 22.

[B2001a] Dines Bjørner. *Software engineering, theory & practice. Topic 6: A simple "market" model*. Technical University of Denmark, DK-2800 Lyngby, Denmark. April 5, 2001.

[B2001b] Mario Bunge. *Philosophy in crisis*. Prometheus Books, 2001.

[BETA1992] O.L. Madsen, B. Moller-Pedersen, K. Nygaard. *Object-oriented programming in the BETA programming language*. (Draft. August 11, 1992.)

[BK1999] O. Bernet and H. Kilov. From box-and-line diagrams to precise specifications: Using RM-ODP and GRM to specify semantics. In *Proceedings of the*

Eighth OOPSLA Workshop on Behavioral Semantics (Denver, Colorado, USA). Northeastern University, 1999, pp. 11-21.

[BS1999] G.C. Bowker and S.L. Star. *Sorting things out: Classification and its consequences.* MIT Press, 1999.

[BW1982] Friedrich L. Bauer, Hans Wössner. *Algorithmic language and program development.* Springer Verlag, 1982.

[BZN2000] Dines Bjørner, Li Zhu, and Nicolai Dufva Nielsen. *A Basis for E-Commerce Semantics: The Market Domain; Flow, Function and Data Semantics.* The Technical University of Denmark, DK-2800 Lyngby, Denmark. November 22, 2000.

[C1865] Lewis Carroll. *Alice's Adventures in Wonderland.* Macmillan, London, 1865.

[C1872] Lewis Carroll. *Through the Looking Glass, and What Alice Found There.* Macmillan, London, 1872.

[C1876] Lewis Carroll. *The Hunting of the Snark.* Macmillan, London, 1876.

[C1887] Lewis Carroll. *The Game of Logic.* Macmillan, London, 1887.

[C1915] *Chemists' Windows.* An Illustrated Treatise on the Art of Displaying Pharmaceutical and Allied Goods in Chemists' Shop Windows. The Chemist & Druggist, London and Melbourne, 1915.

[C1970] E.F. Codd. A relational model of data for large shared data banks. *Communications of the ACM*, Vol. 13 (1970), No. 6, pp. 377-387.

[C1982a] B. Cohen. Justification of formal methods for system specifcation. *IEE Software and Microsystems*, Vol. 5, August 1982.

[C1982] E.F. Codd. Relational Database: A Practical Foundation for Productivity (1981 Turing Award Lecture). *Communications of the ACM*, Vol. 25, No. 2 (February 1982), pp. 109-117.

[C1997] B. Cohen. Set theory as a semantic framework for object-oriented modeling. In *Proceedings of the ECOOP'97 Workshop on precise semantics of object-oriented modeling techniques* (Jyväskylä, Finland, 9-13 June 1997). (Eds. H. Kilov, B. Rumpe). Munich University of Technology, TUM-I9725, pp. 61-68.

[CHJ1986] B. Cohen, W.T. Harwood, M.I. Jackson. *The specification of complex systems.* Addison-Wesley, 1986.

[CS1990] Robert N. Corley, Peter J. Shedd. *Fundamentals of business law*, fifth edition. Prentice-Hall, 1990, pp. 893-979.

[D1901] Charles F. Dunbar. *Chapters on the theory and history of banking.* (Second edition, enlarged and edited by O.M.W. Sprague). G.P. Putnams Sons, New York and London, 1901.

[D1961] E.W. Dijkstra. *On the design of machine-independent programming languages*. Report MR34. Mathematisch Centrum, Amsterdam, October 1961.

[D1963] E.W. Dijkstra. Some meditations on advanced programming. *Proceedings of the IFIP Congress 1962*, North Holland, 1963, pp. 535-538.

[D1969] E.W. Dijkstra. *The programming task considered as an intellectual challenge*. EWD273. Eindhoven, December 1969.

[D1972] E.W. Dijkstra. The humble programmer. (Turing Award Lecture). *Communications of the ACM*, Vol. 15(1972), No. 10, pp. 859-886.

[D1976] E.W. Dijkstra. A discipline of programming. Prentice-Hall, 1976.

[D1976a] E.W. Dijkstra. The teaching of programming, i.e. the teaching of thinking. In *Language hierarchies and interfaces. (Eds. F.L. Bauer and K. Samelson), Lecture Notes in Computer Science*, Vol. 46 (1976), pp. 1-10, Springer Verlag.

[D1982] R.G. Dromey. *How to solve it by computer*. Prentice-Hall, 1982.

[D1984] E.W. Dijkstra. *The threats to computing science*. EWD 898. The University of Texas at Austin, 1984.

[D1986] E.W. Dijkstra. *Who is your "target audience"?* EWD 976. The University of Texas at Austin, 1986.

[D1990] Mike Dillinger. On the concept of 'a language.' In *Studies on Mario Bunge's **Treatise***. (Eds. Paul Weingartner and Georg J.W. Dorn). Rodopi, Amsterdam-Atlanta, 1990, pp. 5-26.

[D1997] E.W. Dijkstra. *The Mathematical Divide*. EWD1268. The University of Texas at Austin, 1997.

[D1998] Jean Dieudonné. *Mathematics—the music of reason*. Springer Verlag, 1998. (Translation from French: *Pour l'honneur de l'esprit humain*).

[D1999] Marcel Danesi. The dimensionality of metaphor. *Sign Systems Studies (Σημειοττκη)*, Vol. 27. Tartu University Press, Tartu, Estonia, 1999, pp. 60-87.

[D2000] E.W. Dijkstra. *Under the spell of Leibniz's dream*. EWD1298. The University of Texas at Austin, 2000.

[D2001] Peter Drucker. The next society. *The Economist*, Vol. 361, No. 8246 (November 3rd-9th, 2001).

[E2001] Off with their beards. *The Economist*, Vol. 359, No. 8224 (June 2nd - 8th 2001), p.64.

[EDOC2001] A UML Profile for Enterprise Distributed Object Computing Joint Final Submission Part I. 18 June 2001. OMG Document Number: ad/2001-06-09. 3.6. The Relationship Profile.

[EV2001] Information Technology—Open Distributed Processing—Reference Model—Enterprise Language. Committee Draft ISO/IEC 15414 (ITU-T X.911).

[F1990] Frank Forman. Virtue, the missing link to the last volume of the *Treatise*. In *Studies on Mario Bunge's **Treatise***. (Eds. Paul Weingartner and Georg J.W. Dorn). Rodopi, Amsterdam-Atlanta, 1990, pp. 491-509.

[G1979] James J. Gibson. *The Ecological Approach to Visual Perception*, Boston, Houghton Mifflin Company, 1979.

[G1998] Joseph Goguen. Tossing algebraic flowers down the Great Divide. In *People and ideas in theoretical computer science*. (Ed. C.S. Calude). Springer Verlag, 1998, pp. 93-129.

[G1999] Joseph Goguen. An Introduction to Algebraic Semiotics, with Application to User Interface Design. In *Computation for Metaphor, Analogy and Agents*. (Ed. Chrystopher Nehaniv), Lecture Notes in Artificial Intelligence, Volume 1562. Springer Verlag, 1999, pp. 242-291.

[G2000] M.L. Gasparov. *Writings and Excerpts (Zapisi i Vypiski—in Russian)*. Moscow, NLO Publishers, 2000.

[G2000a] Dinda Gorlée. Text semiotics: Textology as survival-machine. *Sign Systems Studies (Σημειοττκη)*, Vol. 28. Tartu University Press, Tartu, Estonia, 2000, pp. 134-157.

[G2001] Joseph Goguen. *Are agents an answer or a question?* Department of Computer Science and Engineering, University of California at San Diego, 2001.

[G2001] James S. Garrison. Business specifications: Using UML to specify the trading of foreign exchange options. *Proceedings of the 10th OOPSLA workshop on behavioral semantics (Back to Basics)* (Eds. K. Baclawski and H. Kilov). Northeastern University, Boston, 2001, pp. 79-84.

[GF1999] Joseph Goguen, Kokichi Futatsugi. *Semiotic redesign of a computer language*. Department of Computer Science and Engineering, University of California at San Diego, 1999.

[GRM] ISO/IEC JTC1/SC21, Information Technology. Open Systems Interconnection—Management Information Services—Structure of Management Information—Part 7: General Relationship Model, 1995. ISO/IEC 10165- 7.2.

[GS1993] D. Gries, F. Schneider. *A logical approach to discrete math*. Springer Verlag, 1993.

[GSCC] http://www.gscc.com/netting_and_settlement_frame.html

[GW1977] T. Gilb, G. Weinberg. *Humanized Input*. Winthrop, 1977.

[H1755] Francis Hutcheson. *A system of moral philosophy.* Foulis, Glasgow & Millar, London, 1755.

[H1937] Friedrich Hayek. Economics and knowledge. Presidential address delivered before the London Economic Club, November 10, 1936. *Economica* IV (new ser., 1937), 33-54.

[H1940] G.H. Hardy. *A Mathematician's Apology.* Cambridge University Press, 1940; especially sections 22-25.

[H1945] Friedrich Hayek. The use of knowledge in society. *American Economic Review*, XXXV, No. 4. September, 1945, pp. 519-30.

[H1957] Grace Hopper. Automatic Programming for Business Applications. In *Proceedings of the 4th Annual computer applications symposium*, October 24-25, 1957, Armour Research Foundation, Chicago.

[H1964] F.A. Hayek. The theory of complex phenomena. In *The critical approach to science and technology (In honor of Karl R. Popper).* (Ed. Mario Bunge). The Free Press of Glencoe, 1964, pp. 332-349.

[H1989] C.A.R. Hoare. Notes on an approach to category theory for computer scientists. In *Constructive methods in computing science.* International Summer School directed by F.L. Bauer, M. Broy, E.W. Dijkstra, C.A.R. Hoare. (Ed. Manfred Broy). Springer Verlag, 1989, pp. 243-305.

[H1994] C.A.R. Hoare. *Mathematical Models for Computing Science.* Notes, Oxford University Computing Laboratory, August 1994.

[H1997] Andrew Herbert. *Annotated tour of RM-ODP.* A presentation and commentary for the OMG/ODP workshop sponsored by APM and OMG in Cambridge, England, November 1997. ANSA, Cambridge, UK, 1997.

[H1999] C.A.R. Hoare. *Software—Barrier or frontier?* Oxford University Computing Laboratory, November 23, 1999.

[HJ1998] C.A.R. Hoare, He Jifeng. *Unifying theories of programming.* Prentice-Hall, 1998.

[HKOS1996] W. Harrison, H. Kilov, H. Ossher, I. Simmonds. *From dynamic supertypes to objects: A natural way to specify and develop systems.* IBM Systems Journal, Vol. 35, No. 2 (June 1996), pp. 244-256.

[HSB1999] B. Henderson-Sellers, F. Barbier. Black and white diamonds. In *Proceedings of the Second International Conference on the Unified Modeling Language (UML'99)—Beyond the Standard (Eds. R. France, B. Rumpe), Fort Collins, CO, October 28-30, Lecture Notes in Computer Science,* Vol. 1723. Springer Verlag, Berlin, 1999.

[H2001] Philip Hensher. What do they know of English. *The Spectator*, 17 February 2001.

[I2002] Wes Isberg. Get test-inoculated! *Software Development*, Vol. 10, No. 5 (May 2002), pp. 40-43, 76.

[I2002a] In search of a better Web. *Information Week*, March 25, 2002, p. 18.

[K1979] William Kent. *Data and Reality.* North-Holland, 1979. Also reprinted by 1stBooks, 2000.

[K1999] H. Kilov. *Business specifications.* Prentice-Hall, 1999.

[K2000] H. Kilov. Business specifications and RM-ODP. In *Proceedings of the 34th International Conference on Technology of Object-oriented Languages and Systems (TOOLS 34)* (Santa Barbara, CA, July 30 - August 4, 2000). IEEE Computer Society, 2000, pp. 411-420.

[K2000a] Kristiina Karvonen. The beauty of simplicity. In *Conference on Universal Usability (CUU2000)*, ACM Press, 2000, pp. 85-90.

[K2000b] H. Kilov. Representing business specifications in UML. In *Proceedings of the 9th OOPSLA workshop on behavioral semantics.* (Eds. K. Baclawski and H. Kilov). Northeastern University, Boston, 2000, pp. 102-111.

[K2001] H. Kilov. Introduction to a financial services business information model. In *Proceedings of the 10th OOPSLA workshop on Behavioral Semantics—Back to basics.* (Tampa, Florida, 15 October 2001), pp. 140-149.

[K2001a] Thomas Kudrass. Coping with semantics in XML document management. In *Proceedings of the 10th OOPSLA workshop on Behavioral Semantics—Back to basics.* (Tampa, Florida, 15 October 2001), pp. 150-161.

[KA1997] H. Kilov, A. Ash. How to ask questions: Handling complexity in a business specification. In *Proceedings of the OOPSLA97 Workshop on object-oriented behavioral semantics* (Atlanta, October 6th, 1997). (Eds. H. Kilov, B. Rumpe, I. Simmonds). Munich University of Technology, TUM-I9737, pp. 99-114.

[KA1998] H. Kilov, A. Ash. An information management project: What to do when your business specification is ready. In *Proceedings of the Second ECOOP Workshop on Precise behavioral semantics* (Brussels, Belgium, 1998). (Eds. H. Kilov and B. Rumpe). Munich University of Technology, pp.95-104.

[KA1999] H. Kilov, A. Ash. On the structure of convincing specifications. In *Behavioral specifications of businesses and systems.* (Eds. H. Kilov, B. Rumpe, I. Simmonds). Kluwer Academic Publishers, 1999, pp.141-160.

[KLR2002] Viktor Kuncak, Patrick Lam, and Martin Rinard. Role analysis. In *Proceedings of the 2002 SIGPLAN-SIGACT Symposium on Principles of Programming Languages (POPL '02)*, ACM, 2002, pp. 17-32.

[KR1994] H. Kilov, J. Ross. *Information modeling: An object-oriented approach.* Prentice-Hall, 1994.

[KRS1999] Preface to *Behavioral specifications of businesses and systems.* (Eds. H. Kilov, B. Rumpe, I. Simmonds), Kluwer Academic Publishers, 1999.

[KS1996] H. Kilov, I. Simmonds. Business patterns: reusable abstract constructs for business specification. In *Implementing Systems for Supporting Management Decisions: Concepts, methods and experiences.* (Eds. Patrick Humphreys et al). Chapman and Hall, 1996, pp. 225-248.

[KS1996a] H. Kilov, I. Simmonds. How to correctly refine business specifications, and know it. In: *Proceedings of the Fifth Workshop on Specification of Behavioral Semantics (at OOPSLA '96).* (Eds. H. Kilov and V.J. Harvey). Robert Morris College, 1996, pp. 57-69.

[KS1997] H. Kilov, I. Simmonds. Business rules: from business specification to design. *Proceedings of ECOOP '97 Workshop on Precise Semantics of Object-oriented Modeling Techniques,* Jyväskylä, Finland, May 1997, (Eds. H. Kilov and B. Rumpe), pp. 101-109.

[L1964] Yuri Lotman. Lectures on structural poetics (in Russian). *Sign Systems Studies (Σημειοττκη)*, Vol. 1 (1964), Tartu.

[L1990] Yuri M. Lotman. *Universe of the mind. A semiotic theory of culture.* Indiana University Press, 1990.

[L1992] Yuri Lotman. On the dynamics of culture. *Semiotics and History. Sign Systems Studies (Σημειοττκη)*, Vol. 25 (1992), Tartu, pp. 5-22.

[L2001] Herbert W. Lovelace. The medium is more than the message. *Information Week*, July 16, 2001, p. 74.

[L2001a] Robert Langreth. Machine gunner. *Forbes*, November 26, 2001.

[LS1997] F.W. Lawvere, S.H. Schanuel, *Conceptual Mathematics: A first introduction to categories.* Cambridge University Press, 1997.

[M1835] *Proposals of the Massachusetts Hospital Life Insurance Company, to make insurance on lives, to grant annuities on lives and in trust, and endowments for children*, James Loring printer, Boston, 1835.

[M1944] Ludwig von Mises. *Bureaucracy.* New Haven, Yale University Press, 1944.

[M1949] Ludwig von Mises. *Human Action: A treatise on economics.* New Haven, Yale University Press, 1949.

[MS2000] Grady Means, David Schneider. *Metacapitalism*. John Wiley & Sons, Inc., 2000.

[N2001] Kathy Nottingham. Clearing the myths of supply chain automation. *Electronic Commerce World*, November 2001, pp. 40-42.

[N2002] Peter G. Neumann and contributors. Risks to the public in computers and related systems. *ACM Software Engineering Notes*, Vol. 27, No. 2 (March 2002), pp. 5-19.

[O1949] George Orwell. *Nineteen Eighty-Four*. Secker & Warburg, London, 1949.

[ON1947] William F. Ogburn, Meyer F. Nimkoff. *A handbook of sociology*. Kegan Paul, Trench, Trubner & Co., Ltd., London, 1947.

[OODBTG1991] *Object Data Management Reference Model*. (ANSI Accredited Standards Committee. X3, Information Processing Systems.) Document Number OODB 89-01R8. 17 September 1991. (Also in *Computer Standards and Interfaces*, Vol. 15 (1993), pp. 124-142.)

[P1931] Charles Saunders Peirce. *Collected papers of Charles Saunders Peirce, Vols. 1-8*. The Belknap Press of Harvard University Press, 1931-1961.

[P1999] Henry Petroski. *The book on the bookshelf*. Alfred A. Knopf, 1999.

[P2000] Roland Posner. Semiotic pollution: deliberations towards ecology of signs. *Sign Systems Studies (Σημειοττκη)*, Vol. 28. Tartu University Press, Tartu, Estonia, 2000, pp. 290-308.

[P2001a] Roger Pearson. Artificial paradises. *The Times Literary Supplement*, 27 April 2001, p. 8-9.

[P2001] David Parnas. *Software fundamentals. Collected papers by David L. Parnas* (Eds. Daniel M. Hoffman and David M. Weiss). Addison-Wesley, 2001.

[PO2001] H. Van Dyke Parunak and James Odell. Representing social structures in UML. In *Autonomous Agents '01*, May 28-June 1, 2001, Montreal, Canada.

[PST1990] Ben Potter, Jane Sinclair, David Till. *An introduction to formal specification and Z*. Prentice-Hall, 1990.

[R2001] Jim Reeds. Book review. *ACM SIGACT News*, Vol. 32, No. 2, p. 8.

[RM-ODP2] ISO/IEC JTC1/SC21. Open Distributed Processing - Reference Model: Part 2: Foundations (ITU-T Recommendation X.902 | ISO/IEC 10746-2).

[RM-ODP3] ISO/IEC JTC1/SC21. Open Distributed Processing - Reference Model: Part 3: Architecture (ITU-T Recommendation X.903 | ISO/IEC 10746-3).

[S1759] Adam Smith. *The Theory of Moral Sentiments*. London, 1759.

[S1776] Adam Smith. *An Inquiry into the Nature and Causes of the Wealth of Nations*. London: Printed for W. Strahan; and T. Cadell, 1776.

[S1904] *Specifications for Architects, Surveyors and Engineers when Specifying: and for All Interested in Building.* Annually. No. 7, 1904. Published by the proprietors of The Builders' Journal and Architectural Record (Weekly) and The Architectural Review (Monthly). Great New Street, London.

[S1999] Göran Sonesson. The life of signs in society and out of it: Critique of the communication critique. *Sign Systems Studies (Σημειοττκη)*, Vol. 27. Tartu University Press, Tartu, Estonia, 1999, pp. 88-127.

[S2000] Ronald Stamper. New directions for systems analysis and design. In *Enterprise information systems.* (Ed. Joaquim Felipe). Kluwer Academic Publishers, 2000, pp. 14-39.

[S2000a] Paul Strassman. How e-business affects knowledge capital. *Knowledge Management*, November 2000, pp. 18-19.

[S2001] Steve Seiden. Can a computer proof be elegant? *ACM SIGACT News*, Vol. 32, No. 1 (March 2001), pp. 110-114.

[S2001a] Robert L. Scheier. Stabilizing your risk. *Computerworld ROI*, Vol. 1, No, 2 (2001), pp. 16-22.

[S2001b] Harry J. Saddler. Understanding design representations. *Interactions*, Vol. viii, No. 4 (July-August 2001), pp. 17-24.

[S2001c] Paul Strassman. KM, IT, and organizational capital. *Knowledge Management,* April 2001.

[S2002] Michael Stonebraker. Too much middleware. *SIGMOD Record*, Vol. 31, No. 1 (March 2002), pp. 97-106.

[SE1969] *Software Engineering.* Report on a Conference sponsored by the NATO Science Committee, Garmisch, Germany, 7th to 11th October 1968. (Chairman: Professor Dr. F.L. Bauer, Co-chairmen: Professor L. Bolliet, Dr. H.J. Helms; Editors: Peter Naur and Brian Randell). January 1969.

[SE1970] *Software Engineering Techniques.* Report on a Conference sponsored by the NATO Science Committee, Rome, Italy, 27th to 31st October 1969. (Chairman: Professor P. Ercoli, Co-Chairman: Professor Dr. F.L. Bauer, Editors: J.N. Buxton and B. Randell) April 1970.

[SKB2001] Lawrence E. Sweeney, Enrique V. Kortright and Robert J. Buckley. Developing an RM-ODP-based architecture for the Defense Integrated Military Human Resource System. *Proceedings of the WOODPECKER-2001 (Open Distributed Processing: Enterprise, Computation, Knowledge, Engineering and Realisation) in conjunction with ICEIS '01*, Setubal, Portugal, July 2001, pp. 110-123.

[SS1977] J.M. Smith and D.C.P. Smith. Database abstractions: aggregation and generalization. *ACM Transactions on Database Systems*, Vol. 2, No. 2 (June 1977).

[T1996] ISO/IEC JTC1/SC21. Information technology—Open Distributed Processing—ODP Trading Function. IS 13235. 1996.

[T1999] Paul Taylor. *Practical foundations of mathematics.* Cambridge University Press, 1999.

[T2000] Wladyslaw M. Turski. An essay on software engineering at the turn of century. In *Fundamental approaches to software engineering. (Ed. Tom Maibaum.) Third International Conference, FASE 2000* (LNCS, Vol. 1783). Springer Verlag, 2000, pp. 1-20.

[T2001] Michael Totty. The researcher. *The Wall Street Journal*, July 16, 2001, p. R20.

[TM1987] Wladyslaw M. Turski, Thomas S.E. Maibaum. *The specification of computer programs.* Addison-Wesley, 1987.

[TS1999] A. Thalassinidis, I. Sack. Initiating Business Strategies for the E-Publishing Industry—A Case Study. In *Proceedings of the 8th OOPSLA workshop on behavioral semantics.* (Eds. K. Baclawski, H. Kilov, A. Thalassinidis, K. Tyson). Northeastern University, 1999, pp. 221-226.

[U1999] Daniel H. Ullman. Book review: Proofs from THE BOOK. *Notices of the American Mathematical Society,* August 1999, pp. 789-791.

[UML 1.3] *Unified Modeling Language Specification, Version 1.3.* June 1999. `http://cgi.omg.org/cgi-bin/doc?ad/99-06-08`

[UML 1.4] *Unified Modeling Language Specification, Version 1.4.* 2001. `http://www.omg.org/cgi-bin/doc?formal/01-09-67`

[V1990] Gerhard Vollmer. Against instrumentalism. In *Studies on Mario Bunge's* **Treatise**. (Eds. Paul Weingartner and Georg J.W. Dorn). Rodopi, Amsterdam-Atlanta, 1990, pp. 245-259.

[vG1990] A.J.M. van Gasteren. *On the Shape of Mathematical Arguments.* Lecture Notes in Computer Science, Vol. 445 (1990). Springer-Verlag.

[VJ2000] M. Vaziri and D. Jackson. Some Shortcomings of OCL, the Object Constraint Language of UML. *Proceedings of TOOLS USA 34—the 34th International Conference on Technology of Object-oriented languages and systems,* IEEE Computer Society Press, 2000, pp. 555-560.

[W1933] Ludwig Wittgenstein. *Tractatus Logico-Philosophicus.* 2nd corrected reprint. New York: Harcourt, Brace and Company; London: Kegan Paul, Trench, Trubner & Co. Ltd., 1933.

[W1956] B.L. Whorf. *Language, Thought, and Reality: Selected Writings of Benjamin Lee Whorf.* (Ed. J. B. Carroll). MIT Press, Cambridge, MA, 1956.

[W1985] Niklaus Wirth. From programming language design to compiler construction. *Communications of the ACM*, Vol. 28 (1985), No. 2.

[W1996] Jeannette M. Wing. Hints to specifiers. In *Teaching and learning formal methods.* (Eds. C. Neville Dean and Michael G. Hinchey). Academic Press, 1996, pp.57-77.

[W2000] Michael Wolff. Got it? *Forbes ASAP*, October 2 2000, p. 37.

[W2001] The faces of e-commerce: The people who make it all work. *The Wall Street Journal*, July 16, 2001, p. R1-R24.

[WD1996] Jim Woodcock, Jim Davies. *Using Z: Specification, refinement, and proof.* Prentice-Hall, 1996.

[Z1999] A.K. Zholkovsky. *Mikhail Zoshchenko: A poetics of mistrust.* (In Russian). Moscow, 1999.

[Z2001] Carl Zetie. Context is King. *Information Week,* November 19, 2001.

[Z2001a] Paula Throckmorton Zakaria. Book review of *The Myth of Excellence* by Fred Crawford and Ryan Matthews. *The Wall Street Journal,* July 16, 2001, p. A20.

Index

V

valuation, 4, 72, 83, 114-115, 138, 176
virtual machine, specifics of, 2, *See also* technological virtual machines

W

warm and fuzzy feelings, 40, 128, 181, 187
write-only specification, 8, 19

Z

Z, 118, 217, 227, 230